HOLY
HEATHEN

HOLY HEATHEN

a spiritual memoir

KATHERINE NORTH

Holy Heathen: A Spiritual Memoir
Copyright © 2020 by Declare Dominion, Inc.
ISBN: 978-1-7349529-0-2

Declare Dominion Publishing
Book design by HR Hegnauer

For Adventure,
who first turned my heart into a cathedral.

And for all the kindred spirits
who've shown me your true, raw, fierce and tender hearts.
Here's mine.

PREFACE, PLUS DISCLAIMERS

My mother clears her throat.

"I've been wanting to talk to you about something."

My arms prickle and I grip the steering wheel. Trapped!

My daughter is snoozing in her car seat. My father lets out a tiny snore from the back, possibly staged. Instantly I am twelve again, sitting on my parents' bed, dying a thousand deaths as my mother talks to me about sex and how True Love Waits, and all I can think is THIS IS THE BED WHERE MY PARENTS HAVE SEX.

"Oh?" I say, breathing into the knot in my belly, reminding myself that I am an adult, I am 36 years old, I am a total bad-ass life coach with ninja diplomacy skills. I wish I still smoked. I wish I did drugs. I wonder if maybe I should get into a nice little fender-bender—nothing serious, just enough to shift the laser beam of her attention.

"I'm a little nervous about this memoir you're writing," she says.

"Ah." Okay, better. Better. It could have been about my parenting or my sex life.

"You wrote something on your blog the other day about going to church—about how you had to go sixteen times a week—"

"Mom," I interrupt, "I said sixteen to be funny. It was hyperbole. No one really thought I meant sixteen, don't worry."

She blinks, truly baffled. "But we never went more than once a week."

I concentrate on the road. I think of the thousands of hours I spent in

I

various churches of all stripes, from the soaring gold and red cathedrals of Indianapolis to the dank tatami rooms in Tokyo, to the little awkward circle that met in our home and sat in the creaking metal chairs just below my bedroom.

At least sixteen times a week, I swear.

We look at each other.

"Once?" I say lightly, pretending that I am going to be diplomatic, that I can handle this, that I am an enlightened motherfucking grownup. "ONCE????"

"Well yes! Once! I mean, occasionally when we were living in the States you'd go to Pioneer Girls, or there'd be Bible Study, but in Japan we only did things on Sunday!"

"What about the cooking classes at our house? And the English classes? And the summer camps and the Christmas caroling in front of KFC with the Colonel Sanders Santa Claus??? What about the ladies coming over to do the church flowers and practicing the organ and having to go to church even on Christmas MORNING"—my eight-year-old outrage flares up faithfully—"and the potlucks and the baptisms and the prayer meetings?????"

She stares at me, so gentle, so loving. "But honey," she says kindly, "those aren't really church."

I breathe. And steer. Innnn and out, calm and peace, eyes on the road. I have learned a few things.

There is so much love between us, great deep wide oceans of love, and just as much mysterious space. We might as well be from different planets: two aliens who bewilder and love each other in equal measure.

I glance in the rearview mirror at my dad, whose eyes are steadfastly closed. He is definitely faking. My mother continues: "I want to support you, honey, it's just that I worry that we remember things so differently."

And there it is, the impossible problem of this story.

This book contains the truest truth I know how to tell. But you might say I'm lying about it all, and you might not be wrong. I am going to tell you *my* story, a true one, the one I remember. But it's tricky to tell a story when it touches other people's stories, so I want to acknowledge that this telling is also my own creation. The people in it are characters who live in my memory and my imagination, and in an effort to protect their real-life privacy and anonymity while still telling my own truth, I have disguised identities and used pseudonyms. So it is also true to say that this is a story I have made up entirely. A fiction, as all memory is fiction. The more I try to be accurate about the heart of what happened and what it meant, the more false it may seem.

I'm ok with that.

It's inevitable, actually.

How many times a week did we go to church?

Sixteen, I say, meaning five. Maybe two or three, says my brother. Just the once! says my mother. I don't want to fight, says my sister. My father can't answer because he's deep in a Tom Clancy novel.

So how many times a week did we go to church, really?

Here is the real answer—more than I wanted to.

INTRODUCTION

I never go to church now. I have left the faith of my parents completely, and I am a joyful heathen mystic; my new religion is beauty, and flowers, and swearing. If we're going to be absolutely specific, though, I'm something much worse than a heathen—at least according to the people I grew up with. Heathens, see, are people who never *heard* the gospel in the first place, so even though they are *probably* still going to hell, there's a tiny sliver of liberal theology that allows a slim possibility that perhaps they get out on account of never having had a chance. But what I am is an apostate. An apostate is someone who knew the truth, who was shown the light, and who chose to walk away into the darkness.

That's me.

Oh, I am so *definitely* going to hell!

I don't mind so much, though, because here's what being doomed to hell looks like on any average day:

I walk my daughter to school. She is six, she is in first grade, she wears a backpack. She has blue eyes and golden curls and she looks like Jesus's blonde little sister, at least the Jesus on the cover of my childhood Bible— Jesus imagined by a bunch of white Americans, shorn of his beard and peyot.

Her eyes are oceans.

She has already had one meltdown over her shoes, another meltdown when I tried to comb her hair, and yet another meltdown over her cereal.

I am using the voice that sounds like I'm calm except that it's calm like a tyrannosaurus is calm. Right before it chomps you.

"My socks!" she wails. "My socks hurt me just so much!"

We are out the door finally, approximately three hours after I started *trying* to get us out the door, and we step into the green swaying bowl of Portland and without even meaning to we both begin to breathe again. She grabs my hand; the sidewalk has transformed me from meanest-mommy-in-the-world to her ally.

I'll take it.

I hang on to my precious cargo, feeling my heart lurch at the audacious fact that she wants to hold my hand. My chest threatens to bloom flowers right through my shirt. It is unreasonable how much I adore this tiny cranky beautiful being; humbling how the sight of her little face shoots off sparklers in my chest. Her bright head bobs next to me as we cross the street into the park. We walk the winding path between cherries and camellias, past the eager yelps of the dogs. The park buzzes as families converge toward the school, people wearing clogs and Frye boots and suits, plus dreads and tattoos and Tory Burch flats. I have never seen a place so friendly and blooming: in defiance of all laws of season and nature, the daphne, tulips, crocus, and rhododendron bloom all at once in an exuberant burst of color.

We walk past the swings, past the jungle gym nestled on bark chips, underneath the dogwood tree budding in the soft spring air.

Up the school stairs, into the joyful chaos of the classroom, coat and backpack and green folder and brrrrrring goes the bell, and I kiss my girl's freckles and make my escape.

Back outside again, the park is quiet and gilded with sunlight. I feel my feet against the ground. A thousand points of dew glisten with ridiculous extravagance. I breathe in, soft damp sweetness, and without meaning to my eyes have closed and I am grinning. I linger, pretend to check my phone, and when most of the parents have trickled out of the green golden space, I walk to a tree and casually lean against it. I try to look cool, nonchalant. But as soon as my forehead leans against the bark I can feel it: the humming sap of the tree's life force swirling, bubbling, rolling down into its roots like the tree is doing yoga, turning its wrists and ankles lazily.

Oh hello! the tree greets me. It does not use words to do this, but I can feel its eager greeting through my shoulder.

Hey dearheart, I say back. I don't use words either, because I don't want to mess with my passable imitation of an ordinary adult. I hear birds. And I can feel the flowers; they are blooming their hearts out, practically contorting with joy, the low shimmering of their hum joining the sound of the trees. Up above me the sky is humming too, the clouds coming in and out, alto and soprano, the dirt underneath us a deep cello note.

I cannot pretend that I am anything other than deeply beloved. The rich thrum of all this humming is undeniable. It trickles into me and I tilt back my head, let it pour down my throat, and I drink and I drink of the magical world around me with the shameless abandon of a mystic. It's all right here, this ridiculous world, loving us, dancing its heart out for us.

I can't imagine how I couldn't feel it before.

But I didn't, for a long time.

I spent the first couple decades of my life thirsty. Parched. Cracked with longing. And pretty certain I was batshit crazy.

HOLY
HEATHEN

CHAPTER 1

The thing, the horrible thing—it's trying to get in through the window again. It's coming for me, silent but buzzing, and I squeeze everything closed to keep it out—blue curtains shut, my grandmother's quilt under my chin, dollies clutched to my chest, my eyes screwed tight.

No good. It comes anyway. It's always the same.

In the nightmare, I am standing on an enormous tarmac holding a bundle of string. There are thousands of airplanes overhead, and they zoom in to land, one after another, down a long runway. Relentless. Each airplane has a string, like a kite, and I am holding the strings. It is my job, apparently, to see that the airplanes land without getting snarled. I tug and cajole, trying to get them to be orderly, begging them to fly better. But they lurch and twirl like drunk toddlers. Their threads twist, they come in too fast, it's a disaster—and there I stand, yanking on my handful of threads, trying with all my might to control the enormous metal monsters as they begin to crash into each other.

Then I wake twisted in my Strawberry Shortcake sheets, weeping because I couldn't control the planes and the lines were getting tangled. The unbelievable tragedy of it. A strange buzzing sound in my arms, a clutch of panic in my chest. I am four years old. Never been on an airplane. Never flown a kite.

To put it nicely, the way the Bible study ladies would have, with lots of compassion swirled into their euphemisms, you could say that I was a rather intense child. I had Lots Of Feelings. In fact, I was so full of fears and terrors you'd think I'd grown up in a refugee camp, not in the home of my gentle, happy-go-lucky hippie Jesus-loving parents. I could see them watching me sometimes, loving but puzzled. I was a spiky pterodactyl mysteriously landed in the midst of their fuzzy, loving nest, and they didn't know what to do with me.

On the nights when I had the airplane dream, I'd crawl down the stairs until I reached the heavy door at the bottom. There I'd curl into a ball with my nose pressed into the brown carpet. I liked it there, I could hear the singing from the Bible studies they had in the living room, and the faint vomitous smell of the carpet was weirdly reassuring. I loved the sound of all those grownups laughing and singing, the guitar nudging them along, someone playing the spoons, the rest of them clapping, making a joyful noise unto the Lord. I knew my parents wouldn't spank me for sleeping on the stairs.

Bless their hearts, they gave me more leeway than most Christian parents would have. They hadn't found the Focus On The Family parenting books yet, lucky for me, and so they often agreed to unusual arrangements. For one thing, they let me keep the lights blazing in my room all night long, even though in my bedtime storybooks the good little girls always slept docilely in the dark after they said their prayers. Unfortunately the dark sent me into a rigid, comatose horror that no cajoling or threat of punishment could reason me out of, and my parents, with the good sense that God gave them, decided to pick their goddamn battles.

Maybe they hoped that my sleeping on the stairs or with the lights on would turn out to be a phase, like the year I refused to wear pants—at all, ever—because pants weren't *pretty*. My mother had flapped my new corduroy bell-bottoms at me, indignantly pointing out the hand-stitched applique she'd added, but I was not to be moved. I wanted dresses. Long, frilly dresses.

My dad worked in management at the JC Penneys department store, going off to work every day in a scratchy brown suit, and my mom cooked, cleaned, gardened, and baked. In the summer we could walk down the ticklish green grass behind our Indianapolis home, past the kiddie pool and homemade sandbox, and pick our own grapes right off the arbor. My mother whirled circles around the kitchen, dancing on the yellow-and-gold kitchen linoleum with my brother on her hip, turning the grapes into deep purple jam in clear jars. She moved fast, her hair curling in the steam, listening seriously to my opinions on things.

"Mommy? Why don't my Laura Ingalls paper dolls look like yours?"

"I've had a lot more practice, sweetie."

"But I asked God to make mine better, and He didn't. I can't make their braids right."

"Do you want your hot dog cooked, honey?"

"No, I want it cold. And I want it with cottage cheese. And ketchup."

"Yuck. That sounds disgusting. Maybe God likes your paper dolls just the way they are. Say please, honey."

My mother kissed me as she handed me my cold hot dog. We held hands and closed our eyes for grace.

"Thank you Jesus for this good food, and for my sweet children who I love so much, and please let Virgil have a good day at work. In Jesus's name, Amen."

"Amen," I chorused. I narrowed my eyes at my brother, Jake. "He didn't say amen."

"He's two." My mother wiped a smear of applesauce off his metal high chair tray. The light streamed into the white breakfast nook through the trailing green plant in its handmade macramé hanger. Orange and brown rattan place mats were stacked neatly on the table, but I got to use my very own plastic Cookie Monster place mat.

"Will you help me make Mary and Laura after lunch?"

"No, sweetie, I'm baking bread this afternoon, and then I've got boxes to pack."

There were boxes everywhere. Our whole house was being taken over by boxes. One by one our things were disappearing into them, the way laundry disappeared down the laundry chute and fell into the basement. I had helpfully suggested that we could put my brother in a box as well, but

I had been voted down. My big Raggedy Ann doll went into a box, and so did all my books.

Now at bedtime we didn't read the Little House books or the Sesame Street book about Biff building his house, or *Lyle, Lyle, Crocodile*. Instead, my mother read me stories about a girl named Mieko. She wore a long straight dress with sleeves that hung down to the ground, and socks under her sandals. She lived in a place called "Japan," where bright lanterns stretched across the sky and goldfish swam around in tiny stone ponds and everyone had black hair.

I had learned to spell both our last name and the word "Japan" by listening to my father repeat it over and over on the phone.

"J-A-P-A—yup, that's right, moving the whole family. Got to do God's work. Yes sir, thank you for that. It's spelled P-F-I-F... yeah, I know, it's a funny one...F-E..."

After stories that night, my mom tucked me in and kissed my cheek. She smelled like flowers. I played with the tiny pink cameo ring on her right hand and tried to think how I could convince her of my new plan.

"Mommy? I have an idea. I think we should stay here instead of going to Japan."

She smiled at me and twirled my hair around her finger. "It's a big adjustment, huh? I bet you feel a little bit nervous. But you know what? It's God who wants us to go to Japan. He's sending us, and He'll take care of us. There are so many people in the world who don't know about how much God loves them, and it's our job to go and tell them. Just like we talked about in Sunday School, remember? You don't need to worry. It'll be interesting! We're all going to learn Japanese together."

I pondered this. We had had this same conversation many, many times. "Can I take my dollhouse?"

"No, sweetie. The dollhouse is too big."

I turned my face into my pillow.

"Please leave the light on, Mommy."

After my mother sang "Jesus Loves Me" and patted my back, she carried my sleepy brother back downstairs, where he would sleep in the yellow nursery. It was right across the hall from their bedroom with the big brass bed covered in the brown and cream quilt.

I lay there squinting up at the bright overhead light, then tiptoed into my big walk-in closet and stared at my dollhouse.

My parents had collaborated the Christmas before to make it. It was an exact tiny replica of our own home, with its yellow-beige siding and chocolate-brown trim, the white walls and brown carpet inside, my own little blue muslin curtains flying out of my room upstairs. I crouched down and tucked the dolly into her bed. I pulled the curtains closed. I shut the front door tight, and pushed the open side with the missing walls back against the closet wall so the dollies would feel safe and so nothing could get in. During the day, I felt so loving toward my little house. I felt like I was its kindly guardian, and I took good care of it and its inhabitants, keeping their rooms neat and coloring all the bedclothes pink so that they would be happy.

But at night, I was afraid.

There was another dream I often dreamed, sometimes together with the airplane dream: I would be handed an enormous book, wider than I was tall, and told to fill it out. But I didn't know yet how to read or write, and so I would wake not just anxious but deeply, horribly ashamed. I could hardly stand the sick hotness in my throat. Clearly I was a wretched worm; I was not fit to live; I had failed. My performance as a successful four-year-old was a big fake, and everyone would find out the truth about me—I was an impostor. I wasn't really a good little girl. I was something else. Something so, so wrong.

I am certain that this particular golf bag of guilt did not come from my parents; this was long before the insanity of toddler phonics. Not one person in my life thought I should be reading or writing. No one had even tried to teach me my letters yet—Sesame Street was just for fun. And yet I simply believed, with total manic certainty, that I was doomed because I couldn't fill out that enormous book. I felt panicky every time I thought about it, and I thought about it a lot even when I was awake. It was urgent, I sensed—they were waiting for it.

They?

Just—they. Out there, that circle of people. The ones that watch us. Can't you see them?

Oh.

The grownups say that I have a very good imagination.

I knew the circle of watchers couldn't be angels, because I'd learned all about angels at church. Angels were tall blonde men with enormous wings who were very scary and blinded people with a bright shining light. They didn't come to earth anymore; they'd only come back in Bible times, either to punish someone who had been bad or else to deliver an important message, like the message to Mary that she was going to have baby Jesus. It was a big honor to be visited by an angel, except that it scared people so badly that sometimes they wet their pants or turned to salt. I very much hoped they would never visit me. When my Sunday School teachers moved the Bible figures around on the felt board during Story Hour, the angels always had big swirls of light around them. There was one angel who wasn't sticky any more, and he kept falling off in the middle of the story. We giggled each time he fell off, and the teacher laughed too. It was okay to laugh if the angels fell off the green felt, but not if Jesus did. That would be sacrilege. We talked about Jesus every Sunday; He was after the sand table, right before the apple juice and graham crackers.

Jesus lived in our hearts. Jesus loved us. Jesus was God's son. I didn't really know what all this meant, but it was very important to the adults that we fold our hands into little church shapes and bow our heads when they prayed to Jesus. They talked to Jesus like he was right there in the room with us, even though he never answered back.

I knew that if you didn't have Jesus in your heart, you would go to hell. Everyone in my family knew that; even my dumb baby brother probably knew that. Across the street at my best friend Dawn's house, they didn't have hell—they had a Slip 'N' Slide instead.

Dawn would throw herself down the slick yellow rubber with abandon, squealing with glee as her mother cheered her on.

"Okay, kiddo, your turn!" April was tall and thin and beautiful, with a kind of bouncy energy that no one at my house had. Her hair puffed out around her head in a frizzy halo, and she squirted extra water on the Slip 'N' Slide for me. I so badly wanted to slide down it on my stomach like Dawn did, feeling that rush of speed and fearlessness. But I knew that I would come away welted and scratched, each little bump under the thin plastic making its mark on my skin.

"You're like the princess and the pea, sweetie," said April with concern as I showed her my red smarting limbs. She was so kind and loving, but I was afraid of her because she and Dawn's dad were divorced, and I felt such a heavy wetness in my chest whenever Dawn talked about her dad, who she now saw only once a week. I wanted to be brave and full of laughter like April and Dawn were, and at their house I sometimes felt brighter, with the two silly sausage dogs skittering around on the dark blue kitchen tile and their long fluffy cats drifting through the house like ghosts when you weren't looking.

April always said that we could tell her anything, so one evening as she flipped grilled cheese sandwiches for us, I asked her a question.

"April? How come you don't believe in God?"

She waved the spatula back and forth slowly before she replied.

"Well, I do, sort of, but not the way your mom and dad do."

"But I don't want you and Dawn to go to hell."

Dawn looked at me and tugged on her earlobe. "Hell is where it's hot and they poke you."

April stared at her daughter in amazement. "What?! Where did you hear that? There is NO such thing as hell."

I felt a rush of terror for these beloveds, and I jumped in: "Oh, but there is! And you'll go there if you don't believe in Jesus!"

Dawn began to cry. "I don't want to go to hell!"

April picked her up.

"We're taking you home." She marched me across the street and I heard her and my mother talking in the kitchen while Dawn and I played with blocks in the living room. Then they left, Dawn waving sadly at me over her mother's shoulder as they walked away.

"Mommy? Isn't it true that they should believe in Jesus? So they don't go to hell?"

My mother sighed and pulled me on to her lap. "Yes, honey, it is true. But it's not always a good idea to talk about it." I could feel something twisting in her, something that was knotted and couldn't untangle. I sat there on her lap, soaking up her warmth and soft smell, until my brother began to cry and she put me down.

—⁓—

At Christmas all the church kids were commissioned to be an angel choir, and kindly Eleanor Smithson with the shining dark hair had fastened white capes and deep red ribbons around our shoulders. We filed down the sanctuary under the gracious, soaring arch of the ceiling. I felt so important walking down that aisle in my red plaid dress and my white angel cape, and then I felt it—God's love! Oh, I could feel it in my heart for the first time!

Thank goodness.

We sang in the candlelight, and the rosy walls of the sanctuary glowed, and the smiling congregation beamed at us. The enormous Christmas tree twinkled its white lights in the corner and I knew then that we were holy, we were God's children, and I felt enveloped in the warm cocoon of light, buoyed up by our singing. I blurred my eyes so that the world softened and the sounds slowed down. I felt myself float a little.

Then the pastor went up to the pulpit, and something strange happened. He called my mom and dad's names, and they stood up in their shiny wooden pew, shy and proud. My mother reached into the angel choir, took me by the hand, and led me out of the group of children and up the red carpeted steps toward the pulpit.

Suddenly the lights came on and hit me in the eye. We were up there on the stage and everyone was looking, and I felt naked and tried to hide behind my mother. My dad picked me up and cradled me against his chest, and then, to my utmost dismay, he started speaking into the microphone. I curled into a tiny ball.

"Merry Christmas." You could hear the grin in his voice. My daddy was always grinning.

From out in the dark the congregation chorused back, "Merry Christmas!"

"I'm not a pastor, you know—I'm just a businessman. I understand accounting and numbers, not preaching and leading a church. But here at Trinity Missionary Church, you know we're all about spreading God's word. And I had this strange feeling that I was supposed to go. But it didn't make any sense. Was I supposed to go be a pastor? That didn't seem right—I've got no business being up in this pulpit!" The congregation's low chuckle rolled toward us, and I burrowed deeper. "And then that night our missionary from Africa talked about how preachers and pastors were trying to run their missions, trying to keep track of their finances and find people houses and schools, and I thought—well, I could do that. And then Elizabeth here"—he put his arm around my mother and she smiled at him and boosted my brother higher on her hip—"she told me that God had laid it on her heart, too, that we should be missionaries. And we'd both thought we were crazy! But God had been speaking to us separately. It seems almost like a miracle, that two Kentucky country kids like us would end up going someplace like Japan. But we got the call." There was a murmur of approval from the congregation. "So here we are. We're going to go, and we'll spread God's word doing a job I know how to do, supporting those missionaries so that they can build their churches and spread the truth. Thank you so much for raising the money to send us. We'll miss you. God bless you."

The congregation hurled applause at us, and the pastor came over and laid his hand on my mother and father. I could feel his warm breath on my hair.

"Father God, we ask your blessing on your faithful children, Virgil and Elizabeth, as they follow your commandment to spread the gospel to all the corners of the earth. We know that you'll keep them safe, and their little children, even as they travel to the other side of the world. We pray

11

for all those souls around the world living in darkness. We pray, Lord God, that they will see the light. We pray for every soul who is living without your love and we ask that they may find the Truth and turn from the error of their ways. We send these faithful servants, Lord, to do Your will. Bless them and keep them, and make your face shine upon them. Amen, Lord. Thank you. Amen."

In my father's arms, scalded in the bright lights, I tried my very best to disappear.

CHAPTER 2

The world had tilted. We were getting off an airplane in Japan.

It was just after my fifth birthday. I had received a raincoat and umbrella for my big present, which made me feel very grown up. I would need to think about things like rain now. Also maybe something called bills.

We burst out of the Narita Airport customs gate like soda out of a bottle, spraying our luggage and stroller everywhere. I was amazed and unhappy to see my parents standing in the middle of an enormous crowd of people and turning around and around trying to get their bearings. Things were whirling too fast, like a merry-go-round commandeered by mean kids, and I felt like I might spin right off the edge.

Suddenly two enormously tall old people swooped down. They hugged and patted and exclaimed and piled the luggage higher on the little cart and herded us into an elevator. They had oddly dashing hair, and I studied them closely, because they were the first real live "missionaries" I'd ever seen up close. I wondered if my parents would have to cut their hair like that too, if maybe it was part of becoming missionaries. They stuffed the four of us and our luggage into a battered van, and we were off. Everything felt backward, and I realized the steering wheel was on the wrong side of the car. The roads were tiny, ridiculous, obviously too narrow to contain our careening load. I could hear my mother suck in air every time they rounded a corner, and I thought we'd all be bashed to pieces. Instead, the happy old people passed back goody bags.

"These are for you two. Our own kids are all too big for all this stuff now! We are just, oh my goodness, *so* glad you're here—there aren't enough children at The Center! Do you know what The Center is?"

I nodded. It was where we would be living.

"You're just gonna love it. There's a playroom, and a big yard, and there's even a library...." They kept talking, but I was too enthralled by my goody bag to pay attention.

There were miniature boxes of chocolate cereal in there. There were waxy, oily crayons in colors that weren't Crayola. There was even a pad of drawing paper with pink bunnies on the front. I stared more closely; even though I couldn't read, I could tell that none of the writing looked right. It was a pretty serious haul, considering that we hadn't seen most of our toys in weeks. Our family's things wouldn't be coming for months-- they were traveling to Japan in something called a container, which I imagined floating across the ocean like a big yellow raft.

"Whoooah," my dad said jovially a few times, in his "I'm being a good sport" voice, peering out the window at the telephone pole inches from his face. I could tell from the way she was staring straight ahead that my mother was trying not to get carsick. Then we pulled up an impossibly steep hill and rolled to a stop in front of a building covered in ivy.

It was huge, like a castle made of brown rocks. I gripped my mother's hand. My dad hoisted two suitcases. Jake had his first two fingers shoved solidly in his mouth. We all walked down a wide gravel path with flower-beds on either side and came to the entryway. The great door was made of shining red wood, and it was thick as a tree when it swung open. A whole host of kindly people beckoned us in, murmuring and welcoming, and so I stepped shyly forward by myself.

A sweet-faced woman with pointy glasses on a chain around her neck smiled at me. But something strange happened. Although she kept smiling, her voice stabbed at me. I felt little cold needles thud into my chest.

"Oh dear, the children will have to learn to take their shoes off, won't they," she said, and all eyes swung down to my cherry-red Mary Janes. Oh! My whole body went hot. Unthinkingly, I had stepped up from the gray flat stones of the entryway onto the glossy wooden floor. "But I did know," I wanted to say, "I just forgot!"

My mother had read me stacks of books about Japan before we came. After Mieko, she had plowed through incredibly boring books filled with pictures of girls holding peaches and spinach, with pale pink flowers and tiny pine trees dancing above their heads. I knew that for "yes" you said "hai," and for "no" you waved your hand in front of your face. There was a word for "no" but you weren't allowed to say it. We were prepared.

Naturally I knew all about this basic yet mystifying rule of our new home: no shoes inside the houses. I had even been practicing. I was so proud of how I could take my shoes off all by my five-year-old self, maneuvering the tiny little buckle closure and stiff leather strap all on my own. I was primed and eager to show off my buckle prowess. But here I was, just a stupid little girl who didn't know any better than to wear her shoes inside.

These warm old white people had beckoned to me, waved me in so that they could hug me and pat me, but even with the best of intentions I had tracked mud onto their floor. Oh dear. Me and the missionaries.

The hubbub was incredible.

"Oh, Virgil and Elizabeth, you sweet things, welcome to Japan!"

"Welcome to the family." My dad was shaking hands with an older man with a white beard.

"We've got everything all ready for you; you'll be too busy with language school to do any cooking for a while!" My mother was being smothered in a huge hug by a big grandmotherly woman.

The gathered group treated my parents like children: clucky and sugary. It was eerie to see my parents take our place, being prodded and beamed at and patted. I felt like I was looking at them from very far away, and they looked smaller than usual.

Eventually the throng picked up our suitcases, watched us all step into green plastic slippers, and took us up a wide gleaming staircase and then down a slippery hall to a door. Deep inside the bowels of that huge behemoth was a little set of rooms for our family. They called it an apartment, but since our door opened out onto the same wide hall where everyone walked to get to the chapel and the phone, it was more like having rooms in a hotel.

My mother stepped in gingerly.

"Do we wear our slippers in here?" she asked.

The grandmother lady laughed. "Of course, honey. You only need to take your slippers off on the tatami mats."

"Oh, I see." My mother looked flattened. It was cramped like a dollhouse in there, but old and mismatched and cold.

"Don't step on that hose, children!" The needles thudded me again. The sweet-faced lady pointed at a heater contraption with a shockingly orange hose. I was suddenly afraid that now I would step on it in spite of myself, out of pure orneriness, even though I'd had no desire to a minute ago.

"And your clothes can go in here—" drawers opening—"and we'll just set your suitcase right here and get it opened up, and—oh, Elizabeth dear—this bag is toiletries, right? I'll just get your medicine cabinet set up." My mother opened her mouth, then closed it again.

Almost every room in the "apartment," as they called it, had a sliding door that opened onto the main hallway thoroughfare. My brother and I were in two bunk beds that butted up against a frosted glass door. On the other side of that door, you could see dim shapes moving as people walked through the hallway.

My mother was standing perfectly still in the room that would be my parents' bedroom.

"Mommy, look!" I scrambled up to the enormous round shape in the wall right by their bed. I opened and closed the paper sliding screens and discovered it was a huge round hole. I hung the whole top half of my body out of it, and gazed out into the same gleaming hallway.

"That's a moon window," said a younger missionary with red curly hair. She winked. "Although it's not like you can see the moon out of it—just the people passing by. I guess they didn't think about the fact that you're a married couple and might want some privacy."

"But it's—it's just paper," whispered my mother. "And you can open it from the outside. From the hallway."

"Yup," grinned the redhead. "Welcome to The Center."

The first night we slept in The Center, we all woke up thrashing back and forth in our beds. My mother appeared in the doorway, and then my dad grabbed me down from the top bunk and I realized it wasn't just my bed but the whole building that was shaking.

"Earthquake!" my dad said excitedly, like this was the best fair ride ever. We lurched out of the bedroom and the four of us scrambled under the kitchen table the way we'd learned in our books, but by the time we got properly wedged under it, the building had stopped shuddering.

I rubbed my eyes. I was starving, and I wondered if my mom would let me eat some of that chocolate cereal. I doubted it; she didn't believe in refined sugar. At home she'd always served oatmeal or homemade granola. My stomach growled, and we were squished together in our pajamas under the spindly table legs. I wondered if everyone else all throughout The Center was under their tables too. The shaking had stopped but the windows and shutters were still chattering, and the noise echoed through the enormous building. Something inside me was still shivering too, but Jake was bouncing up and down because he was still a baby and didn't know that we were obviously in dire danger.

Then, suddenly, my dad began to chuckle. He laughed so hard, big helpless whoops of hilarity, that I started to feel tickly inside too. I understood that we were going to be brave. Jake crowed in glee. In a minute, my mother joined in.

"Okay, Lord," she said, looking up at the underside of the table, "I sure hope You know what You're doing."

"Mommy? Can I have some chocolate cereal?"

"I want some too," said my dad. And so we sat around the table that first night spooning sugary chocolate milky contraband into our mouths.

"I can't believe we're up in the middle of the night!" I marveled.

"It's jet lag, honey," said my mom.

"It's an adventure," said my dad.

The whole building was dark and silent around us, but our little family fit snugly around the yellow circle of our kitchen table.

The Center looked as formidable as its name. It was a sort of halfway house for missionaries who needed to spend several years studying Japanese before they spoke it well enough to preach the gospel and convert the heathen.

It was like a whole village contained in one massive stone building. There was a great sense of hustle and bustle, of things being accomplished, though I didn't exactly know what they were. Even looking back, the whole thing seems like a very complicated Victorian machine that required great amounts of coal and produced enormous amounts of steam, whose sole purpose was to create—well, it wasn't clear. A single gumdrop? A Bible Study? Maybe one convert every few years? Proselytizing in Japan is a daunting prospect. Less than 1 percent of the population identifies as Christian, and most churches, even after years of loving work and dozens of missionaries, have fewer than fifty members. Being a missionary to Japan is a heroic and noble act of thankless service, or a quixotic exercise in futility, depending on how you see the world. But my parents were full of hope and Jesus's love. They were, and are, true believers. They prayed every night for the people of Japan, that they would know of God's great love. I prayed along: yes, yes! God's great love!

I didn't mention that I was still waiting to feel it too.

Down the grand staircase, on the first floor, was the central office, where my father went to work after finishing up his language classes each day. It was strictly off limits, and I would peer longingly through the glass-paned door into an exotic world of copy machines, paper cutters, and a stapler as big as a grown-up's arm. Upstairs was the chapel, which was even more off-limits than the office. There was a communal kitchen: a huge green room with fluorescent light buzzing off the enormous pots and kettles. And there was a twisty and dusty *mono-oki*, a storage space bigger than my imagination, which held luggage and furniture and a woodworking shop.

Although my dad wore a suit every day to go downstairs and through that glass door into the office, in my mind's eye he looked the way he did in my favorite photograph of my parents. It was tucked into our family album and I liked it even better than their wedding photo. In the picture, which I knew had been taken before I was born, my father was wearing his favorite red plaid flannel shirt and my mother wore a crocheted poncho. His hair was longer, dark and curling around his ears, and he didn't have a beard yet. My mother's hair was parted down the middle and hung down almost to her waist. They were both wearing enormously bell-bottomed jeans and grinning. Radiant.

But a muddy layer came over them when we were living in the Center. My mom's shiny hair turned dull and lifeless. (It turned out that she'd been using conditioner instead of shampoo; she couldn't read the label.) My father, usually so full of games and jokes, stolidly carried around little stacks of flashcards on a key ring. These were the size of a pack of gum, and he would flip through them anxiously, trying to imprint himself with the dozens of *kanji* characters he was supposed to be memorizing each week. There was a tightness in the air; a high keening sound like an invisible teakettle.

It felt good to slip out of our pinched apartment and slide out onto the wide slippery hallways. There was a sideboard just outside our entryway with a low pottery dish on it, and out of the dish sprung the most beautiful flowers I had ever seen. They looked so sprightly and alive, and seemed to be almost swaying, as if they were still growing in the ground. I stood there marveling at them one day, and the same sweet-faced woman came up behind me.

"No touching, dear," she smiled. No matter where I was, I seemed to bother her. I couldn't believe that she had made that beautiful flower arrangement. I longed to know how she had done it; when I picked flowers and stuck them in vases, they flopped over and looked dead.

The mystery and forbidden status of the chapel down the hall from us made it irresistible to my brother and me. Sunday mornings and wedding days, it would be lined with rows and rows of folding chairs, but during the week the enormous expanse of smooth gray carpet sat empty, smooth, and inviting. The air in there was holy and quiet and made me sneeze. Jake and I wanted more than anything to run across that huge, empty space in our bare feet, and so that was what we did; we ran. And ran. And ran. We'd run from one end of the room to the other, exhilarating ourselves with our own speed and cunning, or sometimes have races to see who could do a series of somersaults fastest and without getting sick. We could do this for hours. There was only one problem: a watchful old couple lived right across the hall from the door of the chapel, so all of this running and somersaulting had to be done in absolute silence. I wasn't sure what they would do if they found us, but probably they would spank us, I thought. At the very least they would tell our parents, and then *they* would certainly spank us. I dreaded those spankings more than anything: my sweet parents disappeared and something else roared into the room, something that hated us. It would destroy us if it could, I knew; all you could do was hold on and try to survive the annihilation. Then after the spankings my parents came back, and it was time to kiss and hug and make up. I shuddered and vowed to be perfectly quiet so we wouldn't get caught.

This older couple down the hall looked like Mr. and Mrs. Claus, all jolly red cheeks and big bright stories. They had raised five kids in Japan. Back then, all the laundry had to be done by hand. Every missionary family had at least one maid, and the Japanese government required foreigners to bring in three years' worth of food so they wouldn't put a burden on the fragile post-war economy. Back then, missionaries hadn't bothered to learn to read and write Japanese; it was deemed impossibly foreign. They learned to speak Japanese and simply wrote it out phonetically in English. This made sense to everyone, especially Japanese people, because Japan was such a mysterious place that no foreigner could ever be expected to truly comprehend it. Certainly the gauche foreigners with their big noses and embarrassing smells would never be able to speak the ancient and subtle language of Japanese with anything resembling proper pronunciation. And so the foreigners remained respected outsiders, tall giraffes who made cups of tea and taught knitting classes. (Though sometimes they were reviled conquerors, white devils who'd dethroned the emperor and ruined everything. You never knew which it would be.)

These older missionaries seemed continually surprised by what seemed to me to be extreme old age. They wore clothes that had been fashionable in the 1960s, or even the 1940s. This made sense, since no one could fit into the tiny Japanese sizes and all their clothes had to be shipped over in missionary barrels, by boat. You never knew what the good church-folk back home might send: sometimes glamorous furs, sometimes clunky oxfords. Sometimes used tea bags (only used once, though!) for the grateful missionaries. The staunch old guard remembered a time when Tokyo was rebuilding itself from the rubble and people were hungry. They were not impressed by two whippersnappers who liked to investigate places that Children Should Not Go—like the cupboard that held the communion cups (darling tiny little flutes under a great silver dome) and the wedding dress room.

Oh, the wedding dress room! It was a Cinderella fantasy come true, like something out of a fairy tale: pretty, pretty dresses by the dozen. True, it was crawling with bugs and you could hardly go in there without sneezing your head off, but it was full of actual real wedding dresses that the mission would loan out to the young Christian brides getting married in the chapel. I tried on most of them at some point, lugging the heavy beaded bodices to look at my reflection in a mirror, or swishing a long train behind me in the elegant manner of a lady from *Mary Poppins*, one of the only movies I had ever seen.

The Center was made up of long shimmering hallways, and chopping up those hallways were ledges for the fire doors: metal frames covered in layers of thick cream-colored paint that jutted three inches out from the walls, ceiling, and floor. They were good markers for races and games and obstacle courses, for leaping over and balancing on, but agony on the toes, the whole body slammed and reeling, if you forgot to watch for them. It was a beautiful, dangerous place, The Center.

The sweet-faced needle lady, Miss Dorothea, grew all the flowers, and I loved them in a way I had no words for. I loved them so much that it embarrassed me. I would tiptoe into the garden to smell the roses, and feel an incredible comfort fill up my lungs and seep down to my arms and legs. It felt like my whole body was going pink. I was surprised to discover that even the yellow and red roses made my body go pink inside. I puzzled over why this might be.

One day I was letting my body fill up with pink and floating between the rosebushes, making up a little song about the petals and their pink magic.

Suddenly I felt the needles, and there was Miss Dorothea shouting my full name. A name that felt so unlike me, so *not mine*, that as an adult I would change it.

Boom. I swung down to the ground in a jarring panic. I wished my mother had not told the missionaries my middle name—I hated how they flung it at me.

"How dare you walk through my flowerbeds?" Miss Dorothea was striding toward me, and her face was livid. "Don't you have any respect, young lady? You'll trample my flowers."

I just stared at her, feeling the words stop up my mouth. Of course I wasn't going to step on the flowers. I was there to gentle them, to stroke them. I wondered that she could look at me and not see that. We stood there, staring at each other. I still had some of the pink in me, and I felt very calm as I looked at the damp gray cloud swirling around her. But then, bit by bit, my pink drained out and I felt her cold fog seep into me. Before I knew it, tears were running down my face. I ran indoors to find my mother, but I knew I was in disgrace. Miss Dorothea announced at dinner that *children* were no longer allowed in the garden. Hot bile rushed through me as I stared at the purple juice in my cup. Everyone knew it was me. I could tell by the way that they smiled at me, those amused, understanding smiles.

I didn't understand how someone so mean could make so much beauty. I kept sneaking in to look at the flowers even though I knew I wasn't supposed to go there any more. Over by the lilies, there was a murky little *koi* pond with so much green gunk growing in the water that even the orange carp looked faintly moldy. There was a gnarled persimmon tree against the fence. A swath of pristine gravel swept up to the grand main entrance. The gravel had stepping stones in it that you were supposed to step on, but they were too far apart for my feet to reach. Nonetheless, the rule was: don't leave marks in the gravel. So I had to be extra careful when I went to visit the crazy purple cabbages by the front door. They were so ugly, so compelling, such grotesque brittle rubbery shredded excuses for flowers, that I would crouch and stare at them in amazement, losing myself in their whorls and veins.

There were anywhere from fifteen to thirty people living in The Center at any point, and during the day it filled up with more. On a wedding or meeting day, there might be over a hundred. But most of the two years we lived there, my brother and I were the only children in the building. Several nights of the week, the Center staff would cook dinner for everyone, and we would all sit down together in the great dining hall on the first floor. The table was covered in green vinyl, the cups were crackled gold plastic. We had dutifully washed our hands in the icy cold water of the bathroom, scrubbed hard to raise a lather from the slivers of soap in the red plastic netting pouch tied to the faucet.

A mysterious thing: there was a brand new box of pearly pink oval soaps sitting underneath the sink, and I never understood why we had to use cracked gray shards instead of the pretty pink. The whole two years we lived there, those soaps stayed there in their packaging, untouched little gems.

Dinner began with a prayer. I couldn't reach my plate unless I sat up on my knees. Everyone asked me questions and didn't listen to my answers. The dinners went on forever and I watched my parents sit there, making conversation and growing exhausted. After a while I would be excused and I'd go out into the empty big hallway and drink from the ancient drinking fountain. Since no one was watching, I put my mouth right onto the spigot, savoring the delicious taste of the metal. I couldn't get enough of that metallic ice water; I sucked and sucked until my belly ached.

After dinner we would head to one of the two *ofuro* baths; each family could reserve a time slot, and the four of us took our bath together. First there was an icy cold entry room where we stood on wooden slats raised off the concrete. There we took off our clothes and put them in baskets on the shelves. Then we stepped into the even colder tiled *ofuro* room itself.

You were supposed to sit on the little wooden stools, pull big dippers of boiling water out of the big tub, and wash yourself completely before you got in to soak. It was impossible. The water was scalding; enough to turn a grownup's body bright red in seconds. Even my father had to ease in slowly. My mother, however, loved it. Everyone called her "asbestos hands" growing up because she has almost no sensitivity to heat and would sometimes pull hot pans directly out of the oven with her bare hands.

One day someone came to speak to my mother. There were quiet, angry voices, and no one looked at us. My mother sat down with us. Someone had defecated in the bath. This was a very big deal, because they drew a fresh tub only once on bath days, and everyone in the Center shared the same water. The idea was that you scrubbed yourself clean, rinsed off, and only then got into the water to soak. In theory, then, the water was still "clean" for the next people.

It wasn't us, we said.

She said she believed us. But obviously no one else did.

I was furious—I was FIVE years old, not some baby. I wouldn't poop in the tub—I couldn't even get in that scalding water! The missionaries just smiled compassionately at us, forgiving us, being benevolent. I could feel it, all those surreptitious eyes watching us. I hated those eyes.

On laundry day the big laundry room would be hung with white sheets, rows and rows, and the windows let in bars of sunshine and the room was sliced into ribbons of light. This room felt intensely familiar to me. I walked through the rows of laundry, trailing my fingers on the sheets, feeling my vision blur. The light shafted and shifted, and I could feel the floors within me shift with them. I felt like I was an apartment building, with six or seven floors inside me that were usually all squished up into my chest. Something about that room caused things in my body to shift and readjust until the floors tumbled neatly down to the ground in even, orderly stair steps. In the laundry room, I wanted to fold down onto my knees and bow my head. I wouldn't have called it "praying," exactly, but I wanted to sit perfectly still in that vast white fluttering cathedral.

Sometimes when I wandered around the building and the gardens by myself, I could feel something golden and liquid come over me. The crooked pine trees seemed like they were talking to me, and I would sit in the grass and listen. A tiny buzzing part of my mind kept on worrying that a bug would crawl up my leg or that I was going to get in trouble for something, but the rest of me was utterly drunk. The bliss seemed to swoop between the trees, slide down the light, seep up through the flowers, and straight into me. When the golden feeling filled me up, I often felt like someone, or maybe a whole circle of someones, was watching me, but I never felt afraid. They were almost always there at the very edge of my awareness, fuzzy and ignored, but when I sat quietly like this with the light pooling inside me I could feel them. They grew warm and dense and friendly, but they never spoke and they never came closer. Sometimes I would feel so full of the gold that I had to get up and do impromptu dances, and the air swirled through my fingers like a sleepy river.

Even indoors, the old building had spots so quiet, where the sun streamed in so golden and yellow on the wide floorboards, that I would lie down and feel the gold seep right into my soul. *I could fly*, I would think; *this gold could make me fly*. Then I would run down the slippery stairs in my socks, hanging onto the banister for dear life and careening around the corner in a quick twirling spin, half sliding, half jumping, mostly flying. I tried to do all this without being seen, because if I got caught by one of the missionaries, I would get scolded and told to go play in the playroom.

The playroom, a dank musty hole in the back of the building, had nasty teal carpet and ancient mildewed picture books, the kind that talked about "virtue" and "modesty." It was a terrible, terrible place. A rickety bouncy horse was suspended on springs from a hollow metal-tubed frame. When in use, it sounded just like the creaking of bedsprings; sometimes rhythmical and rocking, sometimes violent. When I was in there by myself, I would feel so pressed on, so smothered by a dark gray fog, that I would have to run out like a scared little baby and find my mother.

The world of a child is so narrow. It's a series of tunnels, really, burrowing through the middle of things with no sense of what lies outside. The path to the street, the sidewalk squares that lead to the park, the plants and trees and porches along the way—these make up a child's reality so entirely. I lived, like most children, inside the skin of my family, enclosed in the rhythms and familiar objects of our days. Anything outside of that skin was as incomprehensible as the solar system.

And so when we moved to Japan, all that changed for me was the interior of that tunnel. The immediate world was different: we lived in The Center now. Our walls were dark swirled wood instead of clean white paint. Instead of neighbors, we had missionaries. But I had no real understanding of what it meant to be on the other side of the globe, no context for just how different the world around me was—a different country, culture, continent. I just knew that instead of Indianapolis's square leafy sidewalks, we walked from the dark curlicue maze of the Center down steep winding paths carved between high cement walls, a riot of houses jammed in together everywhere I looked.

It was all different, the smells of fish and sewer and tofu pressing in close and hot. But that skin I touched, the membrane of the world that rose up to meet me, would have been just as different in Pittsburgh, or San Francisco, or Chicago. What I had no way of knowing, no context for possibly comprehending, was that the whole trajectory of my life had just shifted, spinning away from the little square house on the green square block of a square city to take us all somewhere vastly, wildly foreign.

For foreigners we were indeed—my dad towering, my mom the object of constant staring, Jake and me gawked at like we had three heads and twelve eyes.

"*Tenshi mitai*, she looks like an angel!" people would say. "Can I have a strand of her hair?" My mother always smiled graciously, but I felt sick and twisty inside. Still, I usually plucked out a blonde frizzy hair anyway and handed it to the stranger. They would tuck it away in a pocket or a purse.

"*Gaijin da! Gaijin da!*" was the phrase we heard yelled umpteen times a day— the word for foreigner that literally means "one who is outside or other."

That wasn't as irritating as the ubiquitous phrase "*Jees eezu a penn*!!!!"—the only phrase that seemed to remain from the hours of mandatory English study. Total strangers would walk up and yell it at us—children and teens, but also men in suits and ladies in hats. It took us several weeks to figure out that they were saying—"This is a pen" in their best English—but this realization didn't exactly help us come up with a snappy reply.

Today, foreigners in Tokyo are as common a sight as potato chips. Many Japanese people use the less derogatory *gaikokujin* instead of *gaijin*—i.e., someone from another country as opposed to just flat-out alien—but in a dirty little backwater of Yokohama, in 1982, we might as well have been purple elephants lumbering down the streets. We were fair game.

Our part of town was what was called *sabireta*, which means that it was fraying around the edges and decidedly shabby. Grown men picked their noses on the trains and urinated on the side of the streets. There were pictures of half-naked women stapled to every wooden surface. You could smell the sour stink of beer and sake all day long. Men with very curly hair (it was called a "punch perm," a super-fro) walked around in old-lady plastic sandals that were too small for their feet. The gaudy silver webbing stretched over their toes and their heels hung off the back. Even well-dressed people had brown teeth.

But we were the foul and disgusting ones, committing such mortifying breaches of decency as holding our chopsticks wrong and not bowing correctly. Worse was accidentally wearing the bathroom slippers into the rest of the house. There was no pretending it hadn't happened; you'd look down and see the silhouette of the little boy peeing, his tiny penis spurting a big fountain, emblazoned in bright black against the pink plastic slippers.

Sometimes when we were done with our grocery shopping, my mom took us for respite into a little coffee shop for the ultimate treat, warm milk for us and a strong coffee for her. This was long before anyone in Indiana knew about espresso, and my mother winced and poured in loads of milk. "It's so smoky in here," she whispered. "Are you guys okay?" We were more than okay; we were in heaven. Jake and I each got our own mugs of warm milk, oh, the richness of it! And there on the table was a golden glass jar of rock sugar, and we could take the little spoon and dump in heaps of the brown crackly crystals. It was so decadent and elegant, and my brother and I sat there grinning at each other in the warmth, luxuriating in it all, not even minding the people watching us out of the corners of their eyes.

As my mother rushed us past blaring pachinko gambling parlors and fragrant fish stalls, little filaments of beauty still snuck through and tapped me on the shoulder: hydrangeas spilling over walls and moss growing thick, the cherry trees dropping petals like pink snow, the faded orange kerchiefs on the *jizo* statues, the women in *kimono*—rare enough to seem like silk birds—and the tiny lunches called *obento* in their artistic, deep red lacquered boxes. These moments jolted me. A sad, sweet persimmon glow would bloom in my chest.

"Mommy, is the chapel our church?" We were walking up the long hill back to the Center. My mother pulled a wheeled bag of groceries behind her.

"Not exactly. The church is the wooden building next door where we go every Sunday. You know, where they make the curry rice for lunch?"

"So why can't we play in the chapel?"

She sighed and readjusted the handle of the cart, which would come clean off if you didn't hold it at the exact right angle. "It's sort of hard to explain. The chapel is where the missionaries worship."

"Why don't we worship in church?"

"Well, we do that too, but it's all in Japanese. So sometimes we need to talk to God in our own language."

I didn't particularly want to talk to God in any language just then, so I changed the subject.

"How come you can speak Japanese better than Daddy can?"

"Oh, sweetie. I can't, really."

"Yes you can. It sounds better when you do it."

"But Daddy can read and write, and I can't do that yet."

They both spent hours every day hunched over desks, staring at sheets of paper with strange spiky writing on it. They practiced their character strokes on pale gray worksheets and listened to cassette tapes on headphones. My father went off every day to spend even more time at school, and my mother worked twice a week with a tutor, who also taught her Japanese cooking. This was good, because you couldn't buy most American ingredients in the grocery store: no roasts, no spaghetti, no pork chops, no baking powder. We held up unfamiliar vegetables and puzzled over what one might do with *daikon* radishes as long as my arm, lotus and bamboo, and burdock.

Mom was so proud when she showed us her first Japanese dish: a bowl of rice with bonito flakes writhing on top.

"Look, guys! The heat from the rice makes them flutter. And then we pour soy sauce over the top, like this—my teacher says that this is what Japanese kids eat all the time for a snack. Doesn't it look good?"

My brother took a bite and spat it out. Mine tasted salty, and something else, too—a taste that went up into my nose. Fishy.

"Mommy? Can we have a bowl of peanut butter and honey instead?"

We sat at the table as the sun went down, my mother deftly raising the rice and fish flakes to her mouth with her long slender chopsticks, my brother and I stirring our peanut butter and honey into a mad swirl with our spoons.

There is a photograph of me ironing handkerchiefs in our Center apartment. My white-blond fuzzy hair is flowing straight upward in a whorl of crackling energy, brushed into such a halo of frizz and static it looks like it might levitate. But I am focused on ironing a white handkerchief into a perfect white square, folded in quarters, creasing the corners razor sharp. I am standing amidst the rubble of our usual household chaos: bags and papers and coats piled on the ugly rattan sofa picked out by someone else, a pile of laundry mounded on the rug that some other missionary family had left stains on. But in my little kingdom, I am making little squares of order with maniacal fervor.

—m—

My mother had a surprise for me.

She led me through the chapel to a little door right next to the wedding dress room.

"This is going to be our special place, honey. It's going to be a schoolroom for you!"

She slid open the door and revealed a tiny room set up like a miniature schoolhouse. There was a blackboard, a wooden desk for her, and a metal tubing desk for me. Bright alphabet posters circled the room, and there was a brand new pad of paper sitting on my desk.

"I'm going to be your teacher. You'll be speaking Japanese at kindergarten, so I'm going to teach you to read and write English in here. We'll come here for a little bit every day after school."

I looked around. There was a stack of schoolbooks, a pencil sharpener mounted on the wall, a box of colored chalk. She was watching me, beaming.

My whole body itched. I felt hot and feverish and wanted to run outside. I sat down slowly at the desk and ran my fingers over the rough tan paper with its pale blue lines. Everything ached.

"I don't want to," I whispered.

She smiled, but stood up straighter. "Well, you have to."

Our daily lessons were mother-daughter bonding times of mutual loathing and misery. It was so tedious, the rules of phonics so stupid and frustrating, a system made more of aberrations than rules, and I never could get my head around it. And yet at some point, in spite of the whining, the yelling, the spankings, the intense physical wretchedness of sitting in that wooden chair, one day I simply could read.

And the world opened up.

—m—

The street leading up to the Center had small circular indentations pressed into the cement. They were for traction on the steep hill, but they presented a maddening kind of game that could be played two ways. The first way was to *only* step on the rings in set patterns: every other one, or every one in a diagonal zigzag, or every third one. Or, you could play by carefully angling your feet so that the edges of your shoe fit cleanly into the spaces *between* the rings, never touching them. In the mornings, I would start down the hill slowly, setting my feet purposefully down on the ground and feeling my toes slide down the incline until they were jammed against the end of the shoe. Then gradually, no matter what I did, I would pick up speed until I was in a desperate race to keep my feet moving fast enough to catch up with my body. The hill was so steep that if you stood at right angles to the ground your head would be considerably in front of your feet, so that by the bottom of the hill I was literally flying, the rubber on the bottom of my shoes hot, barely touching the ground it seemed, then slowly thudding down to a normal run. My kindergarten bag would bang up and down on my back, and the cup and shoe bag that were slung from it would lurch wildly, knocking into my side.

Kindergarten would mark the time I joined other schoolchildren. Before it started, the supplies had arrived: stacks of Japanese books, *Coupy* colored pencils that were smooth sticks of color with no wood, waxy oil pastels, blue plastic scissors. There were sheets and sheets of tiny nameplate stickers, and my mother carefully wrote my name in Japanese and pasted one on every single crayon and book. Along with the supplies was a stack of instructions for her. I would need a cloth lunchbox case, a smock for art days, a divided holder for my fork and spoon, a book bag, and a dozen other complicated items that had to be made to specific measurements, even down to what size the buttons could be. Naturally, all the instructions were in Japanese. The mothers were to sew these.

I watched my mother weep over her sewing machine. I saw her throw her spool of thread across the room. I saw her painstakingly cut out the blue calico Holly Hobbie silhouette that she hand-stitched onto my brown corduroy book bag. I saw how proud she was of my crisp ironed kindergarten smock that first day, when I donned my uniform hat and squinted into the sun, clutching the regulation bag that held all my mother's handiwork.

When we got there that first day, it turned out that my bag was way too big. The instructions had been in centimeters, not inches. I was appalled that they would do that to my mother.

Still, kindergarten was a place where we took naps every day, played in the dirt with our skirts bundled up with rubber bands, and sang songs in unison while we clapped along on our little blue and red castanets.

With other kids, it was straightforward. Pointing, smacking, crying—clear communication at its finest. I could usually gather what they meant, even if I didn't understand the words.

"Come on!" my new friends called. "Want to swing with us?"

"Coming!" I called back. Then I stopped, amazed at what had just spilled out of my own mouth. Japanese, like it was the most natural thing in the world. Suddenly, it flowed through me with no effort at all.

—⁕—

My first Japanese friend was Chiyoko-*chan*. She had two long glossy braids, front teeth that were brown and scabbed like tree bark, and she lived in a house in the woods, like Laura Ingalls. Chiyoko-*chan*'s woods were bamboo and they whispered in an unkind way as I passed through them. I had this sense that it was the great-grandmother who was having the bamboo rustle at me as I raced through. She didn't like me very much. Their house was at the top of a hill, like The Center. Our hills were neighbors. You could have leapt straight from The Center to her house, if you could fly; and I wouldn't have been surprised if her grandmother actually *could* fly.

Later in my life I did the math and realized that her great-grandmother was surely already dead by the time I knew Chiyoko-*chan*, but in my memory the old woman is there at the edge of the clearing, sweeping, glaring at me. It was scary after dark and on the rare occasion when her father was home.

To get to Chiyoko-*chan*'s house, I had to go down the hill along the twisty road where the rusty metal houses hugged the steep slope. Then past the temple and up the stone stairs along the concrete wall, and then I was into the bamboo forest. More stairs here, but these were crooked and uneven and made of stone. There were thousands of them, and you couldn't drive a car up close to the house. When the green sewage truck came to suck out their septic tank every month, it couldn't get up those massive stairs, so they had to snake the brown-green hose all the way up the hill and through the bamboo like an ambitious caterpillar. It smelled unbelievably vile. But other than that, Chiyoko-*chan*'s house was magic.

There was a little shrine inside the house that Chiyoko-*chan* told me was where her dead ancestors lived. She was quite friendly with their ghosts, who would sometimes help her with her homework, but I knew better than to look at the shrine because obviously it had evil demon spirits in it that could leap out and take over my soul.

Evil was highly contagious. You could catch it, like the measles. The veteran missionaries warned us that the devil's minions were everywhere. They saturated the gentle Shinto shrines, they were most definitely lurking in the rows of *jizo* statues honoring dead babies and aborted spirits, and they could even be in the tiny *omamori* good-luck charms people carried. But especially, they warned us, those demons were clustered thick in the family altars.

A book on Japan would have told you that those altars, with their little bells and sticks of incense and flowers, were the place in every Japanese home where people honored and remembered their beloved ancestors. However, according to the missionaries, the altars tempted people to pray to evil spirits and invite the devil into their homes. I wasn't sure what I was supposed to do—Chiyoko-*chan* always ran in and clapped her hands in front of the altar right away when she got home. I didn't want to be rude, but I knew I wasn't allowed to look at the altar or clap to it. So I did a funny bobbing kind of dance, clasping my hands together in a muffled clap that I told myself could also be interpreted as a kind of prayer to Jesus. And then I tried not to look at the altar, with its dull gold bowl and the sticks of incense. But the strips of paper above it were always fluttering. If I'd known about the sign of the cross, I would have made it, but we were Protestants and didn't have such comforts. So there was nothing to protect me from the tendrils that snuck out from the shrine and snuck up my pant legs. I tried to tuck my knees under me tight. But I was pretty sure it wasn't tight enough; I was pretty sure I was being contaminated. I was too ashamed to tell my mother, and also I loved Chiyoko-*chan* very much. It was a dilemma.

The adults took this business of evil spirits very seriously. A Japanese friend gave my mother an ornate Japanese doll as a welcome present, telling her, "This doll told me that she wanted to come live with Elizabeth-*san*." The specific phrasing spooked my mother so much that she placed the doll deep inside a dark cupboard. The doll wore a beautiful purple *kimono* but she had dark glittery eyes, and I thought that if she was in fact sentient, it might not be a good idea to shut her away in a cupboard. I used to peek inside to look at her sometimes, and my skin would crawl with terror. Sometimes I thought I could hear her snarling.

—⟳—

Every Sunday, church. Every night, family dinner.

The blue cloth was on the table, the gray stoneware plates had their blue flowers pointing straight. The silver candlesticks glinted softly in the candlelight. Pot roast, green beans, and a gravy boat. We reached around the table and all held hands.

"Dear Jesus," my dad prayed, "Thank you for this day, and for Beth and the kids, and thank you for this food. In Jesus's name, amen."

My dad was not one of those missionaries who felt the need to go on and on with his prayers. Which I appreciated.

"This is delicious, Beth," he said, but I could tell that the pot roast was dry and tough. My mom had nearly cried over making dinner that night; the oven was erratic and burnt everything. The beans were wilted, though they had a lovely smidge of sage in them. My mom and dad were so quiet. It was so gray in our house, even though the candles glowed so beautifully. My fork scraped on the stoneware and sent shudders down my whole body. I shivered, shook my arms out dramatically, and said "Brrr!!!" and my parents obligingly chuckled. I breathed a little sigh of relief. It had been worth the shivers to see them smile. Watching their faces eagerly, my brother laughed too and threw his body around his high chair, and then we all giggled at him and he beamed.

The rule was that we had to try one bite of everything on our plate. I wished my mother would cook the delicious food that the Center staff cooked on the communal meal nights—tuna fish casserole with potato chips on top—but she insisted on making complicated homemade meals that sometimes didn't turn out quite right.

After dinner, we moved over to the rattan furniture for family devotions. My father pulled down the pink book off the shelf. Each night there would be a Bible story, followed by a story about a modern regular family with two kids, Minnie and Maxi. In a remarkable coincidence, Minnie and Maxi liked to ask their parents probing questions about the very same Bible story we had just heard, and then the parents would explain things to them in great detail. The fuzzy pastel pictures were cozy, and the family looked so safe and happy, doing American things in a big American house with a green American tree out front. I could see that even in our strange, mismatched living room, we looked just like the family in the Minnie and

Maxi books—the father with his beard and glasses, the mother with the softly curling dark hair, the obedient little girl and boy with pink cheeks listening intently to the Bible story. So wholesome and loving.

But oh my heavens, those family devotions were pure misery. I felt squirmy during the Bible stories, embarrassed and itchy. I couldn't sit still. I felt—I couldn't understand it—almost angry. I swallowed and swallowed, tucking it down. The truth was, I wanted to stand up and scream. I wanted to tear the book apart. I wanted to stab a fork into everything. I had no idea what I could be so furious about, but I knew it meant something very bad about me. Only devils and sinners found the fragrance of God's word to be a stench unto them. Each night, I vowed to do better. After all, God loved us! He sent his only begotten son, that whosoever believeth in him might have eternal life... I knew the whole thing by heart.

I tried to believe as hard as I could. I sat there in the warm glow of my family as faithfully as I could. But I was doing noisy somersaults on the inside. The stories were so scary, and Father God was so capricious, so unfair. People did wrong things even when they didn't mean to, and then they might get turned into a pillar of salt or sent away from their country.

I mean, right off the bat, God had cursed Cain just because his vegetables weren't as nice as Abel's lambs. Poor Cain! No wonder he was so angry that he took up a stone. I was pretty sure he hadn't meant to kill Abel; he had just been so mad that he did something he regretted. I knew about that. I had once pinched my brother and told my mother I didn't know why he was crying. But one mistake and that was IT for Cain. Game over. Every single human after that was doomed to suffering and hard work and childbearing.

But that wasn't even the worst of it.

Sometimes Our Loving Heavenly Father would kill entire countries of people, right down to the babies. I'd heard it in church one day. *Babies?!? Even the babies??* I'd asked my mother. She'd said not to worry about it; that sort of thing didn't happen any more.

But one night, while I chewed on my fingernails and tried to make it through to Minnie and Maxi, my parents read the very worst story of all.

Jehovah—that was God again—told Abraham to sacrifice his own son, Isaac. It took me a minute to figure out what "sacrifice" meant. But then I got it: *cut him open with a knife.* God told him to kill his own child, and Abraham was going to do it. In a dramatic last-minute save, God changed his mind as the knife glittered in the air, and Isaac lived. But Abraham *was going to do it.* I sat there mute with horror.

My dad said, "What's the matter, sweetie?"

"God asked him to kill his own child."

"Yes, sweetheart, just to see if Abraham trusted Him."

"But what if he asked you to kill me?"

My parents looked at me in honest bewilderment. They shook their heads. Why was I focusing on that part? This was supposed to be a story about God's goodness. After all, it was God who had caused for a lamb or goat or some unfortunate animal to suddenly appear in the bushes, so that Abraham and Jehovah could make everything okay by cutting the animal's throat instead of Isaac's. See how good God was???? But there I stood, their wild-haired wild-eyed child, missing the point completely. Minnie and Maxi never asked questions like that.

"God loves you, sweetheart! He would never ask us to kill you." My mother pulled me onto her lap. I could feel that my heart was racing, and to calm myself I touched the little cameo ring on her right hand. Her nails were long and oval, burnished smooth, gleaming quietly without polish.

I let her hug me and her warmth seeped into me. I could tell that she and my dad were smiling at each other above my head. I knew they thought I was being silly again.

But why not me? He did it to Isaac. Poor Isaac! How did he even look at his father after that? I could feel the betrayal in my knees, a little twisting clench.

—∿—

Sometimes we had family Bible nights, where we acted out the stories we'd read. We went all out for these theatricals, but our production of

David and Goliath was particularly dramatic. That's the story where a young shepherd boy challenges the bully Goliath, a bona fide giant, and kills him with a slingshot. My brother Jake played David, of course, and he had a little Nerf ball in a handkerchief for his slingshot. At the crucial moment, my dad as Goliath burst into the room in a *yukata* bathrobe, a belt wrapped around his forehead, and red lightning bolts lipsticked onto his face.

He roared, "Who dares to come to fight me?!?!?"

My mother was laughing, delighted, but Jake's eyes were enormous. He was shaking and flapping like laundry on the line.

"Go on, honey," my mother whispered. "Use your slingshot! It's okay, it's just Daddy!"

Goliath roared again, and I thought David was going to pee his pants. But he finally pulled back his spindly arm and let the Nerf ball fly, and immediately mighty Goliath toppled in a great staggering death lurch, bouncing off the rattan furniture, until at last he was flat on his back on the rug, tongue lolling out and still. Jake's eyes got even wider.

Then my dad sprung up and picked Jake up in his arms. "What a brave boy! That's my Jake—brave as David." Jake smiled shyly, and my father kissed him on both cheeks. Then he put him down, ruffled my hair, and went over and hugged my mom.

"How bout that Goliath, huh?" he grinned. He pulled her in close so her hips were right up against his.

"Virgil!" she protested, as he kissed her. "What did you do to my lipstick?!"

But she had that giggle I hadn't heard in a while, the twinkle back in both of them for one good evening.

My mother loved the Bible intensely. Her Bible had gold-edged pages that were wildly thin and transparent, and the cover was shiny burgundy leather with her name stamped on it in gold letters. She read it every morning for her "quiet time" and wrote in flowered diaries in her dainty looping handwriting.

Perhaps the close clutch of Christianity felt warm and safe to her after a childhood spent with a loving but erratic alcoholic father. The stories that frightened me, of a Heavenly Father who might seem moody or angry, were solace and comfort to her. My dad, more of a pragmatist in theology as well as life, always said, "I don't want to argue theology with anybody. Just give me the virgin birth and the resurrection, and I'll call you my brother."

I longed for such sturdiness. I was mortified of always being so afraid, especially at night in the bedroom I shared with my brother. Occasionally spiders as big as saucers would saunter across our wall. But before we went to bed, we always sang a song that said, "Jesus loves me, this I know; for the Bible tells me so!"

I didn't feel so sure. I sang it anyway, a hopeful, fraudulent declaration.

—◆—

I was officially saved at age five, or at least I gave it a shot. One afternoon in the study, I got down on my knees. I sat still for a minute, thinking of all my sins.

"Dear Jesus," I started. I knew the next part; I had to confess my sins. But I didn't even know how to put words to them—how angry I felt sometimes, how I didn't really want to do God's work at all, how I just wanted to move back to America and be normal, how ferociously I hated my horrible frizzy Brillo pad hair. There was the time I had hit my brother as hard as I could on his leg. But he had kicked me in the middle of the back, first—so did that one count? I wasn't sure. I decided on a blanket statement. "Dear Jesus, I'm so sorry for all my sins, and most of all for just being so bad in my heart and making you get nailed to the cross. Please come into my heart and save me so I can go to heaven." And then, just in case it wasn't clear—"I'm really, REALLY sorry for all my sins, and please don't send me to hell. Amen."

I stood up, and my knees hurt. They had red rashy indentations from the braided wool rag rug. I stood there quietly for a minute, looking out the window at the pine trees, waiting for the relief to wash over me. I was sure I'd gotten it right: it was The Sinner's Prayer, the same one I'd heard a million times. I didn't feel any different, but I was pretty sure I'd checked all the boxes. I walked slowly into the next room.

"Mommy? Daddy? I asked Jesus into my heart." They looked up at me, surprised, caught off guard. My face felt hot, strangely; I felt itchy and embarrassed instead of joyful.

My dad said, "Oh! Wow! That's great, honey." He stood up and came over and hugged me. I felt awkward, strange. My mom made that funny smile that meant she was trying not to cry, and she came over, kneeled down, and kissed my forehead.

"Oh, sweetheart, how wonderful. Jesus loves you so much, you know." Yes. But my heart was racing. I wanted to escape.

"I'm going to play," I whispered, and bounded out into the hall. I could feel them shimmering behind me, great beatific smiles on their faces, their joy like sticky honey pulling me back even as I ran outside.

Later that night, I lay in bed trying to feel Jesus in my heart. If He was there, I should be able to feel something, right? Something should feel different. Only I didn't feel any different. I felt around my body, searching for some sort of new sensation of holiness. I tried to find the part in me that was beloved now. Maybe it hadn't worked!

I sat up again, and prayed the same prayer. *I'm so sorry, please forgive me, please come into my heart.* I waited to feel a glow, a warmth, a sense of love or safety. But I felt nothing. I lay back down again, horrified. I didn't know that this was a possibility. They hadn't addressed this scenario in Sunday School. I'd never heard of anyone else whose salvation prayer didn't work. Worse, I slowly realized that I now knew something my parents didn't know. It turned out that maybe Jesus didn't actually love everybody. Maybe I just wasn't one of his lambs. I tried again. "Please, please, I'm so sorry! I'm reeeeeally sorry—please come into my heart."

Nothing. My heart pounded. What would I do? My mom and dad thought that I was saved now, that I was one of them; but I knew that it wasn't true. I lay back on my pillow, and tears ran down the side of my face and dripped into my ears. Night after night while my brother slept, I tried to coax Jesus into my heart, but He never did come. I never told my parents that I hadn't actually been saved, that it didn't "take."

It was my first real secret.

CHAPTER 3

The secrets came quickly, piling up like snow. In April, I started first grade at the local public school. Me, my frizzy blonde Orphan Annie hair, and a thousand Japanese children.

We had gone to the department store to buy me a *randoseru,* the hard leather backpack that all schoolchildren carry on their backs. My father whistled at the price. Three hundred dollars for the shiny red ones: girls got red, boys got black. Plus we needed a hard boxy pencil case, ten pencils, white canvas *uwabaki* indoor shoes, and a host of other new things.

I stared around at the shininess of the store all around us. There were enormous children's desks with built-in bright lights; there were bunk beds with the desk squished underneath. Desks were a big deal in Japan. Studying was a sacrament. I could tell that this was how you bought okayness; this was the kind of store you could get it in. I knew that it wasn't an option for me: too expensive. We always shopped in the dark little second-hand store down the alley. I knew we had just come to the big department store to look.

But my dad picked up the shiniest, reddest *randoseru* of them all and marched up to the cash register.

"Daddy, what are you doing?"

"Getting you a backpack, sillyhead."

"Isn't it too expensive?"

"Don't worry." He kneeled down and took my chin in his hand. The bright lights glinted off of his glasses and he smiled through his thick beard. "Just don't worry about it, sugarpie. Shall we get you a yellow one instead of red?"

"No, Daddy! It has to be red! They won't let me into school otherwise!" I didn't understand why the store even carried yellow and pink ones when everyone knew that you could only take red and black to school.

He laughed. "I'm just messing with you. Come on. Let's take this monster home."

—⁊⁊—

Two older girls and a boy cornered me as I walked out of the big metal school gate. They were fourth grade giants. I was tiny even among my own classmates, with silly putty arms and feet that tripped each other without anyone else's help.

"You're not allowed to dye your hair blonde. You can get expelled for doing that." The girl dangled her yellow school cap by its elastic chin strap.

"But I didn't dye my hair."

"Of course you did. It's *kimpatsu*."

"I know, that's the way it is naturally," I tried to say, but I did not know the word in Japanese for naturally.

"Also, you're not allowed to have a permanent."

"It's *ten-nen paama*," I said, and realized that I did know the word for natural because I had just spoken it. "It's naturally curly, and it's *ten-nen kimpatsu*," I said, proud of figuring out the new word.

The girl grew very quiet, and narrowed her eyes at me. "It's ten times worse when you lie to a teacher," she said menacingly.

"It's true! It's my own hair, the way it is all by itself."

"Well you're going to get in trouble for it. Also, your eyes. We know they're fake."

I had no idea how on earth anyone would go about changing their eye color, and for the first time felt myself on high moral ground. "Of course my eyes are blue. It's because I'm American! I can't get in trouble for that!"

"Yes you can. They'll pull out your ugly hair and poke out your eyes. They're the wrong color. You're not allowed to have them here. It's the rule." The three stalked off.

I walked home stomping my feet angrily, but frightened. I knew that they could indeed send me away for breaking the school rules, though I hadn't meant to. It was a serious offense to break any of the rules having to do with the way you looked. No nail polish, no makeup, no pierced ears: I had seen the teachers yelling and slapping older girls for these offenses at the morning exercises we all did together in the big courtyard. Even when the girls cried and said they were sorry, the teachers kept yelling while the whole school watched silently. What if I couldn't go to school any more? What if they sent my whole family home? All those people in our American church had given us money to come to Japan, and here I was, messing it all up. More urgently, what would happen at school the next day? What if they pulled me out in front of everyone at the morning *taisou* exercises, and yelled at me for my hair and eyes being wrong? My eyes spurted with imagined humiliation. I would die; I knew that I would die.

I tried to be courageous in moments like that, to stand up to bullies like the spunky girls in stories, like Laura Ingalls. But I felt so small, so weak and afraid. I had no grip; I couldn't grab hold and make the world behave.

Day after day I waited to be called in front of the whole school and yelled at about my hair. It didn't happen, but there were plenty of other public failures as the months went by. In gym class, I was too slow. The yellow sash would not stay in my hair. I couldn't do the frogleap over the wooden horse and kept tumbling on my face. I forgot the rules of the ball-throwing on Sports Day, and when the teacher told all of us that our class should have gotten more balls in, I understood with total psychic clarity that it was probably my fault we had lost. I once forgot to bring my *undou-gi*, my exercise clothes, and I was miserably visible in my dress out on the field with everyone else—one thousand children all dressed in identical white t-shirts and navy blue bloomer panties, and me in bright pink. They wouldn't loan me an extra set; my punishment was for everyone to see how irresponsible I was. I was always trailing behind, trying to keep up, never quite knowing what was going on.

My parents couldn't help me. They knew even less than I did about how things worked. My mom couldn't read the papers the school sent home, so I would turn up with the wrong form, the wrong shoes, the wrong kind of pencil case. (It had to be red. With no writing or pictures on it. The first week of school, my teacher picked up my pink case with the blue flowers, the one I had picked out with my daddy, and held it up in front of the room. "Look at this garbage!" he said. Then he threw it in the trash.) And my parents didn't understand what was at stake. They said it would be fine, not to worry so much.

It was cold in the classrooms, but we weren't allowed to wear sweaters. The cold was supposed to be good for us. Even when it snowed, we did gym class outside in short-sleeved t-shirts and bloomers. My American mother scoffed at the no-sweater rule and insisted that I take one to school when I had a cold. I tried to hide it in my red *randoseru* backpack but it wouldn't fit; the identical cases were designed specifically to hold a few textbooks, a regulation pencil case, and little else. What would a good kid need to hide? Everyone was supposed to be the same. But when the teacher saw me trying to stuff my sweater into my desk, he grabbed it and again held it up in front of the class, who laughed obediently. "This is disgusting," he said. "If I see this thing again, I'll throw it in the furnace."

I wanted to tell him that it was my special one, that it had been a gift, that my mom would be mad; but the week before he'd dragged a girl out of her seat by her pigtail and slammed her into the wall, so I kept my mouth shut.

—⟋⟍—

Everything happened in public. There was no privacy because you weren't supposed to need it. We changed for gym and swimming class all together; the bathroom stalls had low walls that you could see over. The toilets were all Japanese squatty potties, of course, which I loathed; I was always afraid of getting pee on myself, on my socks or shoes; I couldn't figure out how to go without it spraying everywhere. So I would sneak into the one stall with a western commode and a proper door, but it turned out this too was forbidden; that stall was only to be used by the teacher. I was scolded and told to squat like everyone else.

We sang songs. We played little *pianikas*, electric keyboards that you blew air into, like tiny accordions without the bellows. We grew morning glories from seeds. We picked the blossoms, ground them up and made ink, and dyed handkerchiefs. They hung gaily from the clotheslines.

All the missionaries told me how lucky I was to have such a kind teacher. That's what the principal had told my parents when they enrolled me; they would put me in his class because he was the kindest, the gentlest. He might even be the best teacher in the school.

One day I sat frozen at my desk, staring down at the blank worksheet in front of me. I didn't know these characters. I just had no idea; my mind was a total blank. I could hear *Sensei* walking toward me and tried to be invisible, but he stopped next to me. He put a knuckle against each one of my temples and ground them together until tears poured down my face.

In class one day we watched a video about World War II, and it showed piles of charred bodies. "This is what the Americans did," said my teacher. He showed us a picture of a bayonet, and he said, "They used these on children. They would stab little babies in the belly."

The whole class turned and looked at me.

I didn't know there had been a war.

"How was school?" my parents asked me each day when I got home.

"Fine," I said.

It really never occurred to me to say anything else. I'd heard my parents telling the other missionaries how well I was doing, how well I was adjusting. It's true! I was! I hardly ever cried any more when *Sensei* hurt me. I stood there and took it like the others.

Sensei called two boys up to read. One was short and skinny, and the other one was much bigger. Neither of them could read the *kanji* characters in the workbook, and my heart went out to them as they stumbled over the words, for I didn't know them either. From the safety of my desk I entered into their hopeless lostness. If you don't know a *kanji*, you just don't know it, and there's no way to figure it out. They made wild guesses, and each time *Sensei* got madder and madder, banging on his desk with a book every time they messed up. Finally they faltered into silence, and he walked toward them. I was deathly afraid, for sometimes when this happened he would test everyone on the spot to see who else hadn't learned the lesson. If he did that, I knew that I would fail.

Instead he said, "Can't you read? Can't you read anything at all? Are you stupid?" They stood very still.

"What's the matter? Can't you read it? Why can't you read it?" His voice was hard. "This was your homework yesterday, didn't you do it?" He was pacing now, and he was getting loud. I felt my whole body go rigid. "Say something!"

They chorused sorry, *gommennasai*, heads hanging down.

Sensei was standing right behind them. "Why is it always the same thing with you two?" He burst out in a full yell: "What's the matter? Say something!"

Miserably, they both mumbled again, "*Sensei gommennasai, mou yarimasen*. We won't do it again."

"What do you mean you won't do it again? It's that you didn't do it in the first place, you idiots! Say something for yourselves."

What could they say? They didn't know it. They hadn't learned it. They were petrified. Suddenly *Sensei* slapped the back of both of their heads so that their skulls bobbed forward in unison. The skinny one was holding back tears of nervousness, and at this they spilled down his cheeks. The bigger one stood stoically, his head up.

"What are you crying about? *Nani naitenda?* You call yourself a boy? *Soredemo otoko ka?*" The skinny kid sniveled and nodded his head emphatically.

"*Kikoenaizo!* I can't hear you!!"

"I am a boy! *Otokodesu!*" he cried out in a high, tremulous voice. The bigger kid cracked a half-smile, and *Sensei* whirled on him.

"What are you laughing at, fatty? You think fat people get to laugh at people?" Sensei looked at the kid, judging the effect of his words. The kid just stared ahead. "You know the rest of the kids are laughing at you, right? They all call you fatty behind your back." He slapped the boy's ear and shouted, "Answer me!"

The kid's face was bright red. "*Shittemasu,*" he whispered. "I know."

"Yeah? You know it? You know that they all hate you?" At this the kid started to cry, big shuddering gasps, although he still held his large body up straight.

"I can't believe these two. A fatso and a wimp."

The whole class sat in stunned, horrified silence. We knew that nothing could save the two now. It was as though they had died right before our eyes, a sacrifice to *Sensei*'s wrath. No one could survive such humiliation and return to the rest of the group. Saturated in our own shame, we wouldn't be able to associate with them. How could you be friends with someone the teacher had thrown to the dogs? You would be like them if you did: contemptible. Ruined. But any one of us could have been up there. I crouched lower in my seat, willing desperately to be invisible. It was one thing I most definitely was not.

Sensei was chanting. "A crybaby and a fatty. A crybaby and a fatty. Hey, you, you're so fat that you've got nipples!" He pinched them, and the boy flinched. "Look at these! I think you're a girl!"

It was true that his chest was round and bouncy, but he shook his head violently.

"Shut up, you do too. Tell me, class, does he have breasts like a woman?"

As if a wave of vomit passed over us, we chorused back, "*Hai, Sensei!*"

He said, "Take your shirt off and show the class your breasts! Don't be ashamed—you have breasts! Oh, I bet they're beautiful breasts. Go on, show them." The fat kid shook his head, and *Sensei* slapped him again on the side of the head. Then, as if he had just remembered the scrawny kid, he switched gears and started in on him. He threw up his hands expansively. "Oh, I get it! I get it now. You two aren't boys, you're girls! Fatty here has boobs, and I bet that you don't have a dick."

"Aru! Aru!" wailed the kid, scrubbing his fists into his streaming eyes. "I do, I do!"

"Wrong. You're both girls. Go on, show them how you don't have a dick."

They both stood weeping now, shaking their heads.

"Show it, if you're boys!" He cuffed them both again and they both fumbled with the top button of their shorts. They unzipped their pants and let them fall around their ankles. They pushed their underwear down. We waited, not breathing. The wild thing in me was flapping, and it took all my strength to tamp it down. *Don't panic, don't run. There's nowhere to run. Just sit still until it is over.*

"You're both pathetic."

Something in the air had broken.

"Shameful. Go sit with the girls." They pulled up their pants, staggered sobbing into seats with the girls, and tried to wipe their snotting noses on their shirts.

That night I curled up into a tight ball under the covers and sang quietly to myself. *Jesus loves me, this I know; for the Bible tells me so. Little ones to him belong; they are weak but he is strong. Yessssss, Jesus loves me...* I mashed my face into my knees and tried to feel Jesus's love. I couldn't feel anything.

I couldn't stop thinking about those boys in my class. It wasn't just that it was horrifying, or that I was afraid. I felt this great deep clench of *guilt*— that I had just sat there, that I hadn't stopped it. I felt their pain, their humiliation, their utter devastation—literally, I could feel it in my body, the deep rasping sobs in the chest, the shielding of the genitals burning with shame, the ache of the heart twisting into a dark corner.

But I'd just sat there. I didn't run out to the principal's office and demand an intervention; I didn't pick up a rock and throw it at *Sensei*'s head; I didn't rush up and pull their pants back up for them and tell him to stand down.

In that moment I didn't feel like a little kid. I felt a helpless fury in my chest, tight bands around my throat, and I sat still and battened down the part of me rising up in a righteous fury. It was utterly clear to me that it was my job to go up there and swoop those boys to safety. And I had failed at it.

—⚊—

Things in pain called to me, whispered to me, reached hooks into me and pulled. I would see a show about missionaries in Africa, see the skinny babies with flies on their faces, and weep.

"Just don't watch," my father would say in frustration, turning the TV off.

I would go to the zoo and see the animals pacing and I would stand there, again, weeping.

"Don't be so dramatic," my babysitter would say. I would see a TV commercial, or hear a story, or see someone else cry, and it wasn't that I was weeping out of compassion, I was weeping for their actual pain, which I could feel in my own body.

My mother understood this phenomenon. She called it her "sympathy knees." Any time someone hurt themselves and she saw it, she would do a funny bouncing dance and grimace.

"Ugh, I feel that in my knees," she would say. "These darned sympathy pains!"

Everyone laughed whenever she did it. I laughed too. That was how I knew something was wildly funny; when the people around me laughed.

Out in the Center garden, my dad called us over.

"Kids! Look! Persimmons!" He handed us pale orange orbs marbled with green. We sniffed them, looked at his eager face, and bit into them.

My whole mouth instantly turned inside out; it was like I had eaten a black hole. My dad was laughing, bent over with mirth.

"They're not ripe yet!" he cackled, and my brother laughed too, drool running out of his mouth onto the ground.

But tears welled up in my eyes.

My dad looked at me with disappointment.

"Oh, honey, you've got to learn to take a joke. That was funny!" But somehow I couldn't seem to find the humor in things. One more flaw in my character to work on.

Dad often told me kindly that I shouldn't be so sensitive; it just wasn't necessary. He hated to see me upset myself over nothing! It was the same thing he would say when he found me looking at World Vision pamphlets and weeping over the starving children. "Honey!" he would say mournfully to me, holding my hand. "Don't be so sennnsitive! Or else just don't look if it's going to make you so upset!"

But I couldn't help it. I tried to hold back my tears and stand up straighter. I tried to walk stiff and straight like I was wearing the armor of God. I thought it might help if somebody would give me a breastplate, preferably with rubies in it. But even when I stayed away from the pamphlets of children with big begging eyes, they came to me in the dark. When I closed my eyes, even in the daytime, I could see them blinking at me, asking me for something. I ground my fists into my eye sockets, but they wouldn't go away.

I couldn't figure out how to bounce my sympathy pains out like my mother did, and I didn't just feel them in my knees. My head ached when I sat behind the old woman at church, and my chest cramped when one of the old missionaries talked about his son who had died. When I looked at the old carpenter who was missing his first finger, I felt a gnawing, hollow pain in my own hand.

Clearly, this was highly self-indulgent and shameful and I was only doing it to get attention.

Everyone agreed on this. The missionaries told my parents that I was too dramatic. It wasn't godly to be so prone to emotion. *Sensei* told me I was a blight, a waste, a nothing. My parents gently told me that I was too sensitive. Just lighten up, honey!

I agreed with them, obviously. I was mortified to be such a totally self-centered greedy attention hog. I tried really hard to be invisible, but I was terrible at it. I drew attention everywhere I went, which was perhaps not surprising given that I was a little frizzy blonde child in a country of Asians. It was also undeniably true that I cried a lot.

But I didn't know how to stop either of those things from happening.

Thirty years later, I now have a phrase to describe what was going on. I was, to use the highly untechnical term, "energetically spongy." It means I pick up on other people's feelings, much like a faithful kitchen sponge, and sometimes mistake them for my own.

But no one in my world had any idea what it was like for me to be so helplessly empathic, so wide open to the world. Besides, if they had, the missionaries would have seen it as a sign of spiritual weakness, a dreadful vulnerability where the devil might get in. So there I was, standing there in this vortex of emotion, feeling it from everywhere, this huge flood of conflicting feelings pouring through my little body, wondering, "Don't you SEE this?? Can't you FEEL how awful it is??? You're the grownups, DO something!!!" And they would glance at me and say, "Oh for heaven's sake, honey, don't be so dramatic."

On days when there was no school, I would spend hours outside on the Center grounds by myself, lost in a reverie and perfectly happy. I was tracking the progress of the tulip buds by the fence. They shot up out of the ground curved and smooth like the handle of a spoon, then they thickened and bulged in the middle, then the leaves folded down to reveal a pointed little bud, and then the green would flush with color and the lips would peel back and there it was, a blossom, a miracle, the petals floating out wide around the stamen, the red so bright that it seemed to bleed into the air around it. I would sit crouched in front of the flower, rapt, and let the colors seep into me. It was like something was talking to me, and I almost understood the words. I would stand up, reeling, dizzy, drunk on the beauty, feeling a deep silence spread throughout me like a gong.

Sometimes I would try to draw the world around me with my markers, but it was a frustrating, demoralizing pursuit. I couldn't capture the way the mouth of the flower curved down to reveal its throat, or the way the pollen fell all over the splayed exuberance of the petals arched to their peak. I asked the adults around me for help me try to draw it, but they were useless: they showed me how to make a U, then add triangle points to the top: see? a tulip! And a green stem and two leaves! There, done!! I could feel their impatience as I tried to explain that I wanted to draw what it really looked like, with all the whorls and petals, and my disappointment at their efforts, and then in the midst of all that misery they would look at my bewilderment and eagerness and just laugh. "You're an intense little kid," they might say. "You aren't satisfied with much, are you?"

I can smell the pollen right now, as I type, the yellow tickle up in my nose, the black powder trickling down my throat, my eager self rising up in greeting, to wave wildly and cry, hello, oh hello! I have been waiting for you so long! And even now I can lose myself in a blossom; I can rest in its folds like I'm coming home.

Those early years in Japan, my whole family was struggling just to hold it together. My parents were trying to learn an impenetrable new language; my brother was learning to use the potty. My father brought home onion rings that turned out to be squid rings. My mother puzzled out the metric conversions and marked her oven dial with the familiar 250, 350, and 400 to get her bearings; then our Japanese babysitter helpfully scrubbed off the offending scrawls.

As I write this, I'm ten years older than my parents were then. I think of those two eager Midwestern kids, picking up their young family and setting out for an unfamiliar island they'd never visited. They'd never even left North America before. They took all the idealism of the sixties, filtered it through Jesus's love, set it to a soundtrack of praise songs, and followed their hearts.

I just love that adventurous, eager spirit in them. They were puppies gamely bounding into an icy lake, going, "This will be fun! How hard can it be?!?" It's so adorable. And holy heck but those sweethearts were woefully unprepared. They had NO idea what they were getting into.

No one back then knew anything about the psychological toll of culture shock; no one had heard of "third culture kids" or imagined that we'd encounter issues of identity, race, culture. I don't think it ever occurred to anyone that maybe Japanese people might not particularly *want* a western religion. After all, missionaries around the world were being welcomed with gratitude and mass conversions, at least if you believed the fundraising letters they sent back home. I doubt my parents had ever imagined their personal loving God having anything to do with the horrors of colonialism throughout history. Certainly no one we knew ever wasted a moment feeling guilty about imposing their own religious views on native populations. Those were accusatory points of view their children would bring up a decade later, from their fancy universities, causing much bewilderment and hurt. In 1983, my parents believed they were doing the loving thing; they were going to save people. After all, if you knew people were in a house on fire, and you had the key that would get them out, wouldn't you do the same? That's how they felt about all those people going to hell; you HAD to get them out of their prison—you just had to set them free. How could you even live with yourself if you didn't?

I wonder what they thought when they realized that this noble and urgent mission meant sitting in folding chairs, talking in halting Japanese about sin to people who had come in for the free English lessons. I wonder if they ever felt uncertain about the efficacy of what they were doing. But their job was to bring love, and that they did wholeheartedly. Over the years they have welcomed in single mothers, divorced people, old people who have been abandoned by their families. In a culture that does not tolerate failure, the Christian church in Japan welcomes in outcasts with kindness and affection. My parents faithfully live out the best parts of that mission: to shine a kindly light into the lonely places of the world.

Nonetheless, our first few years there we were all at sea. Our raft was leaking and the shore was nowhere to be seen. Still we kept praying; we kept going to church; we kept doing everything with a joyful heart, as unto the Lord, goddammit.

Yamanaka-ko translates literally as: "the lake in the middle of the mountains." All the missionary families had traveled to the base of Mount Fuji for an annual retreat. We were smushed willy-nilly into a cluster of shabby holiday cabins, and while the grownups sat in meetings and prayed together, we kids ran riot under the pine trees. It was beautiful and green and the lake was just across the street, but even with the soaring view of Mount Fuji rising up over the lake, things were claustrophobic and fraught. It's a lot of holiness to pack in, with so many missionaries on top of each other.

One evening my family was walking along the boardwalk, looking at the water several feet below. I was dangling on the bars, leaning out over the sand far below, dawdling, musing. This is where memory diverges, and I'm not sure exactly what happened next. Was I in trouble for dawdling? Were my dad and I roughhousing, laughing and joking and threatening to push each other off the boardwalk? We all remember it slightly differently. But suddenly, I was flying through the air and crashing facedown into the sand. I couldn't breathe. I thought I was dying. My chest was collapsing and I couldn't draw a breath; I had never felt such a pain in my middle, and there was sand up my nose and in my mouth. I lay there, stunned.

My dad came running, leaping across the sand, and scooped me up in his terrified arms.

"I'm sorry, oh honey, I'm so sorry," he murmured, holding me against his chest and walking me up the stairs to the boardwalk. I could hear his heart thudding against my ear, loud gongs of panic. I couldn't even catch my breath enough to cry; I had had the wind completely knocked out of me.

These things always happened so fast with my dad. His sense of humor was legendary, but I was—well—sensitive. Tickling was torture. Practical jokes left me in tears. And sometimes, I missed his signals. There were times I would still be grinning, thinking we were playing a game, when the surprise thunk on the head would come or the hot humiliating swat on the rear would shred the day. And then just as quickly he would be smiling again, or saying *sorry, honey, it was just a joke*—and I would nod that *yes, ok, it was fine*, often even before I could register what had just happened. There was a fine line between humor and humiliation, and I always seemed to be on the wrong side of it.

That night at dinner, when all the missionaries were gathered together, he looked at me and said, "Tell them what a terrible father you have."

I looked at him, horrified.

"Go on, tell them how your dad threw you off the seawall." He was grinning, but sheepishly.

I shook my head, staring at him, wanting more than anything to disappear. The fireplace crackled behind the great dining room table where we all sat, and I felt my face grow fiery. There was a banjo string stretched taut between his heart and mine, and there was such sadness pouring into my heart from that string that I thought I couldn't bear it. I knew that he was begging for absolution by confessing in front of everyone; partly to punish himself, partly to find the humor in it. This was his way of trying to make it okay, to fold it into the dinner conversation and weave it into a funny story with an ending where everyone was fine in the end.

But I couldn't play along. I just wanted to pretend it never happened.

I could feel the eyes on us, everyone gone awkwardly silent, and I felt a mad urge to leap up and say, "No, that never happened—it was just a joke! It didn't even hurt!" I wanted to defend him from the uncomfortable rustle under the hush that had fallen over the group. I wanted to kick up a nice dust storm that would hide us both. Instead, I just looked at my plate and shook my head.

Dinner moved on, and I dabbed at my food.

I didn't know how to cut the cord between my father and me, and I could feel it reverberating in my chest until I finally fell asleep that night to the high keening sound of it.

CHAPTER FOUR

When I was seven, we went back to the USA for six months. This was standard practice for missionaries—a few years on the field, then six months or a year on furlough to raise more money.

On the first day at the downtown Indianapolis public school, I stood in line braced and ready. But the line wiggled and jostled; no one stood still and no one seemed afraid. The boy in front of me turned and placed his hand on my chest and giggled. I batted his hand away, and he leaned in and whispered, "Let's fuck, white girl." I crossed my arms in front of my chest and lifted my chin in the air. I had no idea what "fuck" meant.

I soon discovered that there was a whole language I didn't speak: whispered words that made some kids giggle and other kids mad; TV shows I'd never heard of; American kid code. But after a while I found myself encircled by a protective group of girls who sat with me at lunch and shouted off the mean boys. I could hardly follow the stream of insults, they flew so fast, and I never learned to hold my own in the fray. But I did learn how to adopt a protective shield of icy silence.

The second week, I got put into a special reading group, and when I told my parents, they nodded unhappily.

"I was afraid you'd be behind, sweetheart," my mom said. "I'm not a real teacher. Don't feel bad, okay? You'll catch up in no time."

But at the first parent-teacher conference they came home glowing. It turned out that I was in a special advanced reading group. Such vindication for the Lord's work. After all, if my parents were taking care of God's work, God would take care of their family. That was the deal.

But I couldn't read the social cues. I couldn't understand what was cool, and what was funny—I couldn't understand who we were friends with that week, and who would sit sadly by herself at lunch. Every morning the kids slapped their hands on their hearts and rattled off a long stream of words I'd never heard before. It was sort of like the Lord's Prayer, but it went, "I plejallegiance, to thaflag, of the Unitedstates Ovamerica." I only understood what we were doing when I read the Ramona Quimby books and she had her epiphany that a "donzer" was not a kind of lamp, but was actually the "dawn's early light."

I was more intimate with the characters in my books than I was with the noisy girls at school. I liked those school girls, with their pigtails and their barrettes, their stompy sneakers and My Little Pony lunchboxes, and I wanted them to like me, but there was so much bouncing, so much constant motion, that I sometimes felt seasick. The school day passed in a blur, with purple mimeographed work sheets and Montessori games at the cold smooth table, and stories in a circle on the carpet.

By Christmas, the blur was slowing down a little. I could understand what my classmates were saying most of the time. I knew when we'd be going to get our folders from our cubby, and when it was time to line up for lunch.

Naturally, it was now time to go back to Japan.

We discovered something terrible. It turned out that I had fallen so behind in my *kanji* characters during the half-year in the U.S. that I couldn't go back to Japanese school.

I kept seeing myself failing to vault over the horse in gym class, that wooden and canvas measure of my failure. I usually ended up with my face smashed into the mat. Laps to run. There I was again, my ass in the air.

The grownups made clicking noises with their teeth and said it was a shame.

I said nothing, but my heart thudded *thankyouthankyouthankyouthankyou*. And if I had known any triumphant bad words, I would have used ALL of them.

So instead of going back to *Sensei*, I finished second grade with a mission-ary family. This family had hired an American teacher to teach their kids, and our one-room schoolhouse was a little prefab room over their carport. Very reminiscent of *Little House on The Prairie*, only with fluorescent lights. I fell deeply in love with the only boy who was my age, and wrote breathless poems to him in my pink diary that locked with a tiny gold key. (I have to remember to burn those.) The only other thing I remem-ber about that schoolroom is that we made papier-mâché models of the moon, with little raised rings for the moon's craters, and I would run my fingers over those rings with dreamy satisfaction, imagining myself on its white poster-paint surface. Me, some newspaper strips, and flour paste, a million miles away. It would be very quiet, I imagined. Very dark and verrrrry quiet. It sounded delicious.

Life at home was whirling and busy. My parents threw themselves into their new work as real, official church planters. I always pictured an enormous seed pinched in big heavenly fingers when I heard that phrase, God planting seeds from up in the sky, and then churches sprouting up like corn or turnips.

We weren't living in The Center any more; they let us live in the church, since the church was really just a house. A seedling Japanese church of a couple dozen people met there every Sunday, in the two big front *tatami* mat rooms, but our family was allowed to live in the rest of it as long as we kept ourselves out of the holy rooms and didn't mind the church ladies using our kitchen.

We tended to spill over a bit, so every Sunday morning we ran around like possessed people to clean up the house and pull our chaos back into our allotted quarters, stashing baskets of toys and clothes and clutter behind closet doors, around corners, and up the stairs. There were al-ways thirty mad minutes of terror as we rushed to get everything into a semblance of order, including the two dozen slippers lined up neatly in our *genkan* entryway. Then someone would ring the doorbell, and we would smile and graciously welcome in the congregation as the Lord's humble servants.

Even though our church was tiny, we had a little pulpit and everything. An organ. Communion cups. A flannel board! It felt so official. At Christmas, we put on extravagant children's programs packed with Real American Christmas Traditions to lure in the neighborhood children. Then we would tell them that Christmas wasn't really about Santa, it was about Jesus. They didn't seem to care; they wanted the candy and hot chocolate.

During the week, baking circles met in our kitchen and my mother would teach the women to bake American-style goodies. She would talk to them in her gentle voice about how knowing Jesus helped her family to be happy and how Jesus helped her husband to come home every night instead of going out drinking with his boss and doing Bad Things.

My mom played the organ every Sunday. Most Sundays the other missionary or a Japanese man would preach, but every now and then my dad had to do it, sweating through a prepared sermon in his labored Japanese. He used to have nightmares about preaching, always the same: he'd get up to the pulpit...and realize he'd forgotten to write a sermon. He made these stories funny, telling us about them at the breakfast table: *Oh!* he'd wail dramatically, *It happened again!*

Each Sunday, the Japanese church people smiled kindly at us, and I smiled back, but I hated having dozens of people walking around our home. Sometimes I would go upstairs and hide in my room to get away from the hubbub.

My dad had built a tall platform for my bed to double the space of my tiny bedroom. I climbed up the ladder, almost to the ceiling, and snuck under my comforter. In a weird way I felt closer to my parents up here than I did when I was downstairs with so many people bustling about. I could feel their love in the physical objects: the bed my dad had built and the sky-blue comforter with the rainbows on it my mother had bought for me even though I knew it was more expensive than the one she'd wanted to get. In an orgy of domesticity I had taken some rainbow-checked gingham and made my whole room full of rainbows. The bright fabric

I'd slathered around the wastebasket and the crooked tissue box cover gave me little jolts of energy, like I was sucking on a color lollipop with my eyes. As I lay quietly horizontal, the light came in cool and bright and healing, and the long cellophane tail of my rainbow kite rippled and crinkled against the wall where it hung. The kite was a memento of a perfect day with my dad: we'd gone and bought these enormous kites, the big extravagant kind with long swooping tails, and sent them up in the sky for an entire humming afternoon. I felt all these things holding me up as I lay in my bed, and my bookshelf was there too, like a ring of grinning friends: there was my Trixie Belden, my Anne Shirley, my Pippi and Heidi and Pollyanna. But after a few minutes in this sanctuary, I obediently tiptoed back downstairs. We weren't supposed to hide when church people were there. The church was the most important thing that happened in our house, the whole reason we were in Japan.

———❦———

The next year, I started third grade at a brand new school run by some charismatic Christian missionaries. Just to be clear, that's "charismatic," as in holy rolling, snake handling, and speaking in tongues, not charming and friendly. Though the snakes, in this case, were invisible.

The school was one big room with light gray carpet and white plasterboard walls. It felt like the Japanese office it had originally been: two small windows, twitchy fluorescent lights. The twenty students sat in a big circle around the perimeter of the room, each student facing the wall. Our desks were one long continuous piece of varnished wood, but wooden dividers reared up between each student so that we couldn't see each other or anything else. Solitary in our little cubicles, we worked in complete silence on workbooks called Paces. There was a Pace for reading, another Pace for science, another for math. That was school.

The Paces had bright colors and cartoon instruction bubbles. We practiced writing sentences like "Would you like an almond?" but also "Your parents deserve honor," and "I will call upon the Lord." Cute insets quoted Bible verses like "Go to the ant, thy sluggard, and consider thy ways," next to pictures of ants. The next page proclaimed, "The righteous shall flourish like a branch," as part of a botany lesson. We used these workbooks instead of dangerous and heathenish textbooks. (I know you'll be happy to learn that this amazing system of screwing up your children isn't just an odd historical anomaly; it's actually still available, if you'd like to try it. Take a gander at the wonders of Accelerated Christian Education online. They're still "reaching the world for Christ...one child at a time." They provide "godly" homeschooling materials, and will even train you to set up your own little child-soul-destroying factory, if you want.)

When we got a new stack of Paces, I would covertly read them cover to cover instead of proceeding properly through and doing the exercises. I knew this was wrong, but the exercises were so itchy, and I felt almost ravenous for the words. I especially loved the ones on History and Science. I would read everything as fast as I could, careful not to get caught, devouring, skimming. Then I would go back and begin the drudgery of filling in all those blank spots and learning all those Bible verses. Let me pause and say that in fairness to the curriculum, about which I spoke so sharply, I should add that it did do a very effective job of teaching me to speed-read, so I can highly recommend it for that purpose, if you don't mind abandoning all other educational goals.

There were little cartoons at the end of some chapters, and these I studied very carefully. There was a blond boy called Ace, who did everything right. There was a character named Susie, who often made mistakes and had to get punished by her parents, whom she addressed as "Sir" and "Ma'am." There was a heavyset kid and a black kid, too, and they often got in trouble as well. But not Ace! I read these studiously, trying to get the joke. I had seen comics in the paper; my dad called them the funnies pages. These were definitely the same thing; they were blocked off in a row of little boxes, with words coming out of the characters' mouths in balloons. But try as I might, I never could get the joke.

When we wanted to ask the teacher a question, we would take the little American flag stuck in its plastic base and put it on the shelf above our heads. Eventually a teacher (who wasn't called a teacher but a "supervisor") would mosey over to see what we needed, but in general it wasn't a good idea to ask for too much help. It was safer to stay under the radar. But one day I came to a section in my Pace that told me to write an essay on a separate piece of paper. I had never seen or heard the word "essay" before, so I put up my flag and when the supervisor came over, I asked what an essay was.

"You know, an essay," she said.

"But I don't know what an essay is," I said.

"An essay is an essay."

I remembered something from the *Little House* books. "Is it like a composition?"

She stared at me in distaste. "Don't sass me. Just do your work."

I was bewildered. I got out a sheet of paper and watched a few tears fall down onto it. The thought of failing terrified me. I don't know what I thought was riding on this; I doubt that anyone was even going to read what I wrote. But I wanted so badly to do well.

Gosh, those supervisors just loved Jesus so much.

"I just love Jesus so much!" cried Miss Jill, with her hands up in the air. Mrs. Brown clapped and smiled, and we all sang along—*Onward Christian Soldiers, marching as to war!*—and songs too about angels and heaven and God's great love.

God loves you so much! Sing along, children!

But then there was a scuffle from the back of the room, and suddenly Mrs. Brown said in a tight voice, "Back to your desks, everyone." We stopped singing, uncertainly.

George hadn't been paying attention during worship time.

Mr. Brown had him by the arm, yanking on him above the elbow, and he marched George down the stairwell. Without making a sound, we scurried to our seats and faced the wall. I sat as still as I possibly could. Out of the corner of my eye, I could see Mrs. Brown step into the office and come out with the paddle. She glanced at us and said, "Silence, everyone." You could have heard a feather drop.

Then she went downstairs too, and a minute later it started.

"No no no please—" and then the sick smack of the wood hitting flesh. George screamed and begged, apologizing over and over, and the thwacks came again and again. We held our pencils and dutifully sat in front of our Paces. "God chastises those He loves," I read. But I couldn't seem to make my fingers move.

"Hey," hissed Miss Jill right behind me, and I jumped. "Do. Your. Own. Work. Unless you want to join George," she whispered softly into my ear, and I felt my heart stop. I tried to write words, but they came out as scribbles that I frantically tried to erase.

The thwacks came again and again, each one followed by a scream. George's sobs went on and on. I knew he was bent over a desk with his pants and underwear down around his ankles; I had accidentally witnessed Mr. and Mrs. Brown delivering one of their "spankings" one time when I'd been coming out of the bathroom. Sometimes kids would brag about their welts and bruises, turning humiliation into bravado, but I was terrified of the paddle. They had even used it on little Lyddie, who was only five.

And the sight of that thick piece of wood unleashed something almost more horrifying in me: a murderous, blood-curdling rage. I wanted to turn that heavy wooden paddle on the teachers; I wanted to smash in their faces. I wanted to smack down their whole wretched school. I wanted to run downstairs and yell, in a voice that sounded like God, "Stop!!!"

And in my fantasy, they actually *would* stop. They'd stop and stare and they would wake up, like it had all been a bad dream, and say as if in surprise— "You're right. This is wrong. We will stop."

But even my vivid imagination could sustain this mirage for only a few seconds; then the image would warp and I could see what would really happen if I ran down the stairs and screamed at them to stop: they would twist their mouths in that look of scorn and pleasure that I knew so well, and then I would be hit. They would pull my pants down and spank my bare vagina. I thought I would die of the degradation of it.

Naturally, I spoke of my horror and rage to no one. This rebellious and uncontrollable anger of mine was just more proof of my own sinful nature. Didn't I welcome God's authority?

Of course I did.

So I sat during the screams, along with everyone else, listening. What they were doing to those kids was wrong, I was sure of it. I didn't care how much they said they did it with love. I didn't care that it was part of God's authority and plan. I didn't know the word "bullshit" back then, but I knew what it felt like in my body. My stomach clenched; I wanted to curl up in a ball; I wanted to throw up. But instead, I sat there silently. And I hated myself for that silence. I felt as guilty as if I were the one swinging the stick. I loathed myself as much as I loathed and feared the supervisors.

School went from Tuesday to Saturday, and our weekend was Sunday and Monday, because Sunday was the busy day for most families, who ran churches. The pastors needed Monday to rest. I dutifully wore skirts every day, since girls weren't allowed to wear pants or shorts, even when it was freezing. I never really understood why. There were so *many* ways you could get in trouble, all of them slightly mysterious. One day, Edie Langley asked to go to the bathroom again and again, but the answer was no. She ended up peeing right in her seat, and we all held our breaths and pretended not to hear the dripping sound and her tears.

But wait! It wasn't all misery and humiliation! In fact, there was a huge bright spot— I finally had a friend. We went to school together every day: a bus and three trains, an hour each way. Estelle and I used to argue pleasurably all the time. Whose hair was longer. Whose watch told better time. Who had to walk farther to get home. We would sit on the bus in gentle mutual exasperated silence after one of these arguments. I loved the drama, the high of fighting and then making up. I'm not sure she enjoyed it as much.

Estelle's parents worked with my parents in the church we lived in, and on Sunday afternoons after the congregation had finally gone home, she and I would go out into the back yard and work on the carnival we were planning. It was going to be a grand affair. I felt something lilt inside of me, after all those hymns and pages of Bible verses, at the prospect of something with gold curly script and flying flags and music like you'd hear on a merry-go-round. It was something out of a storybook, something gay and lighthearted and full of crimson and blue and green streamers. Oh, I couldn't wait for our fair!

We wrote up programs and advertisements and used our best flowered tape to edge their borders. We made up tickets for all the games and rides and used tacks to perforate them down the middle for easy ripping. We practiced our big routines; I was going to perform a combination of Hula Hoop and baton, and Estelle was going to play the piano. She actually knew how to play the piano, both hands working together, whereas I was making up my dance routine from scratch and nothing. So far, it involved a lot of anguished arching of my arms, and big leaps and soulful hugging of the baton, but my plan was to get to the point where I could keep the hoop spinning around my waist while I also tossed and caught the baton. We decided that our little brothers could perform too, but they declined. All they wanted to do was kick a soccer ball against the back wall, again and again and again. Just watching them for a few minutes made me so bored that I wanted to scratch my skin off.

Estelle was tidy and organized and was always kind to everyone. Instead of Barbie dolls, she had Japanese *Rika-chan* dolls at her house, ones with flat chests and demure clothes. (Her mother didn't approve of the scandalous, trampy Barbie.) Estelle did everything perfectly. She made her bed every day and practiced her piano and did her homework as soon as she got home and always prayed and picked out her clothes for the next day before she went to bed. To top it all off, she had smooth shiny hair that was so soft it was always slipping out of its tiny plastic barrettes. My hair, on the other hand, had the texture of steel wool, wiry and frizzy and bright yellow, and it stood out from my head in a huge mortifying clump. I would have been paralyzed by bitterness over her beautiful silky hair and her general perfection, except that I knew that she couldn't sleep sometimes. It was very puzzling—she would cry and cry, but she couldn't sleep. Her mother said she was over-tired, which didn't make any sense to me.

One day Estelle said to me, "Listen, I think we should stop playing carnival. I'd rather play house."

"But it's not a game." I gestured toward the stacks of tickets, the hand-lettered programs, the Hula Hoop.

"It's not a real carnival. It's just pretend."

I stared at her. I could see it so clearly in my mind: the merry-go-round, the flags flying, the big red curtain opening as we stepped on stage for our performances. And then I saw our little stack of tickets, the ones we'd perforated using a tack. I saw how silly it all was. Where would we get a merry-go-round? Where would we hang a big curtain? Estelle was ready to move on, to go play dolls or *Rika-chan* pseudo-Barbies, but I couldn't get up from the grass. I felt like I was fused to the ground and weighed a million pounds.

Other missionaries filtered in and out, mostly young and earnest and eager, or older and cranky. (Those seemed to be the two main flavors.) One young missionary couple was helping out with the church, and they came over once a week to pray and plan with my parents. The young blond man often turned up a few minutes before his Japanese wife did. She was the first Japanese missionary I'd ever met, and I found her intriguing. I hadn't even realized that anyone besides Americans *could* be a missionary. I kept trying to wrap my mind around it. In addition to the gyrations in my head as I tried to grasp the cultural implications, there was something even more fascinating about the two of them. They had been married less than a year, and I'd heard that they were still in the "honeymoon phase." I studied them to see what the honeymoon phase looked like. Mostly it looked pretty normal, and they wouldn't even kiss when she arrived. They sure smiled at each other a lot though. One day he rang our doorbell and I answered.

"Hi, Mark."

"Hey, you! How you doing?"

I stepped into a pair of the guest slippers we kept by the door and used them like toe shoes, popping up into a full pointe and balancing there while he took his shoes off and changed into a pair of slippers. His heels hung off the back; the plastic slippers were made for Japanese feet. When he came into the living room, my mom called out a harried greeting from the kitchen, where she was trying to fix dinner while also entertaining my new baby sister Ruth. Mark stopped suddenly in the doorway.

"Hi Elizabeth," he said politely to my mother. "Is Virgil not home yet?"

"No," she sighed, jiggling my sister, who squirmed to be put down to investigate the new visitor. Ruth couldn't crawl yet, but she was a speedy slitherer.

Mark looked uncomfortable. "Well," he started. "Well, Elizabeth," he tried again. "It's just that uh, well Sachiko and I, we have an agreement. About being in the house with other women. Or men, for her, I mean, now that we're married, we just decided—" He looked embarrassed. "I'll just go for a little walk and come back, okay?"

My mother said with exquisite grace, "Sure, Mark. We'll see you in about half an hour." She saw him out the door and straightened his slippers so they were turned properly, ready for him to step into again when he returned.

Then she came back to the kitchen table and sat down. I hadn't seen her sit still in a long time.

"What's wrong with *him*?" I asked her. I was mortified for my mother. I wasn't sure exactly what she had done wrong, but it must have been bad if Mark didn't even want to be in the same house as her.

"Nothing, honey," my mother said. She pulled me close and kept her arm around my waist. "Beyond reproach," she murmured. I didn't know what that meant, but I stood there feeling hot and flushed.

My mother was beautiful. Big green eyes, soft wings of dark wavy hair, and full breasts above her small waist. She always dressed modestly; my grandmother had given her a beautiful green blouse for Christmas that she never wore because she said it showed too much of her neck. I wanted her to wear it because it made her look tall and glamorous like the Barbie doll I had finally acquired, and she turned and smiled at herself in the mirror when she tried it on. But she never wore it out, no matter how often I begged. Was that why Mark wouldn't stay? Because she was so pretty? Apparently just being in the house with her was dangerous.

I knew that it was very easy to fall into sin, though I wasn't exactly sure what that meant. I imagined the two of them swooning in an embrace, my mother's head tilted back like Julie Andrews in *The Sound of Music* when she finally kisses the Commandant. That was the raciest thing I'd ever seen, and it made my stomach flutter to think of it. But my mother would never kiss Mark, I knew it. She would only kiss my father. Anyone should know that!

Why couldn't Mark just sit there having coffee while she continued making dinner? The grown-up world was so precarious; they needed a lot of rules to reinforce it. It scared me that grown-ups' promises, their intentions, were so fragile that even a few minutes alone in a room together might blast everything to pieces. It made me sad that my beautiful mother was considered so dangerous. But she couldn't help it; she was a woman. We were the daughters of Eve, the source of sin, and this made us all mothers of evil, even my little baby sister.

—◆—

At school we put on plays and musicals with lovely and subtle evangelical messages. They followed a pattern and were always about children who didn't love Jesus and therefore would go to hell. Where it was hot.

I must confess that I loved being in these plays, loved the costumes, loved the dances and the earnest message and the songs. I danced, sang, and acted my heart out in my best imitation of the woman in *Chitty Chitty Bang Bang*, holding my head high and sweeping my arms as majestically as I could. My favorite part, though, was when I got to play the child who had gone down to hell, and I pretended to cry and wail and writhe in agony. I really threw myself into it; I could almost feel the flames licking around me, red and orange and scathing, and feel myself separated from my mother and father, who would be up in heaven rejoicing and singing hymns. There was a delicious thrill in acting out my own nightmare. I knew that I probably really would go to hell someday, but then and there, for that one moment, I was safe—safe! I writhed in an ecstasy of joy because there I was, beyond reproach, in a play *about* hell. Surely they couldn't send me to hell while I was in a play *warning* people about hellfire, right? I let the terror and the thrill course through me like electricity, and sometimes my body would get carried away and almost seem to shudder on its own. I was awed by my own performance, swirled around by the music, and buoyed by the holy love I saw on the earnest faces of my classmates as the curtain came down and we all took a bow.

But no matter how impassioned our performance, Mrs. Brown would stand there with her arms crossed, shaking her head.

"You guys are just not doing it justice," she would say. "You have to work harder for Jesus."

—m—

Miss Jill had a long straight waterfall of hair, and she was a walking miracle. Literally. During chapel one day, she stood up shyly and went to the front. She twisted the long skein of hair into a rope and wound it around her wrist as she talked.

"Um. So, I want to tell you something you don't know about me. I have this—it's an affliction. It's called epilepsy. It's a sickness that makes people have seizures. It's painful, and it can be dangerous. But children, I'm here to tell you about the will of God. God wants wholeness for you! Our God is a God of healing!"

The other teachers murmured "Amen," and Mrs. Brown raised her hands to the ceiling and said, "Sha-la, sha-la."

"I have been struggling with this my whole life," Miss Jill said. "It's Satan trying to get his claws into me. So last week at worship, I felt the call. And I went forward, and my sister in the Lord Opal laid hands on me, and slayed me in the spirit."

I saw Mrs. Brown with a huge sword. She slashed Miss Jill's chest, and Miss Jill fell down in a faint. I shuddered.

"And I am healed, little ones. I am healed." Miss Jill held up a small plastic bottle. "You know what this used to have inside it? Pills. Medicine. I didn't have enough faith, I wasn't strong enough to trust. But now I know I am healed, and I do have faith—I have so much faith that I flushed every single pill down the toilet." She turned the bottle upside down and shook it. Her face was flushed, and her hair was twisted tight in her fingers.

Mr. and Mrs. Brown went up to her and laid their hands on her head and prayed out loud. "Oh lord, bless our sister, for she has come back into grace. We ask you to honor her new faith and forgive her lack of faith in the past. We ask, oh Lord, that she may be a shining example to all of your grace and glory. In the name of Jesus. Ohhhh, Jesus."

Mrs. Brown was swaying. Her blonde hair was coiled on the back of her head in a cunning, swooping swirl. I couldn't take my eyes off of it. I thought that shining swoop of hair looked like her name, Opal. She wore a tan dress with red piping, and red pumps and red button earrings. Her red pumps warped and stretched as her sways became bigger, her hands in the air. "Shaaaaaa-la," she said again. "Shala mohahikan! Alalalala ele-shaddai nostrakah!" Her eyes were closed, her lips shiny and moist. She was so beautiful. I knew that the strange words coming out of her mouth meant that she was speaking in tongues. It was the fire of the spirit, but I couldn't see any fire and I also couldn't see her tongue.

Several weeks later, we went into a room downstairs that was rarely used. They had desks set up, normal classroom-style desks. I couldn't believe it; if they had real desks, why did we have to sit in our horrible cubbies? They sat us down and placed a gray booklet in front of each one of us. I touched its cover. The paper felt rough and thick, so unlike the smooth, thin Pace textbooks we used every day.

"Don't touch," said Miss Jill. I jerked my hand back. She walked up and down, handing each of us two pencils. The pencils were a deep brownish purple, slick and shiny, with big globs of hard glossy paint at the end. I longed to put one in my mouth, to crack the veneer open with my teeth and sink them into the soft wood inside. I sat on my hands.

Miss Jill told us that these were called Iowa Basic tests. She said that it was very important that we do well, so that they could keep the school open and keep us safe in the Lord. She read us some instructions, told us to open our papers, and then she cried, *Begin!*

The questions were easy. I made little shiny silver ovals with my pencil, one after another, filling in each orange shape completely and fully. I caught myself biting the pencil without having meant to: I could see the telltale curved marks of my teeth sharply etched in the paint. I rubbed them with my thumb, hoping no one would notice.

I felt the sound resonating just above my collarbone before I knew I was even hearing anything. I looked up. Miss Jill had her mouth open, and her eyes looked strange. The odd vibration in my neck was coming from her mouth, and without saying a word she slowly keeled over and crashed onto the floor. We leaped out of our desks and crowded around her. Her eyes were blank white orbs, and her legs were twitching and thrashing. Her long hair caught in the foam that was gathering at the edges of her mouth. A low groaning sound came from her, ululating. Every cell of my body was electric with terror.

"The devil's got Miss Jill!" cried one frantic child as Mr. Brown came dashing into the room.

"Finish your tests!" he bellowed. "Sit down and finish them!"

He dragged Miss Jill by her ankles behind a little partition, and her skirt rode up past her knees. I shut my eyes and tried to breathe. My arms and legs were so rigid, locked and splayed like Miss Jill's, that I didn't think I'd ever be able to move again. Somehow we returned to our seats and picked up our pencils. As Miss Jill continued to thrash and moan at the front of the room, we obediently began coloring in those tiny little ovals, covering up every bit of orange ink with our shimmery gray dots.

It was after that episode that we had the first series of speeches on fear.

Mrs. Brown paced back and forth in front of us.

"You see, children, the devil is after Miss Jill. He's watching her, waiting for his chance. He's a sneaky one, the Prince of Darkness. You must always be watching. You must always be on guard. Satan will slip into the tiniest opening." She stopped and examined us with her all-seeing gaze. "Miss Jill didn't have enough faith. If she had, her seizures wouldn't have come back." She paused and hummed a minute.

"This is the way of the Lord; for our God is a God of healing!" She suddenly thrust her hands up into the air, closed her eyes and swayed for a moment, but then seemed to remember us. "Dear children. Do not be afraid. If you feel fear, that is the devil in you. You must never let the fear in, because that is how you let in the devil."

The fear in my stomach coiled and grinned, reminding me it was there. It was too late for me. It had already gotten inside. My worst secret.

Poor Miss Jill was in disgrace. The whole church was praying for her, and they were going to slay her in the spirit again. I saw the big sword slicing through Miss Jill once more, and I couldn't imagine how that would help. Maybe the sword cut out the sin. But if you cut someone open like that, wouldn't it make it easier for the devil to get in? I was horrified by the thought of opening someone up like that. I could see clear as clear that the sword would slit the membrane around Miss Jill, would leave a gaping wound in her pearly, opalescent covering.

Years later, I actually saw someone get slain in the spirit. A sinner would go up to the front of a church, and a holy person would pray over them. Then, when the whole crowd was at a frenetic peak of *Oh Jesus*, and *We just call on you right now, Lord*, when the music was loud and the whole room was swaying and writhing in rhythm, then the holy person would gently touch the sinner on the head, and the sinner would fall over in a heap. I couldn't see anyone's opalescent covering by the time I was a teenager. But I still didn't like these slayings.

Miss Jill had one other seizure while she was watching us. We were having gym time at the local park that served as our playground, and she was the only adult with us. When she keeled over again, she hit her head on the concrete and a bit of blood oozed from her. Two of us decided to run back to school to get someone, and we dashed back as fast as we could. I felt the wind like ice in my lungs, and my legs burned as they scissored beneath me. I could hardly breathe when we got there, and we panted out that Miss Jill had had another attack. Mrs. Brown said, in what was probably supposed to be a reassuring way, "Don't be afraid, children. Remember, fear is from the devil." I was wrapped in fear, suffocating in it, and I knew at that moment that I was surely doomed, that I would never get the devil out of me, because I could not stop feeling afraid.

—⁓—

If you didn't grow up around fundamentalist Christians, this whole idea of sin and the devil might seem quaint and antiquated, perhaps amusing and camp. For obvious reasons, it wasn't amusing to me as a child, but what you have to understand about the adults around me is that they weren't actually insane. They were proceeding quite logically from a theory as old as time—that there is something so wrong with humans that nothing on earth could fix it. It's a reasonable theory, given the human predilection for violence and cruelty. If you look at the world this way, then everything that happens on earth is kind of a wash. The only important thing is to save the soul, and desperate times call for desperate measures. Compared to the urgent need to rescue someone's soul out of the cesspool of this earthly life, tiny earthly troubles—beatings, cruelty, humiliation, war—are unfortunate but necessary. It's the same way most people think about vaccinating their children: the prick of a needle is a small price to pay for the life-saving power of immunizations.

This is why it's been so easy over the centuries for people to perpetuate horrors—from the Crusades to Catholic strictures on birth control to the proud history of child abuse—in the name of the Father, the Son, and the Holy Ghost. The body has to suffer in order to free the soul. I know that many truly loving and devout Christians reading this are thinking, *No, no! Those horrors are human frailty at work, distorting God's true message!*

It wasn't God who authorized those bad things, it was flawed humans! I agree with them. What we disagree on is how deep the distortion goes: see, they read the Bible and find love in it, whereas I read it and see a warped, culturally distorted hack job with a few rare brilliant gems buried in it. If you dig down deep enough into Christian theology of almost every stripe, it boils down to this belief: that while we humans may do good things and even be capable of beauty and love, none of that is enough to make up for the utter evil of our essence. Only Jesus could do that.

It's almost impossible to convey just how thoroughly we believed that we were steeped in sin. We were the tea bags, the hot water, and the tea itself. Sin was twisted into our very fiber. Every single person I knew in the universe agreed with this fundamental truth: that every single human on earth was sinful. Depending on your denomination, you might talk about our human "sin nature," or if you were a Calvinist you'd just go all in and call it "total depravity."

Somehow my parents could live with this fact, our total fucked-ness, by countering it with the incredible good luck of having been rescued. They lived in the silver lining of being saved.

Everyone I knew agreed on this point: Christians were the lucky ones, because we had been redeemed. That meant that even though we were rotten to our cores, God had relented and punished Jesus instead of us.

All of us kids knew a lot about how that punishment went down. For starters, Our Loving Lord Above had had people whip Jesus with cat o' nine tails (which, as everyone knows, are leather whips with sharp metal bits on the ends), stick thorns into his skull, and beat him with sticks. Even this punishment wasn't enough for the big Daddy-O, though. Jesus had to have big thick pegs pushed through his wrists and ankles, be nailed to a cross, and die.

Apparently Jesus's loving Father had cherry-picked this particular form of death for Jesus because it was the most agonizing one.

That's how bad we were.

At school, we spent a lot of time talking about this. We knew all about the wounds of Jesus. We could recite them in great detail. We sat terrified out of our fucking minds, gorged on images of torture, while the grown-ups swayed, and murmured in tongues, and floated on the gory thrill of it.

The kicker was that all that flagellation and pain that poor old Jesus went through was still hardly enough. We were saved, sure, but only *just barely*. You could step into sin at any moment, easier than stepping in dog poo on the sidewalk. There was a solemn pained look on the faces of the redeemed that meant that they were remembering how sinful they had been, and how narrowly they had squeaked into salvation. They'd better watch out or they'd slip again.

And it was so easy to slip; the devil was wily. He was after Miss Jill, as we'd learned, and he could get you any time you felt afraid or angry. The Browns explained that those sinful feelings opened up a crack in you, and that crack was how the demons got in. To complicate matters, if you felt angry, it was just as bad as committing murder, just like lusting after a woman with your eyes was as bad as adultery. (I wasn't sure what lust meant, but I had figured out that adultery was when married people kissed someone they weren't married to.)

There was an odd plot twist, though; forgiveness, that's a real thing for Christians. Murder was a terrible sin, of course, but if you asked forgiveness, God would forgive you even of that. You could lie and cheat and steal your whole life, and then say sorry on your deathbed, and you were IN. All you had to do to get forgiveness was ask. The only thing you couldn't be forgiven for was something *you didn't say you were sorry for*. Since my wretched feelings rose up in me unbidden all the time, they had to be checked off, forgiven, all the time. I was obsessive about keeping prayed up. Every time I'd feel fear or anger, I'd squinch my eyes shut inside my head and pray, "I'm sorry, please forgive me for being angry." But then instead of a flood of peace, I'd feel another surge of anger, and so I'd have to pray for forgiveness again. Then the fact that I was so sinful, to keep feeling these wrong things, would cause a dreadful gnawing; here was more confirmation that I wasn't really saved after all. I thought of hell and pincers and those spikes they would poke people with. It was terrifying. But terror was of the devil! Just more proof that I wasn't really saved! And around and around I'd go.

I'd pray my desperate prayer silently, fiercely. *Please save me, please let me go to heaven, please love me. I'm so sorry, I'm so sorry. Please give me a sign, I have faith.*

There was never a sign.

The Browns may have been right about the devil. They told us that our fear gave it an opening. But if fear was the chinks in our armor, it was the Browns who wielded a chisel and a hammer on us.

—m—

I was in the car with my mother, telling her about Miss Jill's seizure. "And I know that the fear is how the devil gets in, but I still felt scared."

"Sweetheart, it's perfectly normal to be afraid." My mother's face was flustered, and she was looking at me intensely. I felt the hot vinyl of the car seat sticking to my legs. My throat closed down and a great vise gripped my neck. I squeezed out the words, "I know it's wrong, but I don't know how to stop."

She looked horribly concerned. "Honey, really, it's okay to feel afraid." The two deep curves had appeared between her eyebrows. I stared at her. It was her word against the Browns', and the stakes were high. Something in me yearned toward her so fiercely that I felt my body begin to cant toward her. I almost tilted sideways, as if I would just melt into her lap under the steering wheel. I could feel the sweetness of that softening, how beautiful it would feel to lean into her and have her hold me and let my tears come. I hadn't felt the softness of her chest and arms in a while, and I longed to fall into her the way my baby sister did, to wail all my hurts into her body and be comforted. I could see the fine lines of her neck, the swooping wings of her collarbones under her blouse. She seemed so delicate, so fragile. I could feel the heat in me, the great fiery torrent of terror and rage. I couldn't pour that out onto my sweet mother. It would engulf her, melt her, infect her with my evil. She was so vulnerable, because she didn't even know how easily the devil could seep into you. I stared at her, mute, miserable.

Once again, my parents seemed helpless and unaware in the face of great danger. They had sent me to school to learn about God, and the Browns had told me things about God that even my parents didn't know. My gentle folks just went blithely about their work, teaching classes and holding church services, singing their praise songs, unaware that there was a spiritual battle being waged around us all the time. It scared me to know things they didn't know.

It never occurred to me to tell them how frightening school was. They already knew that the school policy involved spanking; my parents had no problem with spankings; every Christian family we knew spanked their kids. It didn't occur to me that what happened at home—swats with a hand, always over clothes—was very different than the sickening beatings happening at school. I didn't realize that they might have been (would absolutely have been) horrified and appalled.

It came down to this: I loved my parents, and I knew that they loved me—oh, I knew it—but they also loved God. And we were all in Japan for God, and sometimes you had to endure trials for God. That was how God chastened the ones He loved. I mean look what happened to poor Jesus.

Our job was to endure everything with a joyful heart, as unto the Lord. No one else seemed to be having trouble with this.

CHAPTER FIVE

I loved reading Nancy Drew books. My grandmothers would mail them to me in stacks, big brown sea mail packages from Kentucky strapped up with duct tape. I loved Nancy's bravery, her savvy, her cunning, and her ability to take care of herself and take down the bad guys. I didn't mind that they were formulaic; I found it comforting. I longed for a tiny waist, red-gold hair, and a courageous blue roadster.

Halfway through fourth grade, I was reading the one where Nancy is called on to act in a vampire movie to help solve a crime. A killer is pretending to be a real vampire on set, and Nancy goes undercover as an actress to solve the mystery. It turns out to be some crook dressed up in a cape and plastic fangs, of course. (This was my favorite storyline; the scary supernatural things weren't real! It was just bad people! Hurray! Oh, I liked that one a lot.) The cover of the book was dark and dramatic, with Nancy wearing a purple cloak and a vampire lurking in the background, but I felt brave knowing that Nancy would figure it all out.

The Browns pulled me aside at lunch one day. They told me that they were concerned about the demonic books I was reading. I was puzzled, then pulled out the Nancy Drew.

"You mean this one? Oh no, it's just a detective story," I explained. They shook their heads in unison.

"You must be very careful, child. You don't want to let the devil in. He's very crafty. He'll come into any opening you give him." I felt the secret shiver inside, the one that reminded me that the devil was already in me. He had already seeped in so deep I couldn't get him out. Still, I labored to explain to them that in this one instance, they were mistaken.

"It's actually just the set of a *movie* about vampires, it's not really about real vampires at all. Nancy Drew's a detective."

"You don't understand, child. Even carrying around that picture is very, very dangerous. It's like carrying around a satanic symbol. It's an invitation for the devil to take over your body. You don't want that, do you? For the devil to be in control of your body?"

"No, Mrs. Brown. Really, I don't. But see, that vampire is just a costume. It's just a guy wearing plastic fangs and a cloak. See, he's trying to steal the—"

"It can happen in an instant. You must always be on guard, always aware. You must not let there be even the slightest crack. The devil is always after you, always watching you. He knows what you're doing every minute, and he's always waiting for his opportunity."

I had a crazed image of the devil as Santa Claus. *He sees you when you're sleeping, he knows when you're awake...* I could see those horns poking up past the red velvet cap, the rotten leer hidden by a cotton wool beard. I could feel a horrifying, irreverent, disrespectful mad giggle bubble up inside me. I widened my eyes and locked my jaw to yank it back. *No, no, don't laugh*; if I laughed, they would spank me, I knew it. They would pull down my pants and show my vagina to the world and hit me with their heavy wooden paddle. That stopped the giggle.

And then, as they kept talking, talking, talking, something happened. Something amazing. Something that qualifies, in my mind, as a bona fide goddamn miracle. In the midst of my frustration and embarrassment and explanations, some tiny and earnest part of me stepped back and watched the discussion at a slight distance. It cocked its head. *Wait a minute*, it silently noted. *They're not listening to reason. They're not listening at all. They're not paying attention. They're just trying to scare me.*

It was just a moment, just a tiny nanosecond of hesitation. And yet that moment was the beginning of my rebellion, though it would take years to reach its full fury. It was just a tiny seed of straightforward information: *Whaddaya know? These people are a little nuts.*

Instantly I batted it back: *You can't say that.*

Too late!

That knowledge was such a surprising little kernel. It was like a little incredulous bean sprout unfurling in my soul. Seconds later, it withered in a hot blast of shame, of course, but that is the thing about those moments of truth. You can smash them down, but it never works for long. They keep raising their impudent heads and arching their skeptical eyebrows. They keep popping up in the most friendly way, saying, *Hello! What the fuck is going on here?*

CHAPTER SIX

It was the middle of the night. The dark pressed down, and everyone was asleep. I was lying in bed, absolutely bursting, desperately needing to go to the bathroom. I kept telling myself that I could wait until morning, squeezing my thighs together. No good. I climbed down the ladder from my loft, feeling the sharp corners of the wood press reassuringly into my hands and feet. I tiptoed out into the hall and peered down the dark tunnel of the stairs. I could feel the demons with their leathery wings and rotten teeth waiting for me in the darkness. I could hear their faint hissing and the tapping of their talons as they crouched to strike.

I whispered, "Get away in the name of Jesus!"

This, you see, was supposed to be the magic phrase that had power over all things evil. If you said, "I'm a child of Jesus and his protection is over me," then nothing could hurt you. We heard stories of missionaries being attacked by bandits with knives, and how the virtuous missionaries stood there, calmly, and said the magic phrase, and the bandits fell back as though they had been whacked down by big angelic swords. I listened to these stories with my mouth agape, clenched with frenzied longing. I asked a lot of questions about how exactly to get that kind of protection. The teachers explained that it worked because the missionaries had had faith, so I tried to have faith, too.

I truly believed that God had more power than some stupid evil demons. Whether He would use it on my behalf was another matter entirely. I wasn't even totally convinced that the demons looked like the pictures I'd seen, with their claws and evil leers, but I did know for sure that sometimes a heavy blackness pressed me down into the bed so that I couldn't move, blocking my throat and cutting off all air.

That night, one hand touching the wall as I felt my way down the stairs, I had faith as hard as I could. I clenched my teeth and brandished my arm like I was carrying my own angelic sword. I made it to the icy bathroom, let a hot flood of relief pour out of me, and raced back up the stairs, up the ladder, and into the comfort of my bed.

I lay there, heart pounding. I could hear whispers and scuffles just below me. I tried to sing, "Jesus loves me, this I know," but I couldn't make my voice come out. There was just one problem with the magical pronouncements—they only worked if you really were truly a child of Jesus. God protected the virtuous and smote down the wicked. And as hard as I prayed, as many times as I asked Jesus into my heart, I could still feel the things flapping in the dark hallway. I could feel them clutching and scrabbling at me. Then there was the troubling fact of that black smothering darkness that came some nights.

I knew what it all meant: it meant I wasn't really one of Jesus's little lambs. I was a goat. I wasn't Jacob; I was Esau. As the cold certainty of that fact flooded my body, fear would have its way with me.

The movies would start up in my mind. I could see knives, blood, children screaming. I saw torture chambers, red-hot metal pressed against flesh, broken bones. I saw the pictures from the pornographic magazine I had stumbled on in the woods one day, where sharp things had been shoved inside women's vaginas. I saw women thrown down to the ground, their legs pried open, and felt a twist in my belly so deep that I would sometimes retch against my pillow. I would press and press on my eyes in the dark, I would moan and weep, but I could not make the images go away.

Obviously everyone else dealt with this stuff without any problem. They never talked about it. I didn't know why I couldn't just handle it cheerfully like everyone else.

CHAPTER SEVEN

In the midst of all this darkness, in between the cringing and biting my nails, moments of strange joy spiked through— blissful aberrations. They stood out so starkly from the daily horror of school and the warm confusion of home that I didn't know what to do with them, so I just sort of tucked them away, like curios from an exotic journey.

My brother Jake was in Japanese school, and he was being bullied. Bullying is a real problem in Japan; it's so severe that children as young as fourth-graders sometimes kill themselves over it. Jake was athletic, tough, and he spoke perfect Japanese. He was also really good at soccer, which I was completely envious of, since I was hopeless at any sport that involved spheres. This was enough to let him pass through school unharmed, for the most part. He had some good neighborhood friends, and together they'd go off in their little shorts, even in the dead of winter, to kick their soccer balls or use their allowance to buy *Bikkuriman* cards at the Family Mart, or to catch enormous *kabutomushi* beetles in the summer. But there was one boy in his class who wouldn't leave Jake alone. My parents had tried everything: talking to the teacher, talking to the boy's parents, having lots of conversations about forgiveness and turning the other cheek and walking away.

But one day Jake came home with more bruises, again. My dad was done.

"Come here, son." Jake walked over, smearing his eyes with the backs of his hands. "I'm going to show you how to throw a punch."

"Virgil!" My mother was horrified.

"There are some things you just can't understand about being a boy, Beth. Now, Jake, listen. I want you to make a fist. Yes, like that. And then what you do is, you punch him in the belly as hard as you can. Try it. No, harder. Hold your thumb like this. Again. Again. Harder. Good."

I stood there watching, appalled and tantalized. We were never allowed to hit people. (Though grownups could hit children, of course; that was different.) Jake and I punched and kicked each other all the time, but we had a loyal bond: no matter what, you never told on each other to a parent, because what they would dish out would be so much worse than any abuse we could heap on each other. We never ratted each other out, not even the time he choked me until my vision blurred, or I kicked him as hard as I could in the spine.

And here my dad was teaching Jake how to hit! I wished he'd teach me too!

They practiced their punches all afternoon. "You won't get in trouble with me, son. If you hit a kid that's weaker than you, you'll be in big trouble. But if this kid won't stop beating up on you, then it's okay for you to hit him back. You'll only have to do it once."

It was the most heretical thing I'd ever heard my father say. There were special circumstances? The rules didn't always apply? There was so much gentleness in his face as he showed Jake how to hold his fingers just right, how to punch straight forward and through.

The next day we all waited for Jake to come home so we could find out what had happened.

"Well, son? Did you do it?"

"Yeah," was all Jake said, kicking a rock.

The boy never bothered him again; and then they became good friends. I didn't understand this at all, but I found it fascinating. It seemed, weirdly, like good news.

—〰—

When I was still at the religious nutjob school, Mrs. Brown got an idea for a Christmas mural that we would all create together. It involved great big panels of foamboard and an insane quantity of eggshells. For weeks we all came to school with our plastic bags of clean eggshells, and no matter how carefully we had scrubbed them at home with soap, trying not to crush them completely, the smell of sulfur was overwhelming. We were each instructed to sketch a scene from the Nativity story on our foamboard, then we were to glue eggshells on like mosaic tiles, and then paint the whole thing. It would be very beautiful and sacred even though it would surely smell like farts.

My assigned scene in the montage was of Joseph and a very pregnant Mary traveling to Bethlehem. I sketched out a donkey, copying it from a Bible picture, and drew Joseph's rough stocky figure in too. But when I started to draw Mary, an odd sensation started at my fingers and began to creep up my arms. It was like I was little again and lying on the grass outside The Center, the liquid gold streaming into me. I sketched in her gentle face, her hands folded meekly (easier to draw that way) and the sweet bulge of her belly. It was almost like there was music in my head; I felt like I was far away and didn't want to come back.

I looked down at the drawing and hardly knew how I had drawn it so well. In a few soft gray strokes, my pencil had outlined a tired woman gazing down the road ahead, her body heavy but her expression serene. Next to her, the donkey and Joseph looked like crude toddler drawings. My body was still pulsing and pooling with the liquid light as I put down my pencil. I was blissfully, restfully happy, but something else too—I felt like I had done something that would last forever, as if no matter what happened to the drawing itself, it would always exist somewhere, maybe in that golden light. The teacher ended the art lesson and I was startled that an hour had gone by so quickly. I wanted to go somewhere and cry; I wanted to hide in the bathroom and dance. I did neither of those things, but instead took my joy to the park with everyone else until it slowly faded. Eventually, I would obediently cover that holy drawing with crumbled eggshells, obscuring it. But when I thought about that moment, I could still feel a tiny little kernel of gold deep inside my heart.

Now clearly, that precious little gold drop was a seed of wicked heathen joy. After all, only the Catholics worshipped Mary, and everyone knew that they were *definitely* going to hell. I suppose I should have been horrified and prayed for forgiveness that I had accidentally dallied in Mary-worship. The tiny little kernel was certainly the devil in his favorite disguise as an angel of light. After all, everyone knew that God wasn't about crazy good golden bliss; God was piercing and blood and shame and tears. Only the devil could feel that delicious, for the devil was always out to trick us.

If it was beautiful, it was probably evil. I knew that. I really did. The little gold kernel was something I should have apologized for. But here was an odd thing: I didn't want to. I wanted to keep it anyway.

A tiny little missionary popped out of my mind in horror.

"You want to keep it even if you know it's the devil seducing you into heathen Catholic Mary-worshipping sin???" This part of me gesticulated, rolled her eyes, and writhed on the ground. The rest of me watched her calmly.

Yes. That's exactly what I want to do.

And so that little kernel stayed there, yet another secret. But this one was a delicious one. The secret knowledge that I could half-close my eyes, let the world go into soft focus, and feel a golden haze illuminate everything. That even the dust motes in the air would shimmer with an iridescent language I could almost speak. Even though I was a castaway from the true church and the love of God, still, when the dust motes and the golden light on the leaves and petals and buildings spoke to me, I just didn't care as much. That gold feeling was almost worth going to hell for.

CHAPTER EIGHT

The year that my sister Ruth was born, my parents bought a vacation home. They bought it sight unseen, for $2000, from missionaries who were retiring and moving back to the USA. It was Cabin #47 in a mysterious place called Kogayama, a small community of vacation homes owned collectively by a group of missionaries. We packed two weeks' worth of clothes and food into our car, wedged Ruth into her car seat, and drove seven hours northeast along the coast of Japan. We pulled into a gravel parking lot shaded entirely by pine trees and bamboo. The woods were so thick we couldn't see a single cabin, but there was a set of crooked steps and a wheelbarrow, so we gamely started our climb up the hill. About seven hundred hours later, we reached our new cabin. It was at the end of the line, up a dirt path, over roots and rocks, through uncut weeds that stood chest-high. It was a rust-colored, boarded-up wooden cabin ravaged by bugs, small animals, mold, decay, and bird bones.

It immediately became my favorite place in the world.

Over the years, we changed houses, schools, and continents over and over again, but this shabby wooden building was a constant, and my family still returns to it faithfully every summer. We love it the way some families love their Tuscan villa.

The first time my dad wrestled off the rusty padlock and we sidled uncertainly inside, there were weeds growing up through the floorboards. Odd splinters of light streamed through cracks in the wall. It smelled like mildewed dog. But it was huge, and its bones were a strangely majestic blend of Japanese architecture and western adjustments like raised doorways. Rumor had it that the house had been commandeered by a general during World War II, and we found a stash of newspaper clippings from the 1920s. With our stunning grasp of history, my brother and I deduced that there must be pirate loot buried under the floors.

As a bonus, there were barrels and barrels of missionary junk to go through: old padlocked trunks full of musty linens; stacks of ancient magazines piled everywhere; bookshelves crammed with paperbacks; a tool room upstairs filled with rusty, ancient implements. The next year Ruth would toddle around with a flyswatter, joyfully killing the giant bugs we called "hoppers," but that first year Jake and I had to do it. They would crunch and sometimes explode, living up to their name even as we smashed them.

For a kid raised in Yokohama, this wooded hill was like the deepest wildest wilderness. Jake and I thrilled to warnings about poisonous snakes and bears, though the most dangerous thing we actually ever saw was pheasant. There was a freedom about those days that was dreamy and soothing; there were all those trees, trails, and rooms to hide in. I spent most of my time reading, as usual, but I could read in more unusual positions, like draped over the ancient furniture or curled up in the crumbling window seat, that part of the cabin that was inside but only just barely. I romantically adopted it as my "reading spot" because it sounded like something I might find in *Little Women* or *Anne of Green Gables*, my two favorite books. I just had to be wary of the bugs that would drop in from above and the long grass that would poke up through the baseboard and tickle my knees.

Here was a strange thing: it was Miss Dorothea, the mean lady from The Center all those years ago, who had given me my first L.M. Montgomery book. I couldn't believe that someone who obviously disliked me so much would give me a book that I loved with my whole soul. Could she have possibly have *read* it? How could someone like her empathize with someone like Anne, who was all dreams and furious longing and poetry? And how did she know that I would like it too? I had no answers for these questions.

Every day the five of us would adorn ourselves with floaty rings, towels, rubber flip-flops, grass mats, a picnic lunch and sunscreen lotion and trudge down to the beach. It would be awful later, coming back up the hill tired and sandy and sticky with salt, swatting at the mosquitoes that came out at dusk, sliding around in our wet sandals. But that never stopped us. The beach was what I lived for—communing with the water, sitting at the edge and letting it lap at me, feeling like there was a language to the way the water would lick my feet. I was hypnotized by it. Then the sand fleas would bite, those nasty little shrimp-bugs, and I'd sashay into the water, dive into a wave, and feel my hair float out behind me. I felt beautiful there in the water, with my hair streaming down my back instead of spiraling out in a frizz of static. I would swim with my feet pressed together, a mermaid or a dolphin. I kept thinking that I could feel things, sense things—my overblown imagination, I would tell myself, but in the water, half in and half out, half landed and half fluid, I felt something flowing in and out of me, or perhaps I was flowing in and out of *it*. The sky was wide open above me, the pine trees gripped the cliffs like gnarled fingers, and I felt connected to everything the ocean could touch. Sometimes I would be seized with a sudden dark fear, as if a stingray had floated underneath me and I could sense its shadow, and I could feel all the big somber things moving through the water—ships, whales, sharks—or the water around me would suddenly be thick with jellyfish or seaweed, and I would thrash out in a panic to sit, panting, on the hot sand. But soon enough, I'd be back out in the water, perhaps with a raft this time to buoy me, floating on the edge of the earth where the sky met the water, feeling that lapping kiss at my knees, toes, and neck. I was part of something. I was right there where it happened.

Then salty salmon *onigiri* rice balls for lunch, and icy tea from the blue thermos.

One summer, my dad made up an elaborate treasure hunt for Jake and me. Its clues took us all over our hill, down to the beach to count steps and dig holes, and over to the other hill to ask embarrassing questions of kindly missionaries. Each clue led to another until finally we found our booty: two model speedboats that really worked. We spent happy hours cutting, gluing, and painting them, and one glorious day took them down to the ocean for their first trip. We gripped our remote control boxes, speeding our boats across the water, racing and bumping each other, catching the waves so that the little crafts zoomed up into the air, my brother and I cackling with a high, fierce joy.

—m—

On that same beach, I met my first lawyer. I had heard of such things, lawyers, though I wasn't yet old enough to have read *To Kill A Mockingbird* or to see any potential for heroism in the profession. Instead, I was fascinated by the part of the justice system that required even guilty parties to be defended by a lawyer. This just seemed plain wrong. One evening around a community bonfire on the beach, as kids whacked at a watermelon with a stick and the older kids set off fireworks, I approached this man, The Lawyer.

"So. Do some of your friends defend criminals?" I asked, with breathtaking nine-year-old diplomacy. He nodded.

"But you've never defended someone who was guilty, right?" I asked, sure that he would say no. He had, after all, attended Sunday morning church with the missionaries.

"Sure I have," he replied. I stared. I'm sure my mouth was open. He sighed and ran his hand across his chin like he was trying to see if he needed to shave. "Even people who've done something wrong deserve a fair trial, don't you think?"

I thought about this. "Sure, maybe in theory, but as a Christian—"

He actually snorted in disgust, which sent some tiny barely formed antennae climbing up above my ears. I was paying attention with a part of me that usually stayed asleep. He brought it home for the kicker and asked, "Don't you think Jesus loves sinners?"

I paused. "Yes," was the proper answer. But that "yes" meant that Jesus's love for sinners was a kind of sick addiction. He loved them in spite of the fact that they were so loathsome. He was pained by the sinners' sin, felt sorrow for them, and was probably ashamed that he had even made them. It often seemed that Jesus was so sad and forgiving that he sometimes felt a bit faint, so He would let His Father do the punishment part. His Father loved that part. The two of them had a good-cop, bad-cop act going.

I looked up at the lawyer and said, "Yesss?" I didn't usually admit that I had a closely guarded and highly secret heretic hope that something, like some renegade part of God that wasn't allowed into Sunday School, didn't even care about the sins all that much, that he mostly liked the people. I knew better than to voice such a hope. It was called Universalism, and New Age, and I'd get prayed over for being those things.

The man looked at me kindly. "Not everything is black and white," he said. "Lots of things are shades of gray." Then the conversation turned to marshmallows and jackets, and that was it. I kept my eye on him the whole rest of the evening, though. I was pretty sure this man was going to hell, but I wanted to run after him and hug him anyway because when I'd been talking to him there was a pounding in my chest, an eager catching breath like I'd been underwater for a long time and had come up for a brief gasp of air. As he moved through the dark night and in and out of the light of the fire, it was as if faint gray shimmers were rising off of him, as if he was shedding thin skins of silver.

CHAPTER NINE

Between fourth and fifth grade, something impossible happened.

My father performed some sort of diplomatic magic and persuaded the big Christian school in Tokyo to loan us a teacher. Then he cleared out two musty rooms in the very back of The Center and painted the walls yellow. He hauled in desks. He washed the windows. He went in with nails bristling from his mouth and pounded things down until the rooms were tight and clean and the windows opened wide to let in the smell of the pine trees. I hung around, pretending to help, watching, not sure if this really meant what I thought it might. No more Browns, no more paddlings, no more swaying and speaking in tongues? Could it be? I hardly dared hope. I probably looked sullen, and irritated. I was tight and clenched with hope and fear that it might not really happen. Or that somehow it would end up being even worse.

And so one corner of The Center became a two-room schoolhouse, and five of us kids, spanning grades 2 to 5, became our own school. We filed in the first day. Five desks faced a big white board. And standing in front of the white board was a wizened, grinning, skinny man with white hair.

Mr. Wilkins must have been in his fifties, but he seemed ancient to us. Even so, he had a vivaciousness, a zestiness, that I had never encountered in a teacher. He beamed at us. He gave us interesting books to read. He took us outside to collect bugs and make weather stations and go on field trips.

It was very odd.

We tramped all around Yokohama, and everywhere we went, he had us sit down and write in our notebooks about what we had seen. Then—this part blew my mind—he told us we were good writers. Us! Me! He must have been a little eccentric, for I had it on good authority, aside from my brief stint with the advanced reading group in America, that I was in fact a bad student and kind of stupid. But Mr. Wilkins wouldn't stop with the praise; he was relentless. It was like he actually wanted us to be proud of the work we did. I couldn't figure out his angle.

It was a joyful and total mind-fuck. My brain was literally scrambling to make sense of this new world. It was as if I'd gone from educational debtors' prison right up to the castle in one fell swoop, and I hardly trusted the riches. I kept waiting for the boom to fall, for him to start screaming or to brandish a paddle. But he never did.

One time a snake found its way into our classroom from the wild green outdoors, and Mr. Wilkins caught it up with a forked stick and carried it gently out to a tree, letting it slither gracefully into its roots while we gathered round, awestruck. He pointed out its beautiful patterning, showing us how it disappeared among the leaves and dirt. He seemed almost fond of it, and this puzzled me. Didn't he know that snakes were evil? Shouldn't he club it to death? And yet I felt a little stirring of affection, too; the snake seemed gentle, even innocent for a moment; just a little creature that had wandered into the wrong neighborhood. I shook my head. Things were shifting too fast, and I felt like I was losing my balance.

In a small cage in our classroom lived a guinea pig that we named, most imaginatively, Ginny. Plants sat in the windowsills, practically preening with satisfaction. We had stacks of books to read. We had blank lined notebooks to fill. We had hours of silent puttering when we glued, sanded, and painted things. Slowly, in the gentle sunlight, under Mr. Wilkins' eager gaze, something in me tentatively unkinked.

Every morning my brother and I would get in the car with my father and ride with him to work. At a certain point during the trip, my brother would turn green, my father would stop the car, and they would both bolt out the doors so my brother could throw up. My father would wipe

Jake's mouth tenderly with one of the soft white handkerchiefs he always carried, then he would stick it back in his pocket to sour and curdle before herding us back into the car.

When we reached the smooth gravel of the Center yard, my dad would kiss us goodbye, call out, "Love you!" and then he would go through the big polished front door to the office. We would go around the back, through the flowers and pine trees, to the tiny back entrance by the rooms that had become our schoolhouse. The *genkan* entrance was dark and musty, and we would take off our shoes and place them on the wooden shelf. Then we'd step into our classroom and it would be full of light and color. The walls glowed ochre. Posters marched across the wall above the windows. Our weathervanes swirled madly with the colors we'd each picked out: royal blue and gold, red and black, green and silver.

Mr. Wilkins brought with him a full-size puppet theater with red velvet curtains and complicated gold curlicues. We learned about the Punch and Judy shows in history class and molded our own puppet heads out of clay. Then we papier-mâché'd them, painted them, and sewed clothes for them. I don't even remember the story we finally performed, except that it involved an exuberant dragon, but I do remember the happy hours spent with my fingers in wet flour paste, smoothing newspaper strips. The sun streamed through the windows, the pines whispered outside, and as my body industriously shaped things, my mind finally relaxed enough to slip into bliss again. I didn't know it at the time, but making things with my hands has always been one of the ways my wise self heals the things in me that are broken. Those hours were pure and good medicine.

I would wander out from those afternoon creativity sessions totally stoned on joy, stumbling out into the sunshine. While everyone else ran around, I would swing in a kind of daze. There was a wooden rope swing slung from a high tree branch, and we would lug the wooden seat and heavy rope up to the top of the slide-and-swing-set for little kids, twist the rope around and around as tight as it would go, lodge the seat between our knees, and then jump off in a big wide arc. The swing would spin us out into the air and slowly wrap itself around the trunk, and if you timed your twirls just right you could catch yourself with your feet on the bark, push off again, and spin around again the other way, the rope getting shorter on every spiral until you were tight against the bark again. It was joy, it was sheer joy, and it was also escape. As the world blurred and whirled, I felt still and quiet inside, like all the planets were still spinning fast, but I had finally found my place among them.

—◦◦◦—

I was obsessed with Cherry Ames books. I bought them on our rare family trips to the only second-hand English bookstore in Yokohama, and I'd look for them at the annual rummage sale at the big Christian school. I amassed a modest stack of musty hardback copies from the 1950s. I loved the neat efficiency of the nurses, the way they put their hands on their hips, tied on an apron, and handled anything that came their way, including War War II. I found them infinitely comforting. When I told Mr. Wilkins that I wanted to be a nurse, he shook his head at me.

"Oh, for heaven's sake," he said, "You don't need to be a nurse—you can be a doctor!"

I believe that at the time I told him I'd rather be a nurse because of the beautiful white hats they wore, but a very skeptical part of me was listening to him with her mouth hanging open. She was shocked, but she jotted it down anyway in a kind of scandalized glee.

When I rode the train home every day with my brother, the neighborhoods slid by in kaleidoscope colors. We whisked past ripe orange persimmons, crimson maple trees, deep cobalt blue roof tiles. Concrete loomed everywhere, dirty gray and impersonal, but laundry sprinkled even the most institutional-looking apartment blocks. Shirts and socks and *futon* and old men's belly wraps blew around as gay and out of control as confetti. As the world flashed by, all those thousands upon thousands of peoples' lives compressed into each glance, my throat ached. The wild tangled beauty of Japan was sneakily threading its way into my very soul. It stitched in pink lanterns and orange *yakitori* signs and lime green local trains. It quilted in frothy pink *sakura* petals and yellow flames of forsythia and sour red pickled plums. It wove those vivid threads so deeply into me that they would never completely let me go.

—∞—

Every Thursday, after taking the train home from school, I would stop off at Kentucky Fried Chicken, order five nuggets and a small paper packet of fries, and walk to ballet class near the station. It was a perfectly nice but normal suburban dance studio, picked by my parents for its proximity to our home. They had no way of knowing that one of Japan's great dancers happened to be teaching there, and we wouldn't figure it out for quite a while.

Minamoto-*sensei* was unbelievably thin, and her long elongated limbs moved like water. When she pointed her bare feet until the toes curved down toward her heel, a little explosion of joy went off behind my breastbone. She lilted, she leapt, and she issued commands. She had an enormous black mole between her nose and her cheek, but instead of making her ugly, it made her even more beautiful. I adored her, worshipped her, and was terrified of her in equal measure. She forbade toe shoes for her students, because they warped the feet, and what she wanted from us even more than grace and perfect form was *feeling*—she would have us dance trees, or waves, or bugs, or death. It all happened fast, and she spoke in a quick staccato that I couldn't always follow, and I wasn't really all that good—but when it came time to dance things with our feelings, boy oh boy did I have feelings.

I blinked back the tears that oozed out of my eyes as I felt myself become dirt, and then my heart would rise up like sap as I uncurled from a tiny seed, my fingers inching out one by one to unfurl into tight little green leaves, and I was in total and utter bliss. I didn't mind the pulled muscles and the pain of trying to do the splits, or the mortification of always spinning the wrong way whenever we crossed the floor on the diagonal, two by two, my tidy Japanese partner whirling and stepping perfectly, contained and in rhythm, while I flopped and faltered and sometimes even crashed into the wall. I didn't mind the sour smell of feet or the way my tights always frayed at the ankle when we cut off the toes and heels, the way *Sensei* insisted.

I loved the crunch of the rosin, the authoritative way the older girls would press their feet into it, breaking up the little rock crystals into powdery stickiness before twirling and whirling across the room. When we did our stretches and I stuck my feet out and tried, tried, tried to make them go out wide to my sides like the other girls, I would sometimes yank at the canvas and leather ballet slipper in frustration and try to force them out further, until the inside of my thighs burned and my hands would be sticky for the whole evening.

The other girls were kind to me, but I never really felt at ease with them. They asked me again and again where I was from as we changed into our leotards, as though they might understand if they asked me enough times. I always said Indianapolis. They wanted to know whether that was near Disney World. I felt like I was walking around in a brittle glass bubble.

I hated the dark trip home, mostly because of the mortifying buzzer my mother made me wear, the kind that went around my neck on a string like a locket. The idea was that if I encountered any danger, I would grab the buzzer, yank it off its string, and fling it like a grenade. Then it would emit a piercing shriek designed to bring policemen and neighbors rushing to my rescue. But instead somehow the damn thing would always fall off its pin! And start blaring its horrible siren! And then it would inevitably roll into the grass on the side of the road, and I would be down on my knees scrabbling for it in the dark, begging all that was holy that the horrendous noise please NOT bring anyone running. Luckily, it never did. My Japanese neighbors had way better manners than that. If I'd had any sense I would have taken out the batteries. But that was not the kind of sense that I had.

One day I was walking through the train station, weaving through the streams of people trying to be invisible, and heading toward KFC for my regular before-ballet snack. Suddenly Minamoto-*sensei* was standing there, a big bag slung over her shoulder. In her street clothes, she looked even taller, thinner, and more severe. She smiled, but raised her eyebrows and nodded at the friendly Colonel Sanders statue.

"Why don't you come get something healthy with me instead?"

I wasn't sure. Was this allowed? Could I just disappear and pretend she hadn't seen me? But I followed her with a plume of excitement rising inside me as she walked into a dark coffee shop full of smoke and ordered us each a plate of tiny triangular sandwiches.

Heavy red drapes obscured the windows, and muddy oil paintings of European castles hung on the walls. There was a white vinyl lace doily on the table. Men in suits smoked cigarettes and sipped at tiny cups of coffee. Minamoto-*sensei* asked questions and I politely answered, but most of me was buzzing around the room, exploring the heavy glass ashtrays, examining the hand-lettered menus, peeking into the back where the old proprietress was placing one precise sprig of parsley on each of our plates. I tried to concentrate. I gazed at Minamoto-*sensei* with quiet, terrified adoration. I wanted her to scoop me up and swallow me whole. I wanted to disappear into her, to melt into her presence until I too would become elongated and beautiful and have a dark column of hair shimmering down my back.

I could hardly breathe with the intensity of my longing, let alone chew my sandwiches—especially since they were smeared with a fierce green mustard that seared my nose and throat. I tried to swallow but nearly gagged. I wondered if I could sneak some of the sandwich into a napkin and hide it, but there were no napkins, and no glasses of water, either. It was hard to pay attention to what Minamoto-*sensei* was saying when I had this terrible mustard problem to deal with, but suddenly I tuned in. All antennae trembling. She was leaning across the table toward me.

"*Ne*, hey, I think you have a special gift. If you work very hard, you might be able to be a real dancer someday."

I remember her face across the table. I remember how solemn she looked, and how beautifully the mole set off her mouth. I remember nodding.

This was the moment; the very thing I'd longed for; the moment when someone would finally lean in and tell me who I was. It wasn't a finger from the sky, or a flaming bush; it was my elegant teacher and a plate of fiery sandwiches. I waited for the feeling of grace to settle over me. Now I would finally feel safe— now I would be propelled forward by a force greater than myself. I would swoop up to the sky in a golden cloud of purpose, just like in those movies about gymnasts or ice skaters destined to win medals and wear sparkly eye-shadow. Now I would be saved from oblivion, and more importantly, from myself.

I waited for the certainty to kick in. I waited to feel soft and billowy and regal.

Only it wasn't like that at all. Nothing shimmered; my hair didn't straighten out and stream down my back. There was no cloak of safety around me. It was more like Minamoto-*sensei* had handed me a tiny, mysterious creature that wasn't soft and fluffy but scrabbly instead, with sharp claws. I didn't know what to do with it. I tried to sit still and hold it in the palm of my hand, to accept that this conversation was special, and maybe even kind of a secret. That she wanted me to hear something from her.

But I couldn't hold it. I kept gazing raptly at *Sensei*'s beautiful face, still hoping to be rescued and swooped out of my life. I didn't understand that she was talking about a process that would take years. I didn't understand that this little nugget of praise was to be the only one I would get. I would have to eke it out, live off it for years, find a way to feed my own dreams. She wouldn't do it for me. I glossed over the part of her little speech where she said, "If you work hard."

And so I let the awkward poky little creature drop out of my hand instead of holding onto it. I giggled. I ducked my head. I said, "Who, me? Oh, I don't think so." I desperately hoped she would contradict me.

I so wanted for someone to see me and tell me what my gift was, so that I could be absolved of the shame of wanting to have a gift in the first place. I wanted to be both recognized but also told what to do, putting the chicken squarely before the egg.

I wrote in my diary all the time about how much I longed to be an ice skater, or a gymnast, like a character out of those treacly disposable preteen books I'd suck down in a single evening. Yet when someone in real life tried to tell me what would be required, that it meant me deciding, closing my fingers around the sharp scrabbly creature of desire and then working toward it, I didn't hear it. I sat there in the restaurant, feeling like I was sitting with God, and hearing Minamoto-*sensei's* words and being awed by them, but not understanding. I wasn't sure what to do next. Maybe she was just being nice; if she'd meant it, wouldn't she call my parents and demand that I be sent to a special school or given special classes? It never occurred to me that I could tell them myself that I wanted to work toward being a dancer, or to ask what I should do to make that happen. It felt greedy to grab at that; you were supposed to wait, quietly and humbly, and be embarrassed when your destiny was handed to you on a gold platter. Even the joy of sitting with Minamoto-*sensei* at the restaurant was so intense that I was almost glad when it was time to stand up, leave the coffee shop, and go to class.

When it was time for our big annual dance performance, there were no tutus or red satin. Minamoto-*sensei* dressed us younger girls in nude tattered bodysuits, and we danced war and death, birth and grief, to Joan Baez peace ballads. With baskets clutched to our chests, we were soldiers and nurses and angels. We marched, aimed, and fell, and then we would roll over on the ground, pick up our baskets, and become maidens again, gathering flowers. For the grand finale, *Sensei* had all of us poured together on the enormous stage into a great rolling procession that showed the evolution of planet earth. The tiny toddlers wore only little beige panties, and we all danced out the transformation from swimming and squirming to crawling and leaping. The teenagers wore fluttery dresses and climbed a great wooden pyre onstage, the fierce gleam of humanity in their eyes, and there we all were, en masse, with dirt-streaked faces, the whole panoply of creation.

My parents, those wise and generous souls, never gave me a hard time for acting out what I knew was a great heresy: evolution. I never asked them about it, and they never said a word. They just handed over the pale brown envelopes of cash creakily, as if the stacks of bills hurt their joints a little. At first I was bitterly disappointed that there were no pink satin toe shoes or frothy white skirts. My mother must have wondered what all that money was paying for when I brought home my little nude rag of a costume. But once we learned the dances and smeared dirt on our faces, I could feel the thrumming power of the story that *Sensei* was telling. It felt like she was painting a great masterpiece, using our lithe bodies as her paints and brushes. As we pulsed across the wooden stage, rolling and writhing and leaping, I had never felt more in sync with things, as if I was dancing to the very heartbeat of the earth. My teacher watched from the wings, her eyes wet, her gaze steady.

Several months later, in a great and wonderfully unusual act of decadent spending, my mother bought two tickets to Minamoto-*sensei's* solo show. We got dressed up, me in my stiff purple velvet dress, my mother in her soft brown camel coat. We took the train downtown, bought flowers at a fancy downtown flower shop, and walked into the grand theater holding hands.

The dance was called *Tefu-Tefu*, which turned out to be the old Japanese word for butterfly, but as we sat in the fluttering theater trying to decipher the program, my mother and I decided that *tefu-tefu* must be the sound of a butterfly's wings. The lights went down. My heart thudded. And there she was, my teacher, lit up, tiny on the huge stage.

Something seemed wrong. Minamoto-*sensei* was writhing, lurching, moving her body in a way that I found shocking. My beautiful teacher! Why wasn't she showing how gorgeously she could dance? My mother squeezed my hand and whispered, "Do you see? She's being a caterpillar." And then I could see it: there it was, right in front of me. She *was* a caterpillar, rolling and dangling across the stage, twirling and moving as a being with no arms or legs. I was mesmerized.

Eventually she inched her way up to a tree and wound herself in gauze until she was burrowed deep into a cocoon. Then, after a long silence, the whole thing began to tremble. Slowly, so slowly, she began to unfurl the cocoon, struggling and fighting it, until at last she emerged wet, gasping, shaken with tremors and uncertainty. She paused there, breathing, trembling, and I felt myself trembling too, feeling something inside me resonating, like she had found a string deep inside my center and plucked it. Then slowly, bit by tiny bit, she stretched and opened. She became a creature of flight, of leaps and joy and great impossible spirals. I sat there watching with my mother, tears pouring down my face. Some part of me had emerged for the first time, blinking in the brightness, wet and fragile and totally vulnerable. I wanted to cry out with recognition, and I was also clutched with despair that I did not know how to do what Minamoto-*sensei* did, that I did not know how to show magic on a stage or dance a miracle with my body.

Something had happened, some door had been opened, some threshold crossed. I had no words for it, only tears. My mother clasped my hand so that I wouldn't be afraid at the violence of the rending onstage. But I needed to gather myself, to keep a membrane around me so that I didn't fall to pieces, and so I guiltily extricated my hand from hers. After the dance finished, and we had pounded our palms in joy and gratitude, I pulled away from my mother and ran to the bathroom. I was thankful beyond words that she had brought me here. I loved her so much that my heart hurt; I wanted to kiss her on the mouth and curl up in her lap and never leave. And yet I felt in some wordless way that to get where I needed to go, I would need to walk away from her.

Back in real life, I couldn't find my way into the shining beauty of my teacher's dance, nor could I put words to the brilliant thing that had shot into my heart watching her. I was frustrated beyond bearing in dance class. My body felt awkward, stupid; I danced to find transcendence but was clumsy and ugly. My limbs grew heavy. I would hang my head in the middle of lessons and see blackness. I couldn't bear to be so close to that beauty and yet have an impenetrable curtain drawn across it. Minamoto-*sensei* was across a great chasm and I couldn't see how to cross it. I felt like I had finally woken up to the fact that I had been exiled from my true home, and now that I knew it, I couldn't stand to go on. I was in despair, for I believed that my teacher must have been wrong about me; obviously I wasn't a great dancer at all.

I didn't understand that learning is sometimes messy. If I couldn't leap into perfection, I thought, it meant I shouldn't be doing it at all.

Obediently, my body responded to my self-loathing. Shortly thereafter I was always too tired to go to my lesson. I got headaches and cried as I walked to the studio. I felt so cringing and awkward with the other girls that my joints began to ache, so exposed in the bright classroom in the evenings with my blonde hair and awkward self that I began to squint against the lights. I just wanted to crawl behind the velvet curtain where we changed into our leotards and curl into a ball. I wasn't as flexible or controlled as the other girls, and I couldn't find that pure moment I had seen in my teacher onstage; I didn't even have words for what I was longing for. The only words I had for myself were *whiny, dramatic, ungrateful,* and *lazy.*

So I simply quit going.

And I would like to go back to that girl and shake her. I didn't understand then that the purity came from alchemy; I didn't know that the dross could be pushed out through the discipline of practice and turned into gold. I needed a teacher, one who could teach me not just about dance, but about the rhythm of the soul. I had woken up from a kind of dream, and I believed that I was utterly alone. I longed for something, something impossible, something I hardly believed in. It wasn't about being a ballerina; it was about grappling with the world in all its rawness, pain, and transcendence—but I didn't know those words yet, and I simply felt foolish and crazed with longing for I knew not what.

CHAPTER TEN

"Ten minutes!" my mother's panicked cry echoed up the stairs. I fastened the barrette with its dangly feathers into the frizz of my hair, tied the sash of my best Sunday dress, and ran downstairs. I heard the vacuum start up, and I could tell from the violent banging sounds that my father was wielding it. My mother met me at the bottom of the stairs and handed me a laundry basket piled with toys. I carried it up and stashed it just inside the door to my room, along with a pile of dirty laundry, books, and papers. This was our traditional Sunday morning ritual: the frantic house cleaning before the church people arrived for services.

The church was still meeting in our house. The two big adjacent sunny rooms were set up with rows of folding chairs, the kind with shiny metal tubes and brown pleather seats. That Sunday morning we had overslept, and we all five dashed around, hiding the workaday chaos of our family so that things would be tidy when the Japanese congregation arrived. Even my baby sister Ruth helped by stuffing her stack of diapers into the cupboard. My mother was swiping on mascara when the doorbell first rang, and she rushed down the hall fastening an earring.

"Don't forget to check the rabbits," she called out over her shoulder. Flopsy and Mopsy had surprised us by having babies, and they looked like sweet little piglets, curled up against their mother's teats. In an outpouring of love, Ruth would sometimes stuff the rabbits' cage so full of cabbage leaves that they could hardly hop around, so our job was to curtail her eager overfeeding. Every time she did this, Ruth would grin triumphantly, and we'd all explode into laughter, even as my exasperated mother tried to explain about moderation. This was one of the best things about being in my family—we were shameless laughers. We could get tickled by anything, and the giggles would travel from one of us to the next, twining us together in mutual hilarity several times a day. Even over-serious I, with my underdeveloped sense of humor, could get carried along on the waves of my family's riotous mirth. We were easily amused, my dad said.

I followed my brother out to the shed. The light poured through the corrugated plastic roof, and it was hot. Jake was standing strangely still in front of the cage, his video game hanging loose in his fingers. He wore shorts, and his knees had scabs. His eyes were huge and his eyelashes were dark and damp. I stepped next to him and saw that something was wrong. The baby rabbits were stretched out stiff and strange. Their water dish was bone dry.

My mother was already playing the organ when we ran in shouting at her to come. She cradled the tiny furry bodies and tried to put water down their throats with an American Tylenol dropper, but the baby rabbits had died. My mother cried and cried as we huddled around her. Meanwhile, the whole congregation—church abandoned for the moment—looked on with gentle concern. The church ladies helped us decorate a shoebox, and the few rare men who came to church helped us dig a hole to bury them. For the first time, I wasn't sorry that they were all there. Afterward they piled up paper plates full of food for us—cold *somen* salad, deep-fried ginger *karaage* chicken, vinegary *chirashi zushi*, strawberries, cream puffs—and brought them out to the yard, thoughtfully handing us each a set of disposable chopsticks in a thin paper sleeve. Jake and I sat there quietly, eating with our splintery chopsticks, watching each other. The food was delicious. It tasted like love, Japanese flavor.

—⁓—

Once a year or so, we held a church baptism. The church men would drag an empty *ofuro* bath tub to the front of the room, and we'd snake a hose in from outside and fill it with water. White cloth would be draped over the bright blue of the big square plastic tub to make it look elegant and holy.

Sato-*san* was one of the first people baptized at our house. I am sorry to say that I don't remember whether she was nice or kind or what her voice sounded like, but I vividly remember the way her tears made thick tracks through her makeup as she spoke about what Jesus meant to her. She spoke of how sad she had been, how lonely and unloved, and her whole body shook with sobs as she spoke of her new great joy. I watched the tears make great canyons down the putty fields of her face, carving out a glimpse of her skin below the makeup. The tears clung to her chin in great fleshy drops before they would drop, finally, onto her white baptism gown in little ochre spots. I couldn't understand where her emotion was coming from. What had she found that made her so happy? I had found Jesus too, but I sure didn't have tears rolling down my face about it.

In fact, I felt almost allergic to church. I would sit down and feel so squirmy and agitated that I would have to sit on my hands, gnaw on my nails, or compulsively pick at my cuticles to stay in my seat. When everyone sang, it was an aching misery. During the sermon, I could feel myself disconnect and swoop around the room, sleepy and frantic with the suppressed desire to scream, revolt, run away. Obviously, this was evidence of my big secret, that I was possessed by the devil. The Bible says, after all, that the fragrance of beauty and truth will be as a stench to those who are wicked.

I felt almost itchy with my horror at being in that room. The congregation held the thin Japanese hymnbooks, and my mother pounded away at the little organ, and my dad pushed his glasses earnestly up on his nose, and I—I just sat there twitching with misery. It was so boring, and the stories were so awful—Zaccheus up in a tree again, and Paul being blinded on his way to Damascus—the same old stories, again and again, about how we were so bad, and God was so good. And the admonitions. It was relentless, from the pulpit, in Sunday School, in long rambling prayers that were covert mini-sermons. We had to do better, be better. Try harder. Pray harder. Stop being so human! Be holy!

And I couldn't stop. My humanity was everywhere, oozing out of me, all my longings and cravings so frenzied and impossible. So I just twitched, and chewed on my bloody cuticles, and swung my knobby feet against the curved silver of the folding chairs until someone hissed at me to stop kicking, for heaven's sake.

I felt terribly guilty that I was being disloyal to my parents—my eager, earnest, sincere parents. Here they were, working their asses off, doing their best to create a vibrant church. And I was their horrible daughter, the missionary kid who could hardly stand to be there. All those endless church luncheons, with plate after plate of lovingly handcrafted food; all the cups of *mugicha* and orange juice; all the straws, toothpicks, fluted foil cups, all the careful patting of lips with discreet silk handkerchiefs. Even as they set up the long brown folding tables, before any of the Saran Wrap had come off, I was buzzing with irritation and guilt.

But so *much* of what was good and right felt awful to me. For example, take the holy efforts of Christian parenting guru James Dobson. His book *Dare To Discipline* lived on my parents' parenting shelf, and I would flip through it secretly, and with horror. It contained many gems, such as detailed instructions on how to grab a child's neck properly in order to cause the most pain. Dobson explained that if you loved your children, you absolutely must discipline. You must spank, you must hit, you must cause shame and remorse in your child. Only when they understood their own sinful nature could you be successful as a parent. I read the words I knew I wasn't supposed to be reading with fierce puzzlement, because the spankings didn't make me feel more holy or more loving toward my parents; they just made me despise them with a burning hatred. I could see that my parents were faithfully doing everything Dr. Dobson told them to, but it wasn't having the desired effect. I wasn't feeling remorseful or contrite; I was seething.

I am sorry to tell you that this enlightened soul also concocted a series of sex education books and tapes. My mother, bless her heart, bought Dr.

Dobson's offerings. And so it came to pass that on the eve of me turning twelve, she patted a spot next to her on her bed.

I sat down reluctantly. She smiled, but nervously. "So, sweetheart. I thought we could listen to some tapes together. You're, um, going to be a woman soon, and I want you to know what a precious thing that is." She reached over and pushed down the Play button. James Dobson's voice came out of the gray boom box, low, friendly, godly. He began to talk about bodies. Breasts. Virginity. Lust. Marriage. Sex. I looked at my mother. I am quite sure my eyes were bugging out of my head. She kept smiling, her face frozen in panicked determination. There we sat, on the bed she and my father slept in, as this American male voice prattled on about how beautiful sex was between married people, how God's plan was that True Love Waits. I would have plucked out my eyelashes with tweezers, gnawed off my tongue, done anything to get out of there. My mother sat rigid too, her body oozing embarrassment. Finally the voice stopped and the tape clicked off. We sat there for a minute, quietly appalled. I was a mass of writhing grubs inside.

"So, honey? Do you have any questions?" I shook my head so wildly, the feathers on my barrettes flew in front of my face.

"Well, um, have you noticed any changes in your body, sweetheart?" I wanted to place my hands on my poor little hot, itchy breast-buds to hide them. I shook my head again and stared at the quilt with fixed determination.

"Is there anything you want to know about?" My mother was obviously suffering, but determined to do her duty. There was no way I could talk to my mother about my body, its secrets, my fears and feelings. I shook my head again. I thought I might explode into a froth of shame. I wanted to smash the stupid boom box. I wanted to kick James Dobson in the crotch. I wanted to weep on my mother's breast. She finally took pity on me and handed me a book, also by the dear Dr. D.

"Well, honey, I just want you to know that I'm here if you have any questions. I want us to be able to talk about these things." I nodded, stood up, and walked out of the room, pushing my body in front of me, since it had calcified into a stiff mannequin of mortification. I crawled up into my loft bed and shuddered.

Ugh. Awful. Squirmy wretched revoltingness.

Still.

The book was practically ticking, lying next to me, ready to detonate. I closed my eyes. But I couldn't help myself. I pulled the covers up over me, practically buzzing with embarrassment. I don't think I'd breathed in ten minutes.

I already knew the mechanics of sex and babies; I had learned about that from a sweet book called *Susie's Babies*. But I didn't understand why I sometimes felt so hot, so hungry, so furious. Or why it felt so good when I touched myself that certain way at night. Maybe this book would help me figure it out. Wracked with mortification, I began to read it under the covers, occasionally kicking the ceiling inches above my head in frustration.

For the first time, I felt a strange split inside myself. I was reading this book as though there were two of me. One part of me inhaled the words, understood them, and obediently registered the Christian logic of them. Another part of me squinted her eyes in suspicion. The book was all about how our bodies are so precious and we have to guard and protect them, control and rein them in. It echoed the common religious theme regarding a girl's virginity: she is a fragile blossom, and one careless touch will cause her petals to fall to the ground, spoiled and rotten. Great care must be taken to protect this delicate flower, lest she have to walk around the rest of her life as a denuded stamen, vile and hideous.

This was all very lovely, but I was picking up something else from this book. Something under the words was speaking. Its message zinged in as loud and clear as if I had antennae tuned in to a second radio channel. It said, plain as day, that the female body is evil, evil, evil. I felt the two contradictory messages flow into me like two streams running together into a powerful tributary. It was such an odd sensation: I understood the words on the page perfectly, and yet I also could see that they were saying something else entirely.

Through the years I would encounter many such tomes written for and about women, usually by Christian men. They were tangled knots of twisted reasoning, and I felt crazy as I tried to figure them out. Some of their highlights:

- God is not male. He is God. (But we never, ever call God She. Absolutely not.)
- Your body is beautiful. Don't show it off. It is a gift. Don't touch it.
- Sex is beautiful. Sex will ruin you. If you have sex, you'll go to hell.
- Thinking about sex is as bad as having it. Read this book about sex to keep you from thinking about sex.

I didn't know words like "subtext" or have a framework for the kind of postmodern deconstructionist theory that would make so much sense to me in college. All I knew was that these good Christian books said wonderful holy things about how beautiful it was to be a woman. And yet I felt kicked in the stomach by something I couldn't name.

I craved beauty so much. I wanted a blue satin dress and purple suede shoes. I wanted a set of rosebud china I'd once read about. I wanted thick pink velvet curtains on my windows. I wanted a bright yellow watered-silk parasol. I wanted to wear hats with elaborate, cunning feathers on them. If I happened to see a commercial on the VHS tapes our relatives sent from the USA, sometimes I wanted a curling iron and tight jeans, too. But I was more tuned into Louisa May Alcott than to Nickelodeon. I wanted to be beautiful, and I wanted to own lovely, expensive things. But I understood that because we were doing God's will, my family would always be poor. It was what God wanted for us— it was all part of the divine plan. We had to be different: to live in ugly houses and wear hand-me-down clothes and have church in our house every Sunday.

Therefore I hated God.

Therefore I was doomed to hell.

Whee!

Around and around I would go. I would vow to be selfless, to fix my mind upon the things of heaven. Then I would see something beautiful, like the deep rose-colored velvet of the plush carpet at the rug store, and my poor little beauty-loving heart just fell right back into lustful sin. Naturally, the carpet I liked cost ten times more than the practical grayish beige scruff that we ended up with. Why couldn't I just be happy with the beige carpet? My parents stood there in exasperation. Brand new carpet they were buying for me! Out of their limited resources! Why was I so greedy?

Oh my heavens, I didn't know.

It wasn't just that we didn't have the money to buy the beautiful things. It was that the gaping maw in me was so decadent and selfish, so wasteful and sinful, to long for such luxury in the first place. Didn't I care about God's kingdom? What about all the starving children? My parents tried to be kind, but my desires were so ridiculous, so over the top. "Sweetheart, people just don't buy that sort of thing. No one has pink carpet. You could buy a car for the price of that carpet." And so I wept into the ugly scratchy beige floor of my room, scrabbling at it with my fingernails in fury, not understanding why I was so sad about something as venal as carpet. I only knew that my insides were ravaged by a terrible hunger.

I didn't fit in—not in Japan, where I was still a blonde frizzy freak of nature to be ogled, and not within the missionary cocoon at my sweet little school, where I had to constantly hide my true and cranky nature. I wished we could live at our summer cabin at Kogayama year-round; it was the only place that felt like home, the only physical space that had stayed consistent for more than a year or two. There was something else, too: the cabin had all those protective pine trees around it, and farmers' fields rolling away behind. There was a spaciousness inside me there that I never found in the city. I didn't feel as raw there. No one was watching, the air was quiet, and I could rest. It was the only place I could take deep breaths.

Our real house was so cluttered, I felt flattened most of the time. With five of us crammed into a tiny Japanese house, every corner was jammed with furniture, lamps, knickknacks, and craft projects. Every drawer was stuffed full of a strange conglomeration of objects that bore no relation to each other, and you had to shove them back in with all your might to get it closed. Every shelf proudly displayed family photos, pretty vases, candles, and Bible quotes. Each thing individually was lovely, but the overall effect was chaotic. Somehow, even though we didn't have any money, we sure had a lot of things. Sometimes it seemed like we were drowning in them.

I felt most real and most alive when I was escaping to another world through books. The books were rich with color and sheen, dresses and trees, shiny cars and purple-threaded tapestries, a feast of textures and landscapes. And so I read. I read all the time, on trains, walking along the sidewalk, and when I should have been doing homework and chores—sometimes even through the seventh angry call to dinner. I read the same books over and over sometimes, *Nancy Drew* mysteries and *Harriet The Spy*. I even read the ones that induced paroxysms of guilt, like *Treasures In The Snow*, where they were all so good and God loved them so much.

The books saved me, ultimately. My father would make a pilgrimage every few months to the one musty English used-bookstore in train distance and bring home stacks of whatever had turned up in the "Young Reader" section. We still had family story hour every night, though we'd moved on from *Minnie and Maxi* to *The Chronicles of Narnia*. (I liked Aslan a lot more than Jesus, though I never mentioned that, and also I didn't understand how that could be, since clearly Aslan was just code, Jesus disguised as a great lion.) We were a family of readers, my parents always reading silently after dinner, or plowing through book after book with my sister, who was impossibly adorable, and reading horrible endless sports stories to my brother. (It seemed so unfair that Jake was good at sports, in addition to being normal. He had all the luck.) But my dad also brought home everything he could find that he thought I might like, and he piled them willy-nilly into a tall bookshelf: *Babysitters Club* and Judy Blume (oh Margaret!) and *Swallows And Amazons* all mixed in together.

One day when I was supposed to be replacing the paper in the *shoji* screens on the church windows, I found myself sitting cross-legged in front of that shelf. I had pulled out a slim volume I'd never noticed before. It was pale green. The pages were yellowed and swollen. There was a washed-out image of a ball of fire on the front, and in the fire were dozens of eyes. My hands cradled it carefully, like it was a sacred object and not a battered old paperback. I knew it couldn't be possible, but still it seemed that I could hear a faint humming sound coming from my hands. Tentatively, I peeled back the worn cover.

For a few hours, I sat there enthralled while the *shoji* paper stayed rolled up tight, fresh and un-pasted.

The book was *A Wind In The Door* by Madeleine L'Engle, and as I inhaled it page by page, it was like a door literally blew open in my soul and I tasted something new—air that was cold and sweet and full of music. I kept feeling this joyful vibration thrumming deep down in my belly. I recognized these characters! I knew this angry young girl who kept butting heads with everything and everyone! I felt her longing, and I shared her fierce hope that there was something beautiful for her in spite of her awful hair and her bad disposition.

And once again, I felt myself picking up that other radio channel. But this was a broadcast I'd never heard before. It was sweeter than music, deep as a heartbeat. It was utterly new, and yet I felt a sharp crack of relief, as if I'd finally found something I had lost long ago, something I'd given up hope of ever finding, something I'd forced myself to forget.

You are not alone. There is more in the universe than this. There is more to spirit than this. There is more to you than this.

I gulped it down like water.

I chewed on it, I sucked on it, I twirled my fingers in it.

Eventually I returned to the *shoji* screens in a daze, my scissors slicing through the paper, the paste sliding off my brush onto the wooden frame, the paper kissing the paste sweetly and softening the light.

118

In the coming months—oh joyful bounteous universe—I discovered that Madeleine had written other books! I read them all, and then I read them again. And again.

Because I loved her books so much, I kept waiting to be literally transported to another world the way Calvin and Meg were. I waited for a fiery winged orb to appear, or time to wrinkle, or for a unicorn to sweep me away. After all, I had found my people, the strangers like me, and it seemed that this was the sort of thing that happened to people like us. I didn't have anyone to tell me that these things could happen metaphorically, too, so I kept waiting for the literal miracles to happen. A bush would rustle, and I'd hold my breath. The light would shift and bend, and I'd listen for a wing to whoosh in someone magical. Oddly enough, I wasn't particularly disappointed that these things never happened. Just the hope that it might happen, that something wonderful could be just around the corner, was enough to get me through the days.

The children in Madeleine's books were on the side of Light, of Love, working with forces that were incontrovertibly good—and yet there was no familiar Christian language anywhere in them. This made me a little nervous. Was I reading heretical reading material? There was no Father God, no sacrificed Son, no damned creation. This was scandalous and extremely exciting. Madeleine, bless her heathen heart, seemed to believe in a forgiving force that was very big, much bigger than any God I'd ever encountered. She did not call it by any of the names of I knew. If asked, I would have offered a mild theological dismissal (of COURSE she's not referring to the actual God, it's just a story, see) but another deeper part of me was swaying back and forth in silent jubilation.

If I had looked closely, I would have noticed that this part of me was grinning from ear to ear. It was the golden seed, it was the germ, it was a little liquid drop singing revolution.

CHAPTER ELEVEN

While I was lying on *tatami* mats inhaling Madeleine L'Engle, I was unaware that there were books in existence that chronicled the experiences of other missionary kids on the other side of the world. Renee Levann, for example, was raised in Africa by her missionary parents in the 1950s and, as was common back then, spent months at a time away from her parents in boarding school. Naturally, those good missionary kids *didn't mind at all*. At least, that was the party line. I mean, seven-year-olds in a dorm, with strangers: certainly it didn't leave any emotional scars! Why should it? They were doing it for Jesus! I knew many adult missionaries who'd grown up this way, but never spoken to one about their experience.

The now-adult Renee happened to attend my parents' home church in Indianapolis, where we were staying for a one-year furlough. Our whole family went back to the midwest every four years, which meant that I spent my sixth grade year going to public school and sharing a bedroom with my baby sister Ruth in the rented apartment the church found us.

Everyone kept saying we were "home," in a place so unfamiliar I still had whiplash. I'd never heard of Jimmy Buffett and I didn't know how to order a sandwich at Subway. At age twelve, I didn't know what "make out" or "horny" meant. I couldn't dance to Madonna and I was too embarrassed to admit that I secretly liked Amy Grant's music better anyway. We were back in the United States to reconnect with family and friends, but mostly we were back in order to raise the all-important financial support so my parents could continue their mission work.

I had no idea why I was having lunch with Renee, especially alone—I'd never had a scheduled lunch alone with an adult besides my parents. Maybe she wanted to see if we deserved her money. I thought I'd heard that she had been a missionary kid herself, which meant that I was skittish and on my best behavior. Those missionaries from Africa were the most intimidating; they had all the virtue and the hardship, and we were spoiled cushy Tokyo dwellers. Renee seemed nice enough, but I just knew that at any minute she was going to give me the speech about how she had begged God to let her go back to Africa, but God had a harder task for her here in Indianapolis. It always worked like that: if they wanted to stay in the USA and be a doctor, God made them go to Africa. If they wanted to go back to Africa and start a hospital with their childhood friends, God made them stay in America and run the PTA. That was just how it was with God. I was sure that my moment of reckoning would come some day too: I would cry out to God to please, please let me go to college, but God would make me go to Bible school and marry a missionary to Papua New Guinea.

Renee seemed like a nice lady, but I was braced for the strange, awkward dance of holy roller jousting.

We chatted. How were things? Oh, fine. How did I like Japan? Oh, I liked it.

I felt myself running through the glazed script that I had taken up in this strange place, a glossy patter that put up a shell to cover my rawness.

I'd perfected a numb cheerful misery that carried me through school, where I somehow managed to disappear into the edge of the cool girl circle; not popular but not totally persecuted either. But at home I would lash out at my parents, whom I suddenly hated, who seemed to rejoice in my misery and deliberately try to mortify me. Their shoes were awful, our clothes were four years out of date, and my mother gave me a haircut that caused my hair to actually levitate in a tornado of frizz. (Would it have helped to know that this was normal and that preteens all over America were slamming their doors? Maybe. I couldn't blare my angry music, though; Ruth was three, and all she would listen to was Wee Sing Silly Songs.)

So there I sat at this restaurant table with Renee Levann, pretending to be politely bored, waiting for her to start telling me about how lucky I was to be a missionary kid, and how much she missed it. I was as polite and sullen as a little terrified Christian girl could possibly be. My pimply skin itched and my frizzy hair kept kinking out of its plastic clip. Naturally, I was lashing myself silently with misery and self-recrimination. I don't remember what Renee said exactly, because my interior monologue took up most of my attention.

I noticed that she had gone rather quiet. I panicked. Had she asked me a question? Had I missed it? She put her elbows on the table and laced her hands together, watching me. Then she said, without any preliminaries, "You know, I used to be very angry that God had made my family be missionaries."

Crack!

I felt myself shatter before I'd even registered the meaning of her words. I couldn't have been more shocked if she had picked up her fork and flung it at me. And then, to my great horror, I discovered that something impossible was happening, and I seemed to be sobbing. Quite loudly. It happened so fast that I was blindsided by the tears, snot, and guttural sounds pouring out of me. Renee seemed unfazed and handed me a pack of tissues. I honestly didn't know why I was crying, but something was open and I might cry forever. I felt certain my face would peel off from the sheer humiliation of it.

She sat calmly and watched me swab at my face. I tried desperately to stop sobbing. I said jokingly, "This is weird—why am I crying, huh? Weird, huh?" wildly attempting to choke back my sobs. This only resulted in a strange barking sound coming out of my mouth. And then I felt that other radio signal coming in, clear and cool as the clinking of silverware. It was as if Renee was saying, on a frequency I could sense but not pin down, "I see you. I really see you, and I see that you are in agony, and I am totally fine with it. I am not scared of you; I will not try to talk you out of it or shame you for it; I will just sit here and watch you with total peace and acceptance."

I kept crying and crying, and once I let the sobs just come, they felt like a torrent, but a benevolent one. Renee continued to sit there and watch me, untroubled. I felt like I might never stop crying, and I didn't really want to anyhow, because it felt so good to let the tears just come. I went through the entire packet of tissues she'd wisely brought and moved on to my sleeve. I don't remember her saying much; I just remember the incredible relief, the feeling of a thousand pent-up emotions being released. It was the first time I had seen a healer hold space for someone, the way you'd hold a coat up for a small child. It was the most sacred thing I had ever witnessed: a girl at a table littered with tissues, and the woman who sat there calmly watching her.

The cataclysmic weeping I did with Renee was a great gift, but she didn't stop there.

That wonderful woman spoke to my parents. I don't know what she said exactly, but it lit a fire under them. They heard her, and boy oh boy, they mobilized. Things happened impossibly fast.

They made new plans. Then *they asked me how I felt about them.*

What the whaat?!?!?

It was shocking. I didn't understand what was happening.

They asked the big American church for extra money so that my brother and I could go to a real school in Tokyo, an extremely expensive international school. It was unheard of. It was scandalous. My meek, gentle parents! They stood right up there in front of people whose money they needed and said, *This is how important our kids' well-being is to us; we need to do this for them, even though it costs as much as college tuition.* And those good church people gave! For us! For me! You could have knocked me over with a feather. I had no idea that such a thing was possible, let alone permissible. I had no idea that my parents really truly hadn't known how unhappy I was.

We were trying so desperately to make contact, but we were separated by this enormous bewildering space. Renee was our family whisperer. She had one foot in the water and one foot on dry land, and she connected us like a humming telephone line.

CHAPTER TWELVE

That moment of raw grief with Renee in the restaurant had opened up a mystery, and I puzzled over it. Where did all that grief come from? Sure, there was the understandable sadness of a displaced child who felt unmoored at God's request and had no language to talk about it. Then there was the various nastiness of school and the burden of keeping my secret, that I wasn't really loved by Jesus. But was that all? I had sobbed like my heart was going to break, like I would die from it, and that weeping felt better than anything I had ever done in my life. I had so needed to let that torrent out, and yet I was puzzled at its ferocity.

All this went into lockdown, however, as I put on my coolest face and prepared to go to school with the rich kids. I just wanted to pass for normal. But normal, at Kitamachi, was an interesting proposition. It was a school for expatriates living in downtown Tokyo on expat packages, which meant people whose companies would kick out 30 grand a kid in annual tuition without blinking. So my schoolmates were the children of executives, ambassadors, and diplomats. I didn't really understand what that meant, but I did know that they had better clothes than I did.

Yet there was a surprising sweetness to the school, in spite of its pedigree and the expectations for its students (would it be Harvard, Yale, or LSE?). There were mean girls and teasing, but I found a sisterhood there, several other girls who became my fast, close friends. We kept a notebook and wrote to each other in it, slipping it between us during class with great cloak-and-dagger secrecy, somewhere between passing notes and a group diary. We were all, I can say with great love, total dweebs. We would shop in Harajuku for Day-Glo earrings and try on skanky dresses, but we never bought any. We had sleepovers at each other's houses and played Truth or Dare—but the dares were things like "Sing the Beaches song in front of all of us!" or, "Go steal ice cream from your mom's freezer!" Even though many of our classmates smoked cigarettes and drank, there was a kind of innocence about us. We had crushes, kissed boys on rare and thrilling occasion, and felt our hearts swoop and swoon during the slow dances in the basement multi-purpose room. My friends had live-in maids and lived in tall downtown towers or big old Japanese estates and their fathers drove shiny cars I didn't recognize, but they came to my house in the shabby suburbs for sleepovers and never said a thing about the tiny rooms, the threadbare couch, the gray vinyl cabinets in the kitchen. I could see the difference between their homes and mine, and a tiny part of me wanted to die of shame, but the first time my friend Marie came over, she complimented the built-in bookshelves in my tiny closet of a bedroom, and I let myself relax enough to sink into a delirious soup of boy-talk.

My kind Kentucky grandmothers sent me Reeboks from the US so that I could pinch my jeans tight, roll them up, and have my puffy socks show off my brand-name shoes. Guess and Esprit were the only acceptable jeans, but I only really needed one pair to "pass." In class we read books; such books! We watched the Scarlet Pimpernel. We learned to ski on the annual ski trip. We went to art museums, planetariums, history museums. We painted with oil paints and had ice skating lessons and went to the school's cottage in the country to conduct our own science experiments on rocks and water and whatever critters we could find. And, crazy wonder of all wonders, we could check out anything we wanted from the mahogany-paneled library. (At least I assumed it was mahogany, which I'd read about; it was the richest, reddest wood I'd ever seen, and it felt holy to me. I was amazed each time I'd go up to the librarian with my stack and she'd smile kindly and stamp every single book.)

My senses were alive with all the new things I was absorbing. We were asked to take everything we'd learned and swirl it all together into essays and reports, and I did this in a kind of incredulous glee that something that came so naturally was an actual school assignment. I don't believe I saw a single worksheet the entire time I was at Kitamachi. Something inside me bloomed as surely as the purple hydrangea and the ancient pink camellias that clustered around the buildings.

—◇—

I started taking gymnastics lessons at school even though I was thirteen, and the other thirteen-year-olds could already do handsprings and backbends. It was so glorious that I didn't even care that I was grouped with the kindergartners.

They had a parent night and my mom made the 90-minute train trek to come see me, and that's how it came about that she was watching when I went into a simple one-armed cartwheel and heard a funny noise. The next thing I knew my face was smashed into the blue mat. I got up, confused, and saw my right arm jutting out from a new hinge in the middle of my forearm. I ran over to my mom, my arm dangling at a sickening angle. The coach followed, concerned but calm.

He would drive us to the hospital. Plans were quickly made. I pulled him aside.

"Listen," I whispered, "Be careful because my mom sometimes faints."

He raised his eyebrows and said, "You're the one with the broken arm. You don't need to be worrying about your mother." We climbed into the back seat of his car, and I noticed that it was deep blue and very sleek. The afternoon had suddenly turned to evening, and I felt small and nervous sitting in the dark car. Mom sat next to me, gently cradling my strange appendage and smiling at me wobbly. Then suddenly she jerked my arm sharply.

"Stop! That hurts!" I yelped, but her eyes were closed and she was slumped back in the seat. I patted her shoulder. She was out cold.

"See? I told you she'd faint," I said to my coach. He kept driving, and I cradled my own misshaped arm in my lap, but every few minutes I would catch his eyes in his rearview mirror, watching me.

He pulled into a parking lot and turned off the car. There were no streetlamps, and it was very dark. My mother was still unconscious, so we left her in the car and trudged through the quiet gloom of parked cars, toiling toward the bright lights of the hospital. I had never been there before, and I didn't know what part of the city we were in. I turned around and couldn't find my coach's car among the hundreds of identical monsters. But I could feel a faint string still connecting me to my mother, stretched tight and thrumming out to where she was still passed out in an unfamiliar car. I thought about how sad she would be when she woke up, how guilty she would feel. It was very cold and I knew I was supposed to be very brave. I did not feel brave, with my arm moving as two separate pieces inside my skin and my mother sprawled across the back seat of a car in a strange parking lot. I thought about muggers, and whether she would find me once I was whisked into the enormous strangeness of the hospital.

She did find me after a while, and she looked as green as I felt. They were trying to arrange my arm on the X-ray table, and they were frustrated. It wasn't cooperating; it was still bent and wouldn't lie flat. I could barely hold my panic in at the monstrous thing it had become; I wanted to run and escape my own body. Then the tech twisted it angrily and I shrieked.

"You have to turn it," he said. I tried, and cried out again.

"It won't go that way," I explained, so he yanked on it. It felt like things were crunching and grating, but I clenched my jaw and refused to cry. Silently I begged my mother not to pass out again. She didn't.

My coach had disappeared to try to find his wife, who worked in the hospital.

My mother and I sat in a waiting room for a long time, cradling my arm. Then things started happening all at once: my coach came back with his pretty, stern wife; the doctors came; and my mother began arguing with them. There was no one who could set my arm, they said, as it required surgery, and I would have to come back in the morning. They were cold, indifferent, and annoyed. But my mother was on fire.

"That is not acceptable," she said. "*Komari-masu.*" She stood there and held her ground, insisting that they operate on me that night. I'd never seen her talk back to men like that. They weren't sure what to do with the ornery foreign woman and her spawn. I felt safe for a moment, sitting behind her, seeing her silhouetted between me and the doctors.

But when they cut my shirt off and strapped me down to the operating table, she wasn't with me. My itchy little breast nubs were bare for everyone to see, and I felt scalded by the lights. I cried without making a sound. But when they began shifting the bones around with long metal wires poked into my arm I screamed in spite of myself, and the doctor snapped "Oy!" at me.

"Honestly. Have some gumption. *Ganbarinasaiyo*," he said, then he looked down at my chest and saw the tiny swelling orbs. "Oh," he said, "I thought she was a boy." A nurse laid a green paper napkin over my chest.

I tried not to scream any more but I could see them threading thin metal rods into the skin and using them like levers on the bones and then the pain oh the pain and I was thrashing and they were yelling at me to be still and then I blacked out. When I woke up, the green papery cloth had slipped down again and one nipple was poking out. I looked at it for a few seconds, pink and exposed, before I turned my head to the side and closed my eyes. I would not call any more for my mother. I could not stand for her to see me naked and humiliated in the center of a bright-lit circle of male doctors. I did not see her for hours.

When I checked out of the hospital the next morning, they handed me a bundle. I had been wearing my favorite owl sweatshirt, and they had cut it off of me with great shears the night before. But during the night someone had gone back over it, cutting carefully around each embroidered owl, and wrapping their ornate oval bodies in a square sheet of white gauze. As I pulled back the thin white wrapping, their copper threaded eyes blinked up at me.

—ᴟ—

The cast on my arm made for some awkward moments, like slinging it onto the shoulder of the boy I liked during a slow dance. It also meant that I had to sit in the ski lodge sipping cocoa and reading books while my classmates whizzed down the slopes on the annual ski trip. (I tried to look disappointed.) But it broke the ice with my classmates, who all wanted to sign it, and I passed two happy middle school years there at Kitamachi. I experienced plenty of angst, but it was the normal teenage kind: liking a boy who didn't like me back; being liked by a boy who I didn't like; dancing the dance of being popular without becoming part of the group of mean girls.

It was good.

And then it was over.

CHAPTER THIRTEEN

I'd always known that after eighth grade I'd leave Kitamachi and switch to ESJ for high school, the Evangelical School of Japan. I was entering ninth grade and my ninth school.

I'd visited ESJ several times as a child for their annual Thrift Shop, when missionaries exchanged their gently worn goods for each other's gently worn goods, which was pretty much the highlight of my year because we could take home almost anything that we wanted. And the year we'd had our satellite one-room schoolhouse with Mr. Wilkins, I'd met a couple of the other kids. Some of them went to Kogayama every summer, the same place we went, but I didn't know any of them very well.

ESJ was a supremely glamorous place peopled by high schoolers who looked like real adults, who wore high heels and eyeliner and had big hair. ESJ kids were more American than the international Kitamachi crowd, and they were all Christians. This meant I had to take them more seriously. I had watched them at basketball and volleyball games from a distance, noticing their big hairsprayed coifs and pointy black heels. They seemed older, more like people in American TV shows, going steady and wearing promise rings, surly and squinting, with bouncy breasts and manly letterman jackets. Now I was going to be one of those high schoolers. I could hardly believe it.

To ease the transition between the worldly heathen environment of Kitamachi and the moment when I would take my place among the throngs of the faithful, I went to TeeBA summer camp. It was the summer before my freshman year.

TeeBA stands for Teenage Born-Againers. Oh, lordy. I should have known then what I was getting into. But it was so much fun—my beautiful older counselor with her long flaxen hair and tall bangs, the boyfriend she was engaged to, the pictures from her college dorm of well-groomed southern sorority girls playing harmless Bible College pranks and dressed in Jessica McClintock dresses for church.

I didn't know anyone, but the locals were friendly and I was eager and willing to morph myself into almost any shape that would help me fit in. I mean that literally; if it had turned out that they were actually Satan worshippers performing ritual animal sacrifices, I would have dutifully sharpened up my knife. If they'd been doing drugs and mugging old people, I would have merrily joined in. I was absolutely desperate to blend in. To be normal. To *belong*.

This was my chance, my shot; these were my people, fellow missionary kids. (But not the fringe ones who prayed in tongues.) These people were safely devout, but they listened to rock and roll music and wore frosted lipstick: in other words, they were pretty close to the same particular brand of freak I wanted to be! Yes, I knew that I was secretly different—that I was an imposter, not a true child of the Lord—but I had completely given up on actually belonging anywhere for real, and I figured that the trimmings of fitting in, the semblance of belonging, would be good enough.

And so it was that I became pious. I carried around my Bible. I prayed out loud when it was my turn. I sang the songs: "Shine Jesus Shine" and "Refiner's Fire."

I sang phrases like "set apart," "ready to do your will," "my master," and "purify my heart."

And oh, I sang my little heart out. I didn't feel what the others seemed to feel, this love of Jesus—in fact I mostly felt flushed and testy, itchy and angry—but you wouldn't have known it by the way I closed my eyes, tilted my head back, and put my hands in the air along with all the other faithful sheep. I was undercover in Jesus's beloved flock.

It was so, so, so delicious to fit in. I was one of the majority group for the first time in my life. We were weirdoes, sure, but in our own enclave we could forget that there even was an outside world. I loved the bubble.

A big-muscled freshman picked me up on his shoulders at the beach and carried me screaming into the waves. My friends and I whispered at night in our cabin about kissing boys. A popular girl said something cutting to me when I was talking to an older boy, and I felt the thrill of social success: I knew I had made it if I was worthy of her scorn. I was safe, as long as I continued to blend in, so I intentionally gave myself the most wicked case of Stockholm syndrome you've ever seen. I wouldn't learn about the side effects for a good long while.

As part of my ongoing campaign to pretend to be just like everyone else, I dropped my bookish exterior and dove headlong into the shallow end.

Giggling became my main method of self-expression.

I developed crushes on the handsome boys who led Bible study.

I bounced and linked arms with my girlfriends and bobbed my head back and forth like a lollipop doll.

It was pretty over-the-top as a performance, but it was highly effective. No one guessed that there was much going on under my airhead exterior. I even tried out for cheerleading; our pathetic little squad was so bad that the basketball players cringed when we ran out onto the floor. But I gamely curled my bangs every morning with a curling iron, sprayed on grape-smelling Aussie Scrunch Spray, and swung my blonde locks to school on my bike. I sat obediently, oh so obediently, during Bible class and Social Studies. I giggled and passed notes and developed a fetching sort of pique in math class, which I hated with a furious passion.

But in English class it got a little dicey. My act threatened to slip. We were reading *The Scarlet Letter*, for crying out loud, and *Romeo and Juliet*, all these beautiful books that caught me up and twirled me around great spirals of emotion, and my heart thumped and soared with the page and then I would have to clamp down on myself during class. I wanted to spin around and hiss at my giggling friends: "Shut up, this is beautiful! This is real!" But I didn't, of course. My English teacher gave me As on my papers but I worked it into my act: *Oh gosh, gee, I dunno how I did so well, I must just be lucky I guess! Ohhh my gosh, you guys, let's walk past that group of boys and see if they smile at us, 'kay??*

I was insufferable. I was in there somewhere, but I was buried deep.

—⟋⟍⟍⟍—

We were assigned our first research paper and I decided to write about dolphins. I was inspired by Madeleine L'Engle's novel *A Ring Of Endless Light*, in which a teenage girl communicates with a dolphin through a very loving form of telepathy called "kything." I planned to prove my theory that dolphins and whales were at least as smart as people and were trying desperately to communicate with us. I found almost no objective data to support this theory in the school library, but I wrote the paper anyway. It seemed strange to me that I couldn't find any proof of this idea, when I was so sure it was true. I wasn't sure how I had come to believe that; I just had this very calm assurance that it was the truth. And I could feel a longing in myself, a kind of deep pull between my navel and my ribs, right at my solar plexus. The pull seemed to be speaking to me, urging me to do something, but I couldn't tell what it was that I was supposed to do. It certainly didn't magically lead me to the critical piece of evidence I was searching for. As I flipped through my index cards, bored to death with the fiddly bits of scrawled data, I wanted to throw them all away and just scrawl across my paper in big letters, I SIMPLY KNOW IT TO BE TRUE. I managed to restrain myself.

I strove to be good. My body woke, I loved boys, but I stayed pure. This was the magic key, the sure road to God's good graces, and I toed the line. I was chaste, oh so chaste. This was my main responsibility as a girl, the Christians were very clear about that, and I fulfilled it. They told me to be pure; I was. They told me not to swear; I didn't. They told me to do my devotions and pray for forgiveness and be humble and I did all those things faithfully. I would have cut off my fingers if they had told me it would keep me safe. But it wasn't working.

One night I had a dream. I was standing on top of a hilltop, in front of a rough table of rock. I wore long robes and gently cradled a baby. But I was a vampire. I put my face to the baby's and though I kissed it with love, I could tell that I was draining the life from it. I woke weeping, in despair. I could still feel the infant's little desiccated body against my arms, and I got into the shower and scrubbed and scrubbed, trying to wash it off of me.

—ɯɯ—

My family still spent the summers at Kogayama, in our cabin by the beach. There was a new level of intrigue involved now that I was an official part of the ESJ crowd. Sand was thrown, walks along the beach were taken, hearts were broken. I lapped it all up, even when it was my heart being trashed.

There was something about the ocean that made me feel more like myself than anything else. I would stand by the edge of the water as the waves rushed back and forth, scrubbing my insides clean so that I could breathe. I could feel my own feet. My heart thudded in my chest. I looked at my own fingers in amazement. They were so beautiful! Most of the time my body was numb, and horrifying, but when I stood by the ocean I almost felt like inhabiting myself might not be the worst disaster in the world.

One night we had a sleepover at my friend's cabin on the other hill. We ate dinner with her parents, giggled in bed, and fell asleep still whispering. It was all so safe; it was all so normal. I exulted in my ordinariness, in how well I was pretending to fit in.

In the middle of the night, I woke up in the darkness. My friend breathed quietly in her bed next to me. I was pinned to my futon on the floor by something hovering over me. A heavy black form was choking me, tight bands across my neck. I tried to flail and it hissed. There was darkness in my eyes, in my throat, in my heart. I was dying. I tried to pray in my mind: *Jesus, help me!* Then I remembered that I was supposed to be able to cast out demons, so I said the magic phrase silently, in my head: *In the name of Jesus, I command you to be gone!*

I yelled it silently as my eyes bugged out and pinpoints of light prickled all around. There was a deep gurgling laughing, the sound of enjoyment. Whatever it was, it was getting off on my fear. I tried to wake my friend, who slept peacefully just two feet from me, but it pinned my arms down. One hand was over my mouth, one pushed cruelly against my throat. I could tell I was blacking out, and I made one final desperate attempt to escape. There was a great flapping sound, a great fury, and a great piercing pain.

I woke up the next morning before anyone. I lay there silently, feeling my aching limbs, surprised that the room looked exactly the same. I tried to convince myself that I had imagined it, that it was a bad dream. There were no marks on the skin of my neck, but my throat was hoarse, and it hurt to speak. I felt like I was bruised on the inside. I would rather have died than tell anyone.

But I could still feel it, a presence just behind my shoulder. I could hear the chuckle and feel the air move. It trailed me, and no matter how hard I prayed, I couldn't make it leave. Later summers I visited the same cabin, when different people were staying in it, but it felt so menacing, so evil and malevolent, that I could never stay for very long.

—⟋⟋⟍—

There were moments when I slipped out of the wholesome straitjacket of school life and my soul floated. After volleyball or cheerleading or play practice, I would flee the school and whatever boy I was kissing that month. I flung myself on my bicycle and whirred down the street. Dusk would be falling, and I would slide through the tiny streets, taking the smallest roads with the oldest houses, winding my way along the river, and as I went over the tiny bridge I could feel, with the bump of my tires and the caress of the wind, that my soul was there with me, whispering hello. It was flying with me, like we were enveloped in a fluid veil.

I felt alive, I felt like myself, and at the same time I felt like the whole world was gathered there in my heart as I slipped and slid through the cracks between the air.

If I pumped the pedals hard enough I could coast for a good long while, legs out like wings, feeling myself as a part of everything else. In this fluid state my senses uncurled like tendrils. They slipped into windows and smelled what was cooking; I heard the fight between the children down the alley; I heard the river trickling and the reeds whispering and the traffic by the supermarket. I didn't just sense it, I could feel that I was taking part in it, and also that it was all inside of me. I would noodle around the back streets, stretching the ten-minute ride into a timeless hour before finally heading toward home. I would slide into our little driveway still enveloped in that veil, slowing down, hearing the ticking of the tires as the spokes breathed to a stop and I returned to my regular breath. Sometimes as my bike crunched over the leaves and I lurched it into the bike shed, I would startle the enormous toad who lived there and he would hop around like a big pile of dirt. The startle always helped jolt me back into my body, and I would laugh or cry a little as I gathered up my bag full of books. Yellow light streamed from our dining room window out into the evening. Inside the house I would find warmth and food and my most beloved people, but as I slipped out of the fluid world and back into my real life, I felt like a part of me was folding up into a tiny origami of loss.

"*Moshi moshi*?" My dad picked up the phone.

"Hey Dad, it's me. Can you put Mom on the phone?"

"Mom's not here."

"Yes she is! I know she is, put her on the phone!" It was pouring down rain, and I wanted a ride. My dad was heartless; he'd make us ride our bikes home. But my mom was a softie; she'd always come pick us up. She'd even bring us our lunches, uniforms, and anything else we'd forgotten.

"Come on, Dad, let me talk to Mom."

"Mom's in the *ofuro*."

"Daaaad!!!!"

I could hear my mom's voice in the background. "I'm not in the *ofuro*! Virgil, is that one of the kids? Give me that phone!" And then my dad, cackling.

He was the master of the practical joke; his April Fools' Days were legendary. But each year he swore this year he wouldn't do it, so we always fell for it again. Like the time he set all the clocks in the house two hours early and we arrived at school at 6am.

At school we continued to learn about God the Father, his Son Jesus, and that mysterious presence called the Holy Spirit.

"God isn't male, though Jesus was. God is God."

I raised my hand. "Then how come we never say 'Mother God'? Why can't I call God 'She'?"

"Oh no." The teacher visibly shuddered. "That would be heresy. Absolutely not."

I questioned this part of the doctrine often, with unsatisfactory results. True, God wasn't male, but we should still use male pronouns to refer to Him. Why? Well.

Just because.

No kidding, that was the answer. It *just wouldn't be right* to use female ones. Male is neutral; female is the exception. Why not Mother God? Oh no. That would never do. Oh ho ho. Might as well call God Santa Claus. Silly.

It must seem ridiculous that I took this all so seriously, but I did.

The stakes were high. My family, community, and the hellfire demons wielding hot pokers were only part of it. Underneath that was my deep desire to be all right, to be gathered into the fold of something, to feel loved and oh-kay. But the more I tried to merge myself with what I sincerely believed to be The Truth, the more I had to contort myself.

The misogyny was everywhere, from the allocation of funds for sports uniforms to the books that we read. It was there in the way that women gave up their names when they got married and were instructed to submit to their husbands, *as the church submits to the Lord*. It was in the talk about men being "servant leaders," which meant that husbands should smile very benevolently as they bossed around their womenfolk. There was God, there was Jesus the Son, there was Man, and then below that there was Woman.

One of the greatest griefs of my life has been that the women that I loved, looked up to, and trusted, went along with this part. They were so invested in Christianity that they swallowed it whole, even when it poisoned them. I've always understood why it's women who perform female circumcision and foot binding on their own daughters; the hatred of the female runs deep, and gets passed down from generation to generation. And often it's the only way to keep their girls safe in a bizarre world: to do the cutting yourself, first, on your own terms. There were no knives in our case, just words. They kept us small just the same.

To be sure, some of these good Christian women bravely staked out feminist territory in a hostile land. Their feminist version went like this: "God loves women too! Of course He does!! It's a redemptive story about all Creation, and of course women are included too. What Paul says about women being silent in the church? Submission within marriage? Just— well—just don't worry about that part. God loves you just as much as any man. You're just as beloved, it's just that you have a different ROLE to play." The role of a second-class citizen. They twisted themselves inside out, logic and soul, to find room for Daughters of God as well as Sons.

These women made solid biblical arguments for why it was okay that women were subordinate to men. This wasn't a bad thing at all, you see; in fact it was a blessing! They spoke of it as something that was really spiritual and beautiful: God's deepest intent for humanity. Some of them would read the Bible and weep with joy and a sense of being deeply loved.

These smart, loving, vibrant women beckoned to us girls.

Come on in, darlings, the water's fine!

And then we would be blindsided.

I felt betrayed. But ultimately I betrayed those women too when I eventually left the church as an adult. Though we still love each other, there is an enormous rift. They were working hard from within an old and patriarchal system to reshape it slowly and gradually. They were doing revisionist readings of traditional texts; they were learning Greek to add nuance to some of the controversial passages; they were pushing at the edges gently but persistently.

This approach filled me grief and rage and a sense of immense danger.

One day in Bible Study, one of my mentors said, "I just love knowing that I can rest, as a woman. I can rest in the authority of my husband, my God, my church. I'm so glad I don't have to live like a man, taking on the responsibility of all that leadership for a whole life, a whole family, the whole world even." Everyone nodded approvingly.

I tentatively waved my hand. "Um—but what if I wanted to take responsibility for myself? What if the women had something important to contribute too?"

The leader looked at me.

"We do contribute. What we contribute is just as important. But that does not mean we step outside our role. We are to be the helpers, and that is just as valued a role. It's different than what is required of men. That sort of responsibility is not for you, young lady." Everyone looked away, mortified for me. My face was crimson.

I felt deeply ashamed, because I did not want to rest in my husband's authority, arrogant hussy that I was. I couldn't understand why at these intimate moments of sacred communion with my fellow sister Christians, I wanted to tear their heads off, spear their Bibles with carving knives, and jump off a cliff.

—⚬—

One night I had another one of those dreams that felt like more than a dream. I saw Jesus and Satan talking on a dusty road. They stood head to head, two powerful figures faced off as if in battle. Then to my great shock, they embraced, turned, and walked away together. Their two distinct figures began to blur together until it was only one figure with a long coat flapping, and I knew with total certainty that Jesus and Satan were different sides of the same coin, brothers perhaps, or even the same being split into two forms. It was a very gentle dream, and I woke up feeling a deep peace. Yet I could no more have told anyone about this dream than I could have walked up to them and told them that I was handing out sandwiches and condoms to the aliens who visited my backyard. In fact, they would probably have been less horrified by the aliens.

—⁀𝔪⁀—

I nursed my strange, scandalous wonderings and nighttime wanderings on my own, in total secrecy. My friends seemed to feel close to me—in fact even people I didn't know very well would come to me to confide their secrets—but I felt a glass pane between us. It was like always living behind a one-way mirror. I loved them, but it didn't seem like anyone saw inside me.

I was so thirsty. I was so desperately dry that sometimes I felt like I would just crumble into dust and blow away. There was a perforation so deep in my bones, a spiritual osteoporosis so severe, that I thought I might just implode. I wanted—I didn't even know what. I wanted milk and blood and womanhood, I think. I wanted fluidity and laughter and everything feminine. I wanted magic and the deep transformative power of a woman who has unleashed herself. But what we had instead was weekly youth group.

So I would stand with everyone else, swaying back and forth to "Shine Jesus Shine" with my arms in the sky, faking a spiritual orgasm quite successfully, knowing deep down in my bones that I was a fraud.

I didn't think I had a choice. After all, there was nothing else. There was only this God, this angry male deity, and nobody else even seemed to mind it. They were right, of course. I was wrong. Every lurch of dismay, every revolt of will and soul, every yearning, was simply more proof that there was something deeply and fundamentally wrong with me.

Well dammit, I would make myself fit. I would bind my soul until it cracked, bend it over and break it, and totter on the stumps with a big compassionate smile on my face. I was getting so good at that.

CHAPTER FOURTEEN

Though I never tasted spirit in any of my hours of Bible Study, prayer, or fervent supplication, there were strange winds that blew through my life that were spiritual in the extreme. To my intense dismay, however, they never came through the channels they were supposed to come through. Here I was with my mouth up to the spigot, begging and begging for one little drop, and over there someone was dumping buckets of water on my feet. But if you believe that the only good water is the water out of the spigot, you will just be afraid. The water on your feet will be further evidence that you did something wrong.

One summer while I was in high school, we went to Kentucky to visit our extended family. One far-flung relative lived out on a popcorn farm, in an old plank house with an actual potbellied cookstove. In a little barn away from the house was all the precious Civil War memorabilia. I felt nauseated every time I passed it.

While everyone else went to look at the sabers and uniforms, Great-Aunt Vivian took me upstairs to show me her antiques. We stepped into her pretty bedroom with the faded delicate wallpaper and the handmade quilt on the bed.

"This is where Linda killed herself," she told me matter-of-factly. Linda was a cousin several-times-removed who had shot herself in the head when she was sixteen.

Oh, shit, the air was getting thick. No no, I didn't want this, I would back out politely. I edged toward the door. Vivian's voice was low: "Can you believe that she would do that?" The door slammed closed behind me. I wasn't sure how the old lady had closed it from way over there by the bed, but I couldn't breathe. Vivian moved slowly, like she was swimming through deep water. She walked over to the bureau and opened the top drawer.

"There'd been a big fight. She came up here and got her Papaw's gun." She lifted up the slips and nightgowns to show me where it had been hidden. As she spoke, she acted out what she was saying, picking up an imaginary gun and holding it in front of her. "She took it over to the bed, and sat down, right here on my own bed. And she put it in her mouth and she pulled the trigger, right here, do you see?" The old woman lay back on the bed, heaving with dry sobs. "Right here. My grandbaby girl died right here. She had a hard time. Do you hear me? A really, really hard time." She opened her eyes and looked at me imploringly.

I was gripped by something as surely as if she had grabbed my shoulders and shaken them. There was something I was supposed to know, something I was supposed to do, something I was supposed to understand. I could feel it clutching at me, pulling at my hair and pounding at my chest. But I was too afraid. I had to get out. I nodded, mumbled "I'm so sorry," and opened the door. It was heavy and hard to open but I pushed at it in a panic. As I rushed through the hallway and down the stairs, every framed photo on the walls was swinging wildly on its nail. I could see the bright squares of the wallpaper that hadn't been faded by the sun peeping out as the photos lurched back and forth. Later, when I remembered the strange encounter, I decided that surely the swinging photos, at least, must have been my imagination.

Because if it wasn't my imagination, it was something else. And that wasn't allowed. I wasn't supposed to be communing with anything other than Jesus and the Holy Spirit, and for sure that sad, angry presence in that room was neither of those. I imagined it, I decided. I must have imagined it.

—◆—

It was less scary to believe that I was crazy—hallucinating, imagining ridiculous things again—than to believe that spirits of some sort were trying to contact me. There was just one tiny drawback to this good and logical approach: I felt really, really crazy.

I think I hid it pretty well. I had a good cover identity; I was the class airhead. Blonde, bouncy, accommodating, bored—it was a most useful shell. I was cast my sophomore year in a musical production of *Annie*. I was Lily, the dumb, gum-chewing, gin-sipping, greedy little bitch of a girlfriend to Rooster, the man who's willing to kill Annie in order to get his hands on her reward money. I got to play all of it except the gin, and my ditzy, high-pitched rendition got laughs.

This was more intoxicating than alcohol; peoples' eyes glued to me was joy, was bliss. I was clutched in shyness most of the time, my face flushed red when I had to introduce myself, but when I slipped into the skin of someone else onstage, I discovered that I had no fear. I loved the applause, fed on it, could hardly stand to exit. When I belted out the line, "I'm Lily St. Regis—I'm named after a ho-tel," and the boys in the audience cat-called, I didn't even mind that they took to calling me "ho-tel," and then just "ho"—I was enveloped in a heady aura of bliss. Partly this was because backstage, behind the flimsy plywood sets, my onstage boyfriend and I were pressed together, his hands on my back, sliding down my hips into forbidden territory, murmuring endearments as he sucked on my earlobes. This was high school like I'd always hoped it would be.

At night I lay awake with the urgent need he had awakened in my body. This need was a very big problem. I wasn't supposed to have it, obviously, since I was a girl. This was what we learned every week in youth group. Our stalwart leader looked in disapproval at my breasts pointing up through my sweater and spoke about the differences between boys and girls: that boys had physical urges and it was the girls' responsibility to not tempt them. Girls, he went on, only indulged the boys in this because they craved *emotional* comfort, and so any time a girl kissed a boy she was using him, manipulating him, trying to get her emotional needs met by tempting him with her body. And about those bodies—if girls knew how hard it was for boys, he said, running his eye along the line of my long thin adolescent legs—they would never wear bikinis or short shorts. They would understand just how wicked that was, how unfair it was, because those poor boys—and here he frowned at the modest neckline of my t-shirt—those poor boys just can't help themselves. In short, boys had physical needs and girls did not, and if a girl aroused lustful thoughts, it was wicked of her, and if bad things happened to her because of that, it was her own fault.

—⁂—

"I'll go first. This week I really struggled with forgiveness." We had our coffee, our donuts, and our Bibles. "Someone—I won't say who—said something so mean to me, and I am just really struggling to forgive." We all nodded solemnly.

Our accountability group met weekly, usually at Mister Donut.

"I'll go next. This week I am feeling such deep concern about—someone whose name I won't say. But I think you all know who I am talking about. She is really falling away from the Lord. I heard that she and her boyfriend went to second base. I mean it just hurts my heart, her treating herself like trash like that. Once you have sex with somebody, you can never get that back. Your body is programmed so that you love them forever. Her poor husband."

"This week I really hate gossips," said my best friend. She winked at me. "I think you'd all better pray for me."

"All right, everybody talk about your devotions," said our leader. "Who's been faithful?"

The boys were sitting a few tables over with the youth pastor. They were almost certainly talking about masturbation. They talked about how terrible it was, and how often they did it anyway, and how hard they tried to stop, and who they masturbated about, and they always went away deeply penitent for the warped sickness of their minds that kept rooting up that sinful organ between their legs, until first period when they would have the lustful thoughts all over again.

148

At least that's what my boyfriend told me. I thought his group sounded a lot more fun than mine.

We made out obsessively and guiltily. I was still determined to be chaste, and so was he, but see, these bodies of ours had other ideas. We spent hours torturing ourselves right on the edge of The Forbidden Things. We even made rules about what was okay and what wasn't; we drew imaginary lines all over my body like divvying up a corpse. Knees were okay, thighs were iffy, butt and groin were off-limits. My neck was okay but breasts weren't, and there was all that delicious territory in between to be negotiated. Oh, it was tantalizing stuff. It was like tantra, only with more guilt. And each time we'd cross a line, say his tongue would slip below my collarbone, I'd feel a riot of pleasure, my body would nearly explode with desire, and the poor boy would go confess in the donut shop about our wicked, wicked ways.

The youth pastor hated us girls. We were what took his boys away from him. We led them merrily down a path to destruction, as far as he was concerned. And naturally, we did it purely out of the evil in our manipulating, conniving hearts—there was no other explanation for it. It was pure wickedness that made us torture those poor innocent males. Because, after all, girls don't have sexual desires.

They *just don't feel those things*; everyone knows that.

Clearly I had been given a faulty set of equipment to go with my hideous heart. Because I did indeed Feel Things.

I was horrified. I would touch myself at night, come hard and fast, and then weep into my pillow at my own filth. What was wrong with me? I was a girl, dammit! I wasn't supposed to have these urges!

When my mother caught me reading *Gone With The Wind*, she told me awkwardly that I should be careful what I read because certain books could arouse "feelings" that I didn't need. Then we both shuddered with embarrassment and changed the subject.

My parents always spoke earnestly and mortifyingly about how sex within marriage was a beautiful thing, dropping it nonchalantly into conversation like a locker full of bricks. But my mom would follow up these little chats with admonishments about my clothes—my jeans were too tight, my skirt was too short, my tops cut too low. When I look at photos of myself now I see that I dressed like a teenaged old maid, and yet I felt constantly ashamed of my blooming sexuality. No number of frumpy linen pants or oversized sweaters could hide it.

I felt very sad that I couldn't shut down my sexuality completely for Jesus.

Sad, alternated with moments of blinding rage. It's the rage that lets me know that I hadn't completely died in there. I was in there somewhere, buried beneath voluminous sweaters and the thick spackle of guilt. And boy was I seething.

Here's the thing. People had sex anyway. I didn't, but lots of people did. And since most of this sex was accompanied by great billowing clouds of guilt and the fear of a literal hell, it's not surprising that very little of it took place with any kind of birth control. The logic goes like this: I am not going to have sex, because I think it's wrong and sinful and will warp my mind and heart and soul, and because, if I do, I will never be loved by another virgin or anyone else who will be in heaven. Therefore I have no need for condoms or birth control pills.

So you would wear a promise ring or sign an uncomfortable pact with your parents or simply stew in the rich juices of a community that couldn't stop thinking about sex—all the time—because they were so worried that someone might have the wrong kind of sex, which is to say sex that is between anyone other than a man and a woman who were married.

And still everyone was shocked—appalled!—at the pregnancies. Like they were some kind of unexplainable, mysterious pox.

CHAPTER FIFTEEN

Something surprising happened my junior year. A new principal arrived from the states, draped in the allure of "the real world," and he took one look at me and called me a fraud. He ignored my chronic lateness, my forgetfulness, my giggle, and my general swooniness, checked my PSAT scores, and pronounced me smart.

It had been a long time since the days of Mr. Wilkins, when I'd felt somewhat possibly the tiniest bit smart. I had actually done all right at Kitamachi the two years I was there, but everyone did all right there. And I had never studied very hard, except for math, which was still my worst subject. Mr. Jones took me into his office, sat me down, and basically told me that the jig was up, and he would no longer let me get away with pretending to be stupid.

I pretended to have no idea what he was talking about.

I wanted to kiss him.

Years later, I laughed my ass off when this exact storyline showed up in the TV show *The OC*. Summer, the vacuous airhead, suddenly discovers that she is smart after she scores well on the SATs. She runs angrily through the halls, accosting her boyfriend—*Why didn't you TELL me???*

That's how I felt. To be fair, I acted really dumb most of the time. My parents expected me to get good grades, of course, and they wanted me to go to college, but they'd both graduated from the University of Kentucky without fanfare and nobody expected anything different from me.

Suddenly my teachers asked questions and expected me to answer. They read my papers with different eyes, and though I don't think that my work changed so drastically, it was like they saw things there that they hadn't seen before. Suddenly we were talking about college essays and SATs. Mr. Jones called in my parents and talked to them about competitive colleges. He explained that while they are more expensive, they also offer better financial aid. I should try for scholarships, grants. They went away amazed, flabbergasted, and to their great credit, motivated. It is hard to exaggerate how much that one label, "smart," changed my trajectory.

I started paying attention in a different way. This was not good for my social life. I'd been such a butterfly before, so eager to please, flitting and flirting with everyone. Suddenly I saw what a shitty deal the girls were getting. I no longer thought it was cute when the boys called me "ho."

And so, overnight, I earned the lovely label "bitch."

During the ugly transition, the boy who I was to date and love for years threw a plate of food at me across the cafeteria. It smeared into my hair. Can you believe I dated him anyway?

I asked him later to explain it and he blew out air uncomfortably. "It was just—you were so—prickly. And you held your head up. And we didn't like it. And they dared me."

In other words, I had turned into an uppity girl, the lower-caste second sex who no longer knew her place. It cost me.

Mainly it cost me because as I read more and more (I'd always read voraciously, but suddenly instead of Sweet Valley High my teachers were handing me Barbara Kingsolver and C.S. Lewis) I could no longer read the Bible in the same way. I'd always felt afraid of the angry Old Testament god who cut people into pieces and killed whole nations, who'd had Abraham try to kill his own son, but now I discovered that this was just the beginning. I struggled along in my daily devotionals, trying each and every day not to boil over with anger at something. Even the gentle Jesus of the New Testament was a total misogynist (one of my new words). He didn't empower any of the women with the Holy Spirit. He never said one damn thing about slavery or the poor treatment of women in his society. Oh, I thought such angry thoughts, and I waited for the lightning to streak down, and I went from angry to sorry, furious to scared.

I was allowed to join an advanced special class with a venerable teacher-turned-minister, a legend in the community. It was quite an honor for me; I'd never done anything with the smart kids before. We read some of the most beautiful books I'd ever read—the poetry of William Blake, theology by Frederick Beuchner, and *Til We Have Faces* by C.S. Lewis. This latter was a revelation to me, one of the most poetic tellings of the soul's grappling with a faceless god that I had ever read. I still love it; it goes deeper than Lewis's official theology and resonates in my very soul. The only trouble was, the venerable teacher and I didn't think some of Lewis's books meant the same thing.

"But isn't he saying that there might be other paths to God?" I would venture anxiously, seeing a thread there in the writing as plain as day; I could have picked it up with my own fingers, it was so clear to me.

"No, that part of the story isn't meant to be interpreted literally."

"But I thought that it was an allegory, and that meant—"

"Yes, in general, it's an allegory, but you can't take a detail like that out of context."

"But it seems kind of important to me; it seems like he's saying that if people truly worship any god with pure hearts, they're actually loyal to the true God. So wouldn't that mean—"

The thoughtful old scholar was patient up to a point, but finally he'd had enough. He looked at me and said very quietly, "What you are saying is a heresy. And a blasphemy."

The room was silent.

Well, that shut me up pretty good.

The rest of the group sat awkwardly, politely pretending I was invisible, which was very kind of them.

And yet there was this tiny little pip in me that still insisted, in a whisper so tiny only I could hear it: I think Lewis is hinting at *this*. Maybe he doesn't come right out and say it, and maybe he would have answered differently if he'd been asked about it in terms of theology, but otherwise why would he use this metaphor in the first place? (I had started using words like metaphor in my interior dialogue; it was very exciting.) Still, in the face of the old man's certitude, I felt despair.

Why did the world seem so different to me? Why did I get different glasses? What the hell was *wrong* with me?

—⧽⧼—

Then we came to that juicy Biblical plum: the story of Lot offering his virgin daughters to the men outside. I thought I would lose my mind. It was a crossroads for me. There are other stories like this; there is a man who gives a mob his concubine, and after they rape and abuse her and kill her, he cuts her in twelve pieces and sends them to the tribes of Israel. Which is horrifying enough. But in this one, a man of God offers his *own daughters* to strangers to be raped and tortured.

This story burrowed into me like a sick worm, pressed on my heart like a canker. I felt something in me turning. These stories had struck dumb horror into me when I was little, confirming a deepest-darkest-fear nightmare scenario that was beyond my vocabulary. But later, when I railed, impassioned, "How is this pleasing to God?!??! And WHY would I want to give myself over to a God who approves of mobs of men raping and torturing young girls?" I got no answers that satisfied me. The teachers, ministers, and missionaries that I asked said that God probably didn't approve of rape itself. But He approved of the fact that Lot was willing to take care of his guests, even at the expense of his own daughters. They said that there was a strong culture of hospitality. They never quite came out and said that the daughters just weren't as valuable; that part they didn't have to articulate.

When I re-read the story of Jacob and Esau, something clicked. I was Esau. It all made sense. There was no rhyme or reason to God's love: Jacob have I loved, Esau have I hated. I read Katherine Patterson's book *Jacob Have I Loved* and wept with relief and recognition. I felt my spine grow stronger; I began to feel more calm; I began to get in trouble for talking back; and I began planning my escape.

—⚮—

One night at a friend's house, during a cheerful slumber party that involved sweatpants, cookie dough, and Kevin Costner in the movie *Robin Hood*, I woke up after everyone was asleep. I sat up, my heart pounding. My friends slept on, tumbled in sleeping bags around me. But when I looked at them I began to shake, for I could see their bones glowing faintly beneath their skin. I could see the outline of skull and vertebrae, the dark pockets of the eyes. I sat there frozen, trying to believe that I was having a bad dream. I pinched myself, and it hurt. I closed my eyes and popped them open again, trying to get back into normal reality. Still I could see the firmness of the bones through the skin, see the tough angles cradling all the tender humming bits inside. In fact, everything seemed to be humming: even the coffee table and sleeping bags and remote control seemed to be vibrating. I could see it, and also see through everything.

I was certain that I was broken, that there was something in me that had finally snapped and could never be fixed. I felt like I was falling off the earth, like I might throw up. Finally I grabbed hold of my friend's shoulder, shuddering as I saw the bone through the skin. I shook her until the luminous bones dimmed, faded, and became hidden again under her skin.

"What's the matter?"

"I can—I don't know. There's something really wrong with me. I feel like I can see the bones under your skin."

"Ha ha. Shut up. Leave me alone, I was sleeping."

"No, really. I'm really freaking out." My voice sounded like it was coming from miles away, but the glow had faded and I could see her face again. Her eyes were wide.

"Stop it. It's not funny. You're scaring me." She sat up in her sleeping bag.

"I'm sorry, I'm just—" She reached out and grabbed the bottle of Coke and handed it to me. I took a swig.

"Can you see my bones now?"

"No."

"Okay, lie down here and I'll hold your hand. Weirdo. You just had a bad dream." And so we lay there, me and my Southern Baptist friend, among the chip wrappers and the sleeping bags, and I tried to convince myself that it had, indeed, just been a dream.

CHAPTER SIXTEEN

The school librarian, a quiet renegade, saw that I had checked out everything by Madeleine L'Engle. He looked at me quietly. "Would you like to read more books by her?" he asked me. "Uh, *yes*." He asked me if I could be discreet. My heart pounded, and he showed me a secret shelf. "Not everyone can handle this shelf," he told me. "These books aren't in the system." He grinned.

I read Madeleine's books over and over. I was enthralled by her vision of a god who was much bigger than petty religion, who didn't care about sex or theology or profanity as much as pulling the tangled threads of our world back into harmony. I thrilled that she claimed God as her own. I was astonished by her belief that she had as much a right to speak about *her* own understanding of God as anyone else. It gave me wild ideas. (Many years later, I would come to see hurtful, problematic threads in her writing, but compared to the narrow dogma I'd been exposed to up until then, her words were as wide open and generous as the ocean.)

I knew that she had actually come in person to speak at my very own school years before, and that during her speech, people had stood up and angrily walked out of the auditorium in protest. She was labeled a heretic, the worst kind of evildoer—a traitor within the ranks of the church who corrupts the minds of the faithful. In stormy chapels when I just wanted to scream at the hatred and fear that was pouring out of the pulpit, I would quiet my mind by thinking, *Madeleine thinks God loves everyone.*

And it was like a soothing trickle of water ran into my hot heart, and kept me from actually exploding into a flaming apoplectic fit.

Then another book came into my hands, or more accurately, I snatched it out of the hands of my friend who was reading it because I recognized the author's name. Where did I know that name from? And then it clicked. It was Renee Levann, the woman of the fateful lunch in sixth grade, the woman who had helped my parents shift the entire course of our family's life. I had no idea she had written a book.

In fact, Renee had done a very brave thing. She went back to her childhood experiences as a daughter of missionaries and wrote a series of letters from her little-girl self. She voiced the secret thoughts of a generation of missionary children who were routinely sent away so that their parents could go do God's work. In her book, she writes to her parents and tells them how much she misses them. She writes about her confusion about a God who seems so far away and who has chosen her family to be split across countries, who has commanded her parents to love Himself more than their small children. She writes about pining for them from boarding school and of her bewilderment when they return to a USA that is nothing like home but in fact a foreign, and often frightening, country.

These might seem like normal sentiments for a lonely, displaced child, but they were extraordinary in the evangelical world because no one had ever written about them before. Nice Christian ladies just didn't do that. Voicing pain about a childhood that was warped by God's demands was uncomfortably close to criticizing God, or at least God's workers. Renee just came right out and wrote down all the wild feelings that never get airtime in religious homes where faith is also the breadwinner. She talked about the pressure of being on display as her family raised funds in American churches, knowing that one temper tantrum or surly face could jeopardize an entire family's livelihood for the next four years. She named the displacement that is all the more painful for being invisible and seeming ridiculous.

This is now called called the Third Culture Kid experience, the fact that children who grow up in a foreign country aren't quite at home in their parent's home country, since they've hardly lived there, but are still officially foreigners in the place they know best. But they do share a 'neither/nor' world called the "third culture" with other global nomads. They tend to feel most at home with other expats, immigrants, and floaters, in a hovering world defined primarily by being neither here nor there. This explained why, years later, when I went off to university, I felt more at home with the international students pouring in from Seoul, Dubai, Jakarta, and Vietnam than with my fellow Americans.

I smuggled Renee's book home, and read it in total and utter secret. I hid it like it was erotica or a book of witchcraft. The irony was that my mother would have been delighted to see me read it. She had recently learned that her MK (missionary kid) children might need to do some sort of emotional "processing." This was a revelation to her, but she earnestly embraced it and tried, bless her heart, to get us to open up to her about our feelings.

That's precisely why I had to hide it; I was certain that my mother was nowhere near ready to handle the cavalcade of emotions that poured out of me. So I read Renee's book locked in my room and completely dissolved. I cried so hard I thought my head might become permanently dislodged. My tears and snot ran into my pillow. I cried with such abandon that drool fell out of my mouth. And I did it in total silence.

I couldn't figure how this woman's experience growing up in Africa forty years earlier could remind me so much of my own. I'd never been sent away to boarding school; never ridden a freighter across the ocean. And yet at the heart of that book was a profound loneliness, and it set off my own heartbreak like a vibrating string. Why was it that the nature of God seemed to require that something in me be torn apart? I didn't know the answer, but I did know that there was someone out there who had felt the same way. I remembered Renee's kind face, her compassionate hand on my arm, and mostly I remembered how unworried she was by the storm of emotion I had let loose in that restaurant. Far from being embarrassed and helping me to wrap it up, she encouraged my tears to flow. She seemed to care not a whit what people thought. She cared more about me.

I had never dreamed that such an unflappable woman might have once felt the agony in the pages of that book. I wanted to know how she'd gone from the shores of despair to that fearless, loving place. And barely articulated, deep down, there was another wish: once I'd figured it out for myself, I wanted to help others cross over, too.

—⁂—

When I started looking at university, the world suddenly got big and scary. While my fellow students looked at Wheaton, Houghton, Calvin—all those honorable Christian colleges—I was getting packets from farther afield. My parents dipped into their savings to send me to America for a week to visit colleges. I did visit several Christian colleges; I was especially interested in Gordon, the alma mater of two of my favorite Christian adults. I babysat for them sometimes, and they would loan me books afterward and sit and talk to me like an adult. Diane even made me my first gin and tonic; she said that if I was going off to college I needed to start testing out my alcohol tolerance. We grinned at each other in a mad glee and I tottered home the tiniest bit tipsy. Then they helped me edit my college essays.

I loved them very, very much, but I didn't love the college they'd gone to. It was beautiful, a safe vibrant compound filled with smart, engaged, intellectual...Christians. I felt smothered; I couldn't breathe. I looked at the course list, filled with classes like "C.S. Lewis: Oxford Don and Theologian," and "Kiddie Lit: Reading the Redemptive." I had already been accepted into an Honor Society; I was eligible to do a semester at Oxford; I had received a generous scholarship. I wanted so badly to want to go.

Then I went to the University of Chicago and some big state universities for contrast, and I was terrified by the bigness. I could feel myself getting lost in the crowd, not having some visceral thrust of ambition that I could sense was necessary there. And then there was Bryn Mawr.

Quirky, beautiful, terrifying in its own way—I had never met such smart women—and yet in them I recognized something. They were all a little…too much. They talked too fast, argued a little too hard, seemed to feel things intensely in that endearingly awkward way that I knew only too well. They were all like me! I was petrified, though. I didn't know how I could take my place here, either; the classes were notoriously hard, the curriculum rigorous and self-directed, the ideas radical and stringent to me.

I went back to Japan in a haze of ideas and fears. The thought of living in a dorm, walking to get my meals, finding a place in those huge cafeterias—it made me queasy. And yet something in me thrilled to the spires, to the stacks of books, to the intense hand-waving table-pounding conversations that people were having.

When I mentioned that I was thinking about Bryn Mawr, members of my community sat me down with great concern. One of my classmates spread the rumor that I actually believed that homosexuality *might not be a sin*. That's just how far into heathenism I'd slipped. A kind woman warned me with intense anxiety that I would be in great danger there, for I would encounter witches, and covens, and evil spirits, and lesbians, and—worst of all—feminists.

I was sold.

CHAPTER SEVENTEEN

My first month at Bryn Mawr, my English literature professor, Dana Oaktree, called me in for an individual conference in her office. She held up my most recent paper, balancing it carefully on her palm. She said, "You, my dear—" (she called everyone dear) "—are not a child anymore. I don't want to see any more of these formulaic papers—introduction, three main points, blah blah blah. I want more from you." Then she slashed huge red marks into most of my prose, dismissing it, and circled the few adventurous leaps I'd made. "Here. This is good thinking." And the one line of poetry I'd slipped in, hoping she wouldn't notice: "This line, dear one. Write like this." I left her office clutching my eviscerated paper, practically leaping across the lawns with a kind of pure, ethereal joy. No one had ever seen my mind like that before, seen what it could do, seen how much it chafed at the little chastity belts I'd been locking it into.

But I was woefully unprepared for my classes. I'd never even heard of Virginia Woolf or Jane Austen. I began reading to try to catch up, inhaling great stacks of books in total euphoria. I was drunk on words, high on language. I was swooning with the beauty of the campus, the regal bell tower of Taylor Hall, the way that my dorm, Pembroke East, looked like a castle; the quiet old fountain in the cloisters behind the library. But I was afraid of my classmates. They were so fierce, so smart, with their dreadlocks and their shaved scalps, their piercings and their opinions. I had always pressed too hard against the people around me, been too sharp, too intense, and now here I was cringing like a timid little schoolgirl. My clothes were dowdy and prim, I was terrified that I might accidentally turn into a lesbian, and I was thrilled to find that feminism wasn't even radical here, it was just an accepted fact of life—but there was just one little problem.

I wasn't cool enough for the real feminists. I was the country mouse, the missionary kid, plain and shy and ashamed. I didn't like Camille Paglia. I couldn't see porn as empowering. I harbored a secret and shameful love of Laura Ashley curtains. I was lacking a kind of toughness that everyone else seemed to have. And I didn't want to drink or have sex or do any of the fun things they did—or rather, I did want to, desperately, but I was too afraid. They might get away with it, but I was already on the edge; one slip and I'd fall off the edge into outer darkness. I so wanted to be like them, but I couldn't unhook the coil of fear from my guts.

So I ended up hanging out with the very people I'd gone to college to avoid—the Christians. Even knowing how it all turned out, even from this great remove, I still feel sad when I think of how unwillingly but inevitably I ended up going to Bible Study meetings. I wish I'd been braver. I really hated those meetings, but I was too afraid to find my way with the people I really wanted to be with—the theater people, the poets, the people who worked the rape hotline. I watched them from afar, longing to approach them, but I didn't dress like them, or talk like them, and I didn't know how to drink with them. I knew I definitely wasn't supposed to feel so turned on by their unshaved, unwashed lesbian bodies. I was pretty sure that finding myself staring so intently at their nipples showing through their thin tank tops was not a good sign. And besides I missed Japan so badly, and general homesick melancholia kept me small and shy.

So I pined away, watching the cool kids from a distance, resenting my good, kind, wholesome Christian friends, and loathing myself for becoming, once again, a fraud.

I kept reading, and more and more found that I really just couldn't stomach the bible. It wasn't for lack of trying. I actually took a class on "The Bible As Literature," hoping I could fall in love with its language, at least. When we talked about Genesis on the first day of class, the professor opened the class discussion by asking what people thought. One student called out, "That God guy is like a total abusive parent. He's a sicko." I almost burst up out of my seat, gonging with gratitude.

I was not pleased to discover that the collection of scriptures that I knew as The Word Of God had just been arbitrarily decided on by a bunch of sexist dead guys at a council of something or other. In fact, I was *pissed*. Who knew if those guys were even right? Why did *they* get to decide? Most of the religious authorities I'd known were total asshats; I didn't trust a council of people who'd appointed themselves holiest of all.

My skepticism of basic Christian theology did not, surprisingly, endear me to the campus Christian group leader. I wanted to read the other scrolls, the other gospels. Where were the gospels written by women? Well, according to him, those were *the very worst ones*. Nor was he inspired by my insistence that the subjugation of women disguised as submission in marriage was totally blasphemous. I gradually stopped going to meetings.

And yet as I fell away from the church, I found oddly luminous moments that buoyed me up. They fed my soul but couldn't be reconciled with doctrine. I didn't know what to do with them, so I put them in a little container, a little beautiful-but-suspicious bubble. (Because, as we all know, the devil always comes disguised as a being of light, so you should be the most afraid of the things that feel like sweet nectar to your soul.)

The first strange thing was that a dream I had had in high school came true. I had dreamed about a woman I would meet in college. In the dream she told me a terrifically sad story, and I wept with her for hours, until we were both wet with tears. I awoke that morning grieving for someone I'd never met, sad to my bones, and cried until I felt all cleaned out on the inside. A year later, my favorite classmate sat me down one night and sobbed out her deepest, darkest secret. Aside from the intense strangeness of the déjà vu, I knew clearly that I had already grieved her loss so that my own reaction would be out of the way and I could be there for her. And so I was able to listen calmly, hold her in my arms, and hear the story that might otherwise have destroyed me.

The second thing was meeting Madeleine L'Engle. Yes, really, the one who wrote the books that kept my spirit twined to joy, the one whose words had literally saved me from utter despair, she of the cropped hair and long caftans. I went to a conference at Calvin, which is a very nice Christian college, and the whole time she spoke I could feel a burbling in my chest, the quiet sound of recognition, like laughter. I queued up to speak to her afterward, and spilled out a quick version of my missionary upbringing and my horror at the Bible. What did she think? I don't remember the words she used, but I remember her eyes. She looked at me from a deep well of compassion. She saw me. She told me, and it might have been by nonverbal transmission, that God is all around us. And that I would find my own way. I was starry with gratitude. I held onto the feeling for a few weeks, until it faded and dissipated.

But even as I was falling away from the safe structure of the church and my faith, the spirit of the school seemed to be there to catch me. I was caught up in the beauty of the trees at night. I would stand out on the green in the dark, looking up at the stars through bare branches, pressing myself against the trunk of a tree, weeping happily.

That same English professor, Dana Oaktree, had become a kind of mentor to me. (Me and every other English major.) She was not a high-faluting academic, by our college's standards, and wore a little shabby cloak of shame about her lack of publishing, but she was a true teacher. Her generosity toward her students was unbounded, and she sparkled with enthusiasm toward our writing, our thoughts, our questions. During her classes she practically quivered as she laid open Henry James or illuminated Jane Austen and the sexual significance of the tiny pencil. I had never encountered someone like her, who was so unembarrassed about lavish praise and ruthless criticism in equal measure.

I was in her office when she said, "I honestly believe that you could make an academic career if you work hard." My heart pounded. It was a great honor. And yes, an English professor, clearly that's what I was meant to be, and yet—yet.

"I, um. I actually, well I..." my face was hot and my shoes were too tight. "I kind of have always actually wanted to try to be a writer."

She raised her eyebrows and smiled.

"Oh, but writing mere fluff is easy. It's disposable. If you really want to contribute, if you want to be a part on the ongoing majestic ongoing dialogue of great minds and hearts—" she waved her hands about wildly—"you'll become an academic and do something *real*. Something lasting."

And it was so odd. The words coming out of her mouth were so disconnected from who she was, from the great gift she had. Her magic was to engage and motivate, to inspire and delight, not to proclaim or pontificate or write boring footnoted papers. In fact, her most precious gifts to me had nothing at all to do with her academic credentials. She was the best teacher I ever had, and she didn't publish for shit. And so I was able to ignore her words completely and just feel the love that flowed from her. Underneath it all, she was saying, "I want you to be safe. I want you to feel like you've *arrived*." And of course I wanted that too.

Then she died a few weeks later of a stroke, right before term and our intensive tutorial were supposed to begin. And I didn't become an academic, but for the longest time I also didn't become a writer.

I was afraid, you see, that I would do it badly.

And I believed that ridiculous lie, that it's worse to make bad art than no art. It would be years before I would discover Julia Cameron or Anne Lamott, the teachers who would free me to write badly enough, consistently enough, to write at all.

Nonetheless, in a great euphoric act of decadence and gratuitous joy, one semester I summoned all my courage and signed up for a creative writing class. My teacher was vital, sparky, funny and quick. I loved talking about writing. I loved thinking about writing. But when it came time to write our first short story, I quickly discovered that writing was about as soothing as giving birth to a porcupine. All my beautiful thoughts were clunky on the page, awful, cringe-worthy. I went to my first tutorial with the professor, and she held my story on her lap and looked at me kindly. I burst into horrible mortifying tears because it had happened, the worst thing of all: I had tried to write and done it badly. Terribly! *Appallingly.* I wanted to melt into a puddle of shame. But she just handed me some tissues, cheerfully told me to try again, and didn't seem appalled at all. I couldn't believe it. I really thought she would tell me that I should drop the class, because obviously I wasn't cut out for this.

I kept patting my own cheeks, amazed to find that my failure had not caused me to spontaneously combust.

—✴—

Every year during a welcoming ceremony called Lantern Night, the student body dressed in black choir robes, carried glowing lanterns, and walked through the cloisters singing songs, some in Latin. This was the most thrilling and beautiful ritual I had ever imagined. I loved it all—loved the songs about Athena, goddess of wisdom; loved walking in the dark swinging our individual lights; loved the gorgeous, brilliant women walking beside me. Afterward we took our lanterns and gathered around the steps of Taylor Hall. We sang Indigo Girls, Bread and Roses, and old folk songs. I melted into the cluster of women. I was invisible and present in equal measure, taking part in something greater than myself. It was utter joy. It was everything I'd ever wanted from church. My classmates' faces glowed in the candlelight and I was caught up in something so deep, so high, that I felt that I could never fall down again.

CHAPTER EIGHTEEN

Only I did. I fell, not exactly into love, but into desperation. I made a leap into safety. Or so I thought.

I could feel myself pulling away from the church. It was exhilarating, it felt like flying; but I also knew, with the utter certainty of a twenty-year-old, that flying was usually what happened before you crashed and burned and found yourself huddled in a ditch shooting up heroin and having sex with strangers for needle money. (Oddly, this exact scenario didn't seem to be playing out yet for the lovely nonbelievers I knew, but it was surely just a matter of time. If you weren't saved, you were doomed. Doomed!)

I stopped going to church. I stopped going to the Christian girls' rooms for Bible Study. I stopped praying. These things gave me the same terrifying, delicious thrill that most people get when they decide to just NOT file their taxes or check their parachute.

Part of me loved this new sense of liberation, but most of me was dreadfully concerned. Danger, Will Robinson!

I didn't know then that the liquid gold feeling I got when I watched live theater or the vivid awakeness I felt under the stars was my soul trying to guide me toward something good, something you might call my true destiny or my natural path. Nah— I was pretty sure it was my fucked-up sinful nature. I was so conditioned to think that anything that felt good was evil, and vice versa, that I was completely cut off from my own benevolent instincts.

Which is the only explanation I can think of to make sense of the fact that, instead of taking off into the big wide open with my arms spread wide, I got tangled up with a Christian boy.

And then, dear reader, I—

Well. Wait.

If I just tell you the bald facts, I will seem so idiotic, so ridiculous, and so self-sabotaging that you might dismiss me completely. You have to remember, I was only twenty. I bet you made some pretty bad choices too when you were twenty. Don't judge.

I had actually met this boy at a Christian summer camp several years before. He was in Japan as a summer missionary, come from glamorous New York to work at TeeBA (remember, that's Teenage Born-Againers) camp.

I was a camper. Sixteen.

He was a counselor. A cute counselor.

He was studying photography at Pratt. I asked if I could see some of his pictures.

He grinned. "They're not pictures; they're photographs."

We sat side by side on a bench and I flipped slowly through his portfolio. He smelled like art to me. Visions of brownstones and gallery openings swirled in my head.

"Can I write letters to you?" he asked. "We could encourage each other in the faith."

I nodded. Of course, the faith.

He wrote me letters on bits of birch bark that he peeled off trees. They arrived in the mail with that tantalizing return address—New York, New York. He wrote about how he and his hipster Christian friends would go into the nightclubs of New York, those dens of drugs and despair and ruinous sex, and just go and pray as they danced through the throngs of lost souls. His band of Christians were skateboarders (only they were called skaters, I soon learned), models, club promoters, DJs, dancers. They all loved Jesus.

It was the most romantic version of Christianity I'd ever heard.

Two years later, there I was at Bryn Mawr, and he was just a few hours away. Plus, importantly, I was now past the crucial of eighteen, and he wasn't my camp counselor any more.

He drove down to Bryn Mawr from New York a couple of times. I showed him the beautiful old buildings and introduced him to the friends who had the biggest dreads, the hairiest armpits, and the most piercings. He showed me some nifty tricks he could do on his skateboard. We didn't have much to talk about, but it felt glamorous to walk a male around our all-female campus.

After several of these scintillating visits, he invited me to come up and see New York with him. I packed with great angst. Nothing I owned was possibly cool enough, so I went with the not-trying approach: thin white tank tops, loose ragged jeans, old bowling shoes.

Driving across the bridge from Jersey into the city, my heart started pounding. It was HUGE. I felt how tiny, how insignificant, and embarrassing I was. Walking through the streets, the city was terrifying, filthy, loud, dirty, confusing—but it also felt like home. It reminded me of Tokyo, and I felt wildly, jarringly homesick. I would have given anything for a bowl of ramen and the comforting Japanese train announcers.

I met his glamorous friends, slept chastely in a female friend's dorm room, and went to my first real club. The bouncer looked askance at me; I was obviously not part of the cool posse. I got in after a few sharp words from one of the credible New Yorkers. Before they fanned out through the crowd to spread the love, we gathered in a tight huddle.

"Jesus, let us bring your light into this dark place. May we be safe and protected from the evil within, and may we bring solace to those who need it, may we be messengers of your hope and joy to those who are dying inside. Bring your angels around us to keep us safe and pure."

I was too shy to dance; I stood at the side and sipped water. I couldn't feel any angels.

Someone was doing cocaine in the bathroom.

I watched the swaying mass of people from my safe perch against a speaker. They looked out of their minds, most of them—their eyes were wide, they seemed out of control of their bodies—but instead of remembering to pray for them, I found myself longing to be like them. I wanted to hurl myself into the fray, inhale anything that would make me feel free, and throw my body around to the music with wild abandon.

Instead I hugged the speaker all night, and me and my skater boy made out in his 1987 brown Toyota.

Every time we kissed, I felt a tiny little recoil inside me. Maybe it was guilt, I thought. Maybe it was my virtue trying to keep me safe.

—ᴍ—

When he came down to Philadelphia and stayed in my dorm room, he always brought his sleeping bag. Because, naturally, we did not share a bed. Instead, we would twist and contort, trying to get our bodies to tangle together without actually doing the forbidden thing. Sometimes we came so close that we would stop and pray about it, hot flushed prayers of contrition.

One night he whispered, *I love you*.

So I whispered it back.

I felt a puzzling mixture of pity, envy, romance, and longing toward him. I imagined myself marrying him, moving to New York, and how he would show his photographs in art galleries. I imagined myself writing. I imagined us filling our apartment with brilliant, shiny people who were exciting, but still part of the faithful throng. I never quite imagined how it would feel to wake up every morning next to someone whose skin I felt a little allergic to.

It did concern me every now and then that I felt such relief when he drove away every weekend. Also the annoying little fact that I couldn't really talk to him deeply about anything.

But I could feel a deep connection between us!

I didn't understand that the cord that thrummed between us was mainly made up of unarticulated pain. We were feeding off the romance of each other's melancholia. I felt deep and wise when I understood his hurt. He felt strong and manly when I told him mine. Together we touched the special secret truth that most of the world was oblivious to. We had put our finger on the pulse of reality and found an unending thrum of grief, hurt, and woundedness. It made us feel dark and mysterious, like real artists.

He wept as he spoke about his vague memories of the orphanage in Korea, about knowing that his biological mother had given him up, and my heart went out to him—taking my good sense with it.

One night we stood under the willow tree outside my dorm window. A cool spring wind moved the budding branches all around us in a soft dance. It was evening; he would drive back to New York in a few minutes. I leaned against him; he felt warm and solid through his shirt. I felt myself melting a little into the blue twilight, and he picked up my hand and asked me to marry him.

Everything inside me went very still, eons between each heartbeat.

I knew I would say yes. Yes was the correct answer in these situations.

But suddenly I seemed to be a dozen feet above my own body. All I could see was the blue light through the branches. A blue light that tugged and pulled at me to run after it, fly away, get out—the twilight pleaded with me to follow it through the night and away from that promise. I yanked myself back. There was an important moment happening here.

I smiled at him. Yes. This was good and right.

The six months of our engagement are a total blank in my memory. I literally cannot remember how I woke up for 190 days in a row and convinced myself that it would still be a good idea to marry a man who I couldn't talk to, who I'd never lived or slept with, and who I'd never spent more than 48 hours at a time with. I was back in Japan for six months, saving a semester's tuition by graduating in 3.5 years. I worked at a flower shop and planned my wedding while my fiancé stayed in New York, although he had left art school and given up photography to attend a Bible college, a development I found troubling but, like so many other things, managed to ignore. Sort of like the way I found myself avoiding his phone calls and cringing at his emails. Under no circumstances should this relationship have lasted; we grated against each other and would have broken up had we spent a week together. But the distance made it all seem romantic, and the wedding itself was a lovely diversion—creamy roses, gleaming camellia leaves, a hundred votive candles.

Let me just stop for a moment. This marriage is the most mystifying part of my own history. I have NO IDEA why I went through with it. Why did I marry someone I really didn't love?

I still don't know.

But if I had to bet money on it, I'd guess it has something to with inherited beliefs. I didn't encounter this idea for another decade, and even if I had, I would have considered it scandalously New Age, smelling suspiciously of crystals and goddess circles and chakras—and therefore dangerous. Inherited beliefs are those beliefs that are so deep and taken for granted by our particular community that we often don't even realize they're beliefs, they just seem like the way things ARE. In spite of my feminist university education, I had a deep and unconscious inherited belief around sex and marriage. It said that the surest way to ensure my safety on every level was to marry a nice Christian boy before I accidentally had sex and ruined myself for all eternity.

The thing about inherited beliefs, you see, is that they often defy logic and common sense.

There was such a great cognitive dissonance between what I was doing publicly (getting married early and chaste, oh joy! Phew!) and what I knew deep down to be true (that this was a grave, grave mistake and the dumbest thing I had ever done)—that I believe I put myself into a sort of trance.

In fact, I think many people walk around for years of their lives in a numbed-out trance state, trundling through life ignoring the big bundle of uncomfortable feelings they're carrying around.

On the surface, I had rebelled against my Christian upbringing by going to Bryn Mawr, spouting feminist ideals, and fighting with my mother over whether or not we would serve alcohol at my wedding. (She won; we toasted with sparkling apple juice.) But I didn't really want to be a rebel.

I just wanted to be—oh noble aspiration—safe.

And in my world of origin, getting married as a virgin to another virgin was pretty much the slam-dunk way to accomplish that. It was convenient that within the safe cocoon of virgin marriage was a nice decorative streak of rebellion—like the sprinkle of paprika on those deviled eggs. There was something slightly edgy about and cool about getting married to someone so dashing and romantic because—after all—he was *from New York*.

My own parents had married when they were both just 21—around the same age as my fiancé and I—and they were still pretty damn happy about it 25 years later. I looked at their beaming faces in the faded 1970s photos. I didn't feel beaming, but that was surely just because of my flawed character and bad attitude.

My friends back at Bryn Mawr were puzzled but generous. My Christian community was overjoyed. No one seemed concerned that I was twenty years old, a junior in college, and really didn't know this man at all. My dad was concerned that my fiancé had never held down a real job besides stints at Jiffy Lube and Christian summer camps, but I bristled in a delightfully feminist way and declared that I could hold my own. I am sure that I convinced them that it was a wonderful decision. I probably spoke eloquently about how I knew that he was The One. But I don't remember any of it.

I do remember looking at flowers in some wedding magazines, though. Those flowers were so pretty. I figured out how to recreate the $500 bouquets in the magazines using spray roses and camellias from the neighbor's tree.

And so it was that in my junior year of college at one of the most feminist, pro-woman, supportive environments in the world, I got married. To a sweet, wounded, lost man.

I ordered some ivory satin lingerie from the Victoria's Secret catalog. My mother insisted that I go on the Pill. My father carried scores of precious pillar candles in his suitcase from the USA in his suitcase back to Japan, because pillar candles cost $30 apiece in Tokyo. We set the candles in a circle around the spot where my husband-to-be and I would stand. It felt holy, that circle of flickering lights. I felt a surge of hope, setting up the night before the wedding in the little round wooden church, that standing inside something so beautiful in a pure white gown would surely make me beautiful and loving too.

My old home ec teacher handled the wedding cake. My almost-mother-in-law made my dress. My fiancé and his family flew in a few days before the wedding. I kissed him on the lips when he got off the plane, and my upper lip burned. I gripped his hand, hard, and held my breath.

And then I was married.

CHAPTER NINETEEN

We had sex for the first time a few hours after our wedding, in a cold Japanese hotel out by the airport. We were both virgins, had no idea what we were doing, and had neither lube nor passion to ease things along. It hurt. My skin burned, red and rashy, everywhere he touched me. He looked at me with such love. I wanted to curl up and sleep for a million years.

The knot of disappointment in my stomach told me then that I had made a mistake, though I would never have admitted it. It was our first try, I told myself. We were tired; I was overwrought. We would work on the sex.

But it wasn't the sex. It was the loneliness.

We woke up early, got on a plane to Europe, and I tried to convince myself that it was all right, or at least it *would* be all right.

I couldn't understand what had gone wrong.

We had played by the rules; we had both been virgins on our miserable wedding night; we had read the books you were supposed to read; we were married in a Christian ceremony; we had done everything goddamn fucking right. And so I was not prepared for my life to feel so wrong.

I look back on that girl and feel such immense compassion for her. Her grief, and the reckoning before her, were immense.

It's painful to look back and see all the ways my body, intuition, and heart tried to stop me from marrying someone I had no connection to. I was so deeply convinced that my own urges and longings were wrong that I didn't know how to decipher any of my own clues. If it felt uncomfortable and itchy and a little bit wrong, then that was usually the sign that it was "right." And so I blew past all the warnings, all the little signals telling me to call it off. I didn't know that the little twist of uneasiness meant run. That the slight recoil in my gut meant no no no. That the sinking sensation in my heart meant Don't Marry This Person.

I didn't know.

—ɱ—

Oh, it was a pretty good life, though! I attended Bryn Mawr from our light-filled apartment on the Main Line. After school and on weekends, I worked at the most beautiful flower shop in the world. We found a church full of anarchists, artists, and intellectuals. This radical church community met in small groups in people's houses, talked deeply and intensely, and the strands of faith and my yearning seemed to twine together again. My husband was the tech guy at a homeless shelter. Our home was filled with flowers, beautiful wedding dishes, and a quiet, tiptoeing misery.

This is not his book, so I do not want to tell his story for him. But one of the pieces he brought to the table was the memory of his childhood years in an orphanage, and sometimes it seemed that nothing would ease the pain of the abandoned toddler who peered out with such disappointed, accusing eyes.

I myself was a roiling abyss of unmet needs and unacknowledged pain and all sorts of tasty treats.

I graduated with honors, bade a sad farewell to the flower shop, and started working as a peon at a big, prestigious, secular foundation.

We trudged along. Every day I went to work wearing heels, stockings, and blouses. Everyone in my department had at least a master's degree from an Ivy League school, and I was basically their secretary. It wasn't exactly uplifting. But I learned from them, watching the worlds they moved in, learning how they wrote letters to each other, seeing how the money moved from the big foundations to the universities and occasionally trickled down to worthy nonprofits like the one my husband worked at. I once took three days off of my job to sleep on the streets in protest of a mean-spirited law directed at the homeless. Our protest made it to television, and the ACLU took up the case. Then I returned to work, ordering the plates of pastries for meetings, scheduling teleconferences, and editing documents outlining grants for hundreds of thousands of dollars.

My husband and I decided to live "in community," which meant sharing a house, meals, and chores with other people. A small church group, called a "cell," met in our house every week and we cooked dinner for them and led the theological discussions. We were cast in the role of stable married couple, and our friends were other stable married couples. It all looked so lovely!

And I was slowly losing my mind.

It took me a while to figure out what was happening. For one thing, I seemed to be crying a lot. I wasn't sure if most people cried this much. And I hated having sex with my husband.

Something was off, but I couldn't figure out what it was. I tried vacuuming the couch again, but that didn't seem to help. I tried not to be so selfish. So needy. I tried not to want so much space. I tried not to itch where his skin touched mine. I tried to be grateful for my job. I tried to pray for patience, kindness, anything besides the blind rage that threatened to burst around the edges of the lid I was cramming down over it.

One night at a women's Bible Study group, I tentatively raised my hand.

"So, I'm just wondering—how hard is marriage supposed to be? Sometimes I—well, I know I don't really mean this, but—sometimes I don't even really—" my voice dropped to a mortified whisper—"want to be married."

The room erupted with warm, loving support.

Oh, honey, that's normal.

Marriage is hard! It takes work.

Take it to the Lord, sister.

All couples go through rough patches.

You're just coming out of the honeymoon phase.

This is the real deal, the true test of faith.

This is why we make promises, so we're not at the mercy of our emotions.

It's hard, but good.

It's worth it.

Worth it. Worth it. These words tumbled through my mind relentlessly. Worth more than feeling happy. Worth more than whatever juice in me was slowly seeping away. Worth more than my impossible, selfish wantings.

Worth so much more than me.

We had gone the church-sanctioned route, to the great surprise and joy of our new church pastor—wedding-night-virgins are a hot commodity—and so we were asked to mentor young couples who were "struggling." Which was code for the fact that they were tempted to have sex. I didn't feel very confident about being a good example, because living in our example sucked. Could I really tell young women that they should jump into marriage rather than hop in the sack? Wasn't that betraying the sisterhood?

Actually, speaking of the sisterhood, I was pretty mad at my Christian sisters, especially the married ones. Why hadn't anyone told me how awful marriage was going to be? Clearly it was a vast conspiracy.

I would bring it up with the other wives in the kitchen when we were doing the dishes after dinner parties. I'd throw out some carefully edited tidbit from our marital conversations—something irritating but not quite horrifying—and roll my eyes, then hold my breath and wait. I was desperately hoping that someone would burst into tears. I would have done a dance of relief.

(Note: I never found out what would have happened if I myself had burst into tears. I was frantically yearning for someone to open up their armor and show me their tender insides, but I certainly wasn't about to go first.)

But the legendary difficulty of marriage was a source of pride among my sistren, a big hilarious romp requiring stamina and tits of steel.

"Oh, yeah, marriage. *Gosh* it's hard!" they would sympathize, with serene, amused grins. We were all in this together, doing this heroic thing that was—gosh!—hard, but—gee!—so dang worth it.

Yeah. Absolutely. I tried to grin too.

For the life of me, I couldn't believe that I was turning out to be such a wimp. Everyone else was toughing it out; why couldn't I?

The joke among the married women at my church went like this:

"Of course I've never considered divorce. Murder, yes—divorce, no."

Then everyone laughed. Holy laughter. Ha ha ha.

Get it? Because anything—anything—was better than getting divorced. That would put you beyond the pale.

Being married to my husband was like living with a vacuum cleaner that was always turned on, and all the juicy parts of me, the joy, the ideas, the creativity, were sucked out. It wasn't his fault. He didn't know how to turn it off, and neither did I.

One bleak day, I said to him, "I think I'm going to start seeing Helen once a week. She's going to mentor me."

"Why?" he asked.

"Oh, you know. Deepening the faith, spiritual maturity, whatever." I pushed the orange plastic chairs tightly under our Ikea table. "Plus, you know, she's a trained therapist."

"Therapy. What bullshit."

I hitched the chair legs over the warped floorboards. Was it? His father was a counselor, so he had more direct exposure to that world than

I had ever had. And it's true that every book I had ever read by a Christian counselor made me want to eat tacks. Helen seemed different, though.

"Bea went to therapy, and she said it really helped."

"Helped? Yeah, it helps navel-gazing self-involved people be more narcissistic. Don't fall for any of that."

"Bea isn't a narcissist. And Helen is great. You don't have to be a jerk about it."

"Listen." He came over to me and put his arms around me, pinning me gently against his body. "That stuff is dangerous. It'll really mess with you. I just don't want you to get all weird. People who think about their feelings too much get kind of embarrassing."

I tried to relax into him. His long hair tickled my neck, and he was like a heater, warm and moist, making me sweat. I pulled back, and he finally let go. "Whatever," he said, tapping me on the forehead. "We can't afford it anyway."

Suddenly I was boiling, steaming, radiating rage from every pore. I walked into the kitchen to hide my face.

He followed me. "You can't just do whatever you want, you know."

I whirled around, and words flew out of my mouth. "Shut UP!!! You're not my boss, you're not in charge of what I do. I'll talk to Helen if I want to, damn it! I NEED it!!" My throat ached, my eyes burned, and I wanted to throw up.

Suddenly he was the betrayed little boy, backhanded across the face. His face registered hurt, his lips twitched, his eyes brimmed with tears. "Why are you like this? You're being irrational. And awful. And not a good wife."

It was all true. I was wrong. I had hurt him. Lost my temper. Blown up over nothing. I steadied my voice and said, "She's going to mentor me for free." He shrugged the saddest shrug in the world. I knew he would punish me for days with a sulky, injured silence.

My body ached as if I'd beaten it.

—◊—

I grinned cheerfully across the tiny room at Helen. My jaw ached. My legs were crossed. I was on an undercover mission, you see. I had to play my part carefully. My plan was to see Helen for "spiritual mentoring"—a common thing in our community—but see if I could sneak bits of information from her on what was actually wrong with me.

Without ever admitting that anything was really wrong, of course.

She smiled back at me, and I started to cry.

So much for being sneaky.

It took a while for me to see how my current misery was in some ways connected to the childhood events I choked out in tiny snippets. I sat locked into my chair during these sessions, trying not to cry, trying not to scream. It was all tangled in so deep that I couldn't have poured it all out even if I'd wanted to. But there was something in this woman's eyes, this devout, committed woman, who regarded me with such compassion. It was almost more than I could bear, that loving gaze. I was afraid I would fall apart completely under it. I had to keep myself rigid if I was going to keep going. Lord knows what would happen if I loosened my grip for even a second: devastation, catastrophe, public floggings.

But our conversations helped. I found the whole thing so astonishing, how Helen would sit there and listen just to me for a whole hour at a time. And she had some wild ideas about what you were allowed to ask for in a marriage. For instance, I learned a radical new phrase:

"Honey, I love you, but I'd like to be by myself for a while."

I practiced it under my breath. *I'd like to be by myself for a while*. It tasted like milky tea, steamy and delicious.

One Saturday morning, he pulled out his skateboard.

"I'm going to skate today. Why don't you come with me?"

This was a contentious topic between us. I didn't skate. I didn't like to watch other people skate. I didn't like skate parks, bridges, or the grating noise involved as plastic, wood, and bodies slammed into concrete. He thought it would be nice if I would come and watch him skate. He thought it would be even nicer if I actually watched him instead of reading some stupid book.

Which obviously I would *want to do*, if I loved him even a little.

So I had spent several miserable weekends in loyal support, sitting outdoors in the cold next to a stretch of concrete while he and a bunch of other dudes did complicated tricks with their boards. There were no bathrooms. There were no coffee shops. The guys peed in a ditch, but I wasn't up for that. (Apparently, though, women who really loved their skaters didn't mind peeing in ditches.)

So that morning, I said carefully, "Honey, I don't want to come watch you skate today. It's just not very fun for me. I think I'll stay home and read a book instead."

He groused a bit, but then decided that in that case he would stay home with me.

"No, it's fine, you should go."

"But I want to spend my weekend with you. We can hang out here."

"Okay, but I'm going to be reading a book."

"No, come on, hang out with me!"

The moment had come. I took a deep breath.

"Honey? I love you, but I'd like to spend some time by myself today."

He stared at me for a few seconds. I almost starting breathing again. Then it started.

"Why? Why don't you want me around? Don't you even love me? It's like you don't even care about me, you only care about yourself. You're so selfish. Why would you want me to not be here? You're going to kick me out of my OWN apartment? It's my space too, you know. I can be here if I want to. Everyone else gets to spend time with their wives. But not you. You and your precious SPACE." He fluttered his hands in the air. "Wah wah wah, I'm so special, I want to spend time BY MYSELF. Is that one of the phrases Helen gave you? Is that some therapy bullshit? Well you know what? We're married. We're supposed to spend time together. You should want to come watch me. If you cared about me, you'd rather come watch me skate on a Saturday than read some stupid New Age book. Does Helen even know you're reading those? I bet she'd be pissed."

I clutched my precious copy of *The Artist's Way* to my chest. My body had opened up a raw pulpy gaping hole and heaven knew what was about to spill out. The familiar gold and red cover of the book was like a benevolent shield between us. I wasn't sure if it was keeping us apart or holding me together.

"I'm going to go to a coffee shop for a little while," I said finally. He went into the bedroom and slammed the door.

I put on my coat, and then stood in front of the closed bedroom door. "It's just for a little while," I called. "I just want a little time to myself. I love you, it doesn't mean I don't, just because sometimes I want to be by myself."

"Yeah, you'd rather be with strangers, you mean," he called back.

I locked our front door and went down the dingy stairs to the street. Then I stepped out on South Street, where all the coolest parts of Philadelphia converged. People, colors, sounds, smells—they were intense, and busy, and they all were beautiful to me.

Thirty minutes later I was installed in a café, cradling a latte and looking out the plate glass window. I pulled out my journal and felt the humming start. It was the warm, slightly buzzy sensation I always got when I did one of the writing assignments from *The Artist's Way*. It felt so good, I was pretty sure it was a little immoral. And certainly the exercises themselves were appallingly selfish and indulgent. For example, she had you write down ten things that you wanted. Or ten things that make you happy. Can you imagine? The whole idea was completely scandalous. Gluttonous. But it felt so good I could hardly stop myself.

Today's delicious assignment was to list five things I secretly wanted, even though I knew they were impossible.

My hand flew across the page: *A diamond. A baby. To be an actress. To live by myself.* I was breathing hard. I noticed my mouth was open.

I put down my pen. All impossible, of course. The inner lashing started up.

Diamonds cause conflict and children are killed and turned into child soldiers and it's immoral to spend so much money on something so frivolous when there are people starving right here in Philadelphia.

A baby? No WAY would I bring a child into our miserable home. I would never be a good mother; I was too neurotic, too self-absorbed, too selfish. And the thought of having to co-parent with my husband sent actual chills down my spine.

An actress? Please. I was a secretary, and not even a very good one. I hadn't even done theater in college, hadn't done anything since high school. I was too chickenshit even to go to the college auditions.

To live by myself? When I was married? Obviously I was the slime of the earth, the very lowest of the low, an ungrateful disloyal woman. Plus embarrassing.

As I looked in despair at my list, I heard a tap on the café window. There was my husband, grinning at me. "I thought you might want some company!" he said cheerfully.

I felt a pang of guilt. How dare I? Who did I think I was? BY MYSELF? Without him??? The ridiculous list I had just written seemed clear proof: *I* was ridiculous. I was immature and trying to weasel out of my commitments. I put the book away and made room for him at my table.

He sat down, ordered an espresso, and gave me a little loving lecture. Following a proud Christian male tradition, he explained that I shouldn't need to talk to anyone but him about my feelings. He should be enough. Furthermore, feelings are just—sheesh—feelings, not to be indulged too much. Everyone knows you can't go around living your life based on *feelings*. He explained it to me reasonably, kindly. You have to do what's right, not what you feel. Everyone knows that.

I ended up nodding. That was true. Yes, that must surely be true.

But I couldn't stop scribbling in my copy of *The Artist's Way*, furtively and with great guilt. I didn't read it so much as make out with it. I read it when I was pretending to do my devotions, hiding it under my Bible and something by Thomas Merton. I began getting up early every morning and writing my morning pages, three sheets of longhand dumping. I tucked it in the bookshelf behind other books and stuffed it under the mattress of our marriage bed.

Every Friday night when he would go play basketball with the guys, I sat curled up in the big white armchair by the window, reading each week's chapter in the book and going through box after box of tissues. As Julia Cameron's words pulled me out of my haze, I began to see more and more clearly just how much I hated my life. It was almost unbearable to acknowledge. I wept as each impossible dream bloomed on the page and I scratched it out with angry scrawls. Those things were denied me. I had chosen marriage, this excruciating vise, and I had to stay.

—ᴍ—

In an attempt to create closeness between us, I agreed to pose for him. Nude. I still loved the photographer in him—the artist who made such beautiful things with his camera. And after all, Georgia O'Keefe had posed for those incredible nude photos for Alfred Stieglitz. She was a powerful woman; I could do it too. The human body was so gorgeous, and I was past the point of being ashamed, I told myself. His plan was to take photos of different parts of me and then put them together to make them into a tree. I thought it sounded intriguing and beautiful. I took my clothes off, shy and proud.

He unveiled the finished product triumphantly. It was nothing like the gentle, beautiful, sensual nude I'd imagined. Instead of a tree, I was a dissected specimen. My body was chopped up. He had impaled the photos of different parts of me on wire. All my tender parts splayed and pinned apart. My pubic hair on view in our living room when my parents came to visit.

I was horrified. I felt sick. But I was also embarrassed that I was embarrassed. It was art, right? Still, I quietly decided, no more nude photos.

But then he took a photo of my face—one in which I looked rather pretty for a change, I thought—and "worked on it." Which meant that he scratched the negative with a nail so that my face had angry scrawls across it like barbed wire. He printed it, framed it, and showed it to me.

187

"I'm going to hang it in the church art show. I think it's good."

I protested.

"It's not your decision."

"But it's my face!"

"But it's my photograph."

"But you scratched it out. It looks like I've been attacked. It looks like you hate me."

"It's art."

I wish I could tell you that I smashed it. Or hid it. Or put my foot down.

Nope. I wore an elegant boatneck top and a long black skirt to the opening and smiled and smiled and smiled. Someone told me I looked beautiful, but all I could feel was how many lashes it took to make myself keep my head held high.

—m—

While I was doing my best Stepford Wife imitation, there was turmoil in our church. A debate was raging about sex.

Articles were written, discussions were held, sermons were preached. One of the elders of the church, a man in his thirties with a wife and child, wrote a diatribe against the lax morals of the congregation. He laid down the law about how we had to have integrity even in a postmodern, fluid church family.

I read it. And then I just imploded. Something about this article absolutely infuriated me. I couldn't put my finger on it, but I was livid, literally churning with rage. I went over to Bea's house.

"It's just bullshit," I said. I slammed down a glass of wine.

Bea poured me more. "I KNOW," she said. "I mean his reading of the Biblical texts is just so totally flawed and skewed by his hatred of women." Bea had good Biblical reasons why the elder's argument was flawed because she had gone to seminary. (A seminary where women could *attend*, but not actually be ordained. So it was like you could GO to med school, but then you graduated a landscaper.) "Everything he says just reinforces these old sexist, patriarchal readings of the text."

"Okay. Good. Well, I don't really know about that, I just think he's lying." I sat up in surprise. "He's LYING."

"Yeah? How so?"

"I don't know. I have zero evidence. I can't back it up at all. I just— he's just—aw man, he's full of SHIT!"

I stood up, suddenly furious.

I could feel it, right behind my breastbone. It was maddening that I couldn't prove what I absolutely knew to be true. It was a physical sensation so specific, so clear, so calm. When I paid attention to that insistent finger in my chest, I noticed that my anger instantly dissolved. My body felt quiet and soft. Only the information remained, neutral and clear; *he is lying*. I drew a peaceful breath. Huh. Weird.

Almost as quickly, I doubted myself. "Uggggggghhhhhhhh. He's pretty solid with God, though. He's an elder, and plus they live in community, and they volunteer...they're good people. I mean, I really like his wife. I don't know. I think something's wrong with me. Because I just feel like, deep in my bones, that he is LYING."

In fact, I could see the word flashing in front of my eyes: Liar. Liar. Liar.

"Oh, honey, I don't know. I love God so much, but I really can't stand His people sometimes." Bea leaned back. "Listen. I've been thinking. Maybe we should make more pesto this year. Should I plant more basil?"

About a year later, the man would leave his wife and child to go live with his secret male lover in New York City. But at the time I just thought it was more evidence that I must be wrong about everything.

—⁓—

Also, the Bible still made me mad.

This was such a problem. Everyone else I knew read it and felt super inspired and comforted and they really felt God "lay things on their heart," like a funky hippie guru, but not me. Every page had something that sent me into a fury. My poor pastor would get so exasperated; he said it was like I was *looking* for proof that God was bad. It wasn't that I was looking, it was just that I saw it everywhere.

For instance, blaming all the evil in the world on Eve was a good start—one that carried weight years later when Peter or Paul used that as a justification for why women should be under the authority of men.

Other Christian women, even the closet feminists, talked about how inclusive Jesus was; how he was so ahead of his time in being gentle to women, even letting them travel with him. I continued to boil over in anger about him; I thought that with all of eternity to give him some perspective, he might have done better than letting them give him their money and trail along behind the twelve disciples. If Jesus cared so much about women, why hadn't he made six of his twelve confidantes women? Or seven, if you wanted to accurately represent the human population.

If Jesus was bold enough to take on the Pharisees and break down so many religious and cultural assumptions, I wanted a whole lot more from him than letting someone cry on his feet and then wipe her tears off with her hair. (This was supposed to be a very moving scene, see. Jesus let that filthy scrap of womanhood actually touch his feet with her hair. And leak her nasty body juices on him. Jesus was so generous, so loving, so wonderful!)

Where was his sermon about slavery? Nowhere, that's where. I couldn't understand it. And New Testament women still had to obey their husbands and couldn't preach. A lot of revisionist theologians, some of who were in our church, were working very hard to try to find gleams of hopeful stories buried among the misogynistic texts. They wrote reams of text and did deep linguistic excavation. They proved again and again that women are actually loved by God and maybe even (possibly) considered equal human beings in a theological sense. But the very fact that they had to work so hard at it made me feel sad and exhausted. Why would you work so hard to be included in something that obviously didn't want you?

I had a terrifying nightmare over and over again. I dreamed of a little girl, maybe three or four. She was always in a dungeon, filthy and naked. Her body was a horrific patchwork of skin, like something out of a sick serial killer fantasy. The patches of skin were held together by thick black thread. Lines of crude stitching crisscrossed her whole body and face. She would look at me with cold evil blue eyes full of hatred. I would wake crying, screaming, shuddering. I could not shake the terror of those nights. I began to feel like there were angry eyes peering at me from car windows or behind curtains. I felt like something was following me, and I was always afraid.

I kept going to therapy with Helen. (We had given up pretending that it was "mentoring.") We were working on unraveling how God sending my family to Japan as missionaries had gotten twisted into every frightening thing that had happened to me as a child. She kept trying to examine whether my childhood beliefs were really true, that things happened to me because God wanted it to be that way. That the scary things had been part of God's will.

But the whole time I was battling with my faith in the present day—furious at my church community and all the pious conversations about marriage and sexuality and purity. I couldn't stand my own hypocrisy as I pretended that if you followed God's rules and just tried hard enough, you could make it through anything.

I had followed the damn rules, I was trying everything I knew to try, and yet I thought constantly about death. Other women thought about murder, not divorce? Since divorce wasn't an option for me, I thought about dying instead. I watched trucks at intersections; I studied train tracks. Inhaled car exhaust, testing its scent. I lay in bed and imagined never waking up. That one was the sweetest idea of all; it fell inside me like soft rain. Over and over, I imagined myself pulverized in a thousand different ways—my body broken and my soul finally released.

I was filled with rage at God. He had ruined my childhood, and now He was keeping me stuck in this horrific thing called marriage. I had nightmares every night; great flapping demons tried to carry me away, and I clung to the cross. I was trying desperately to hold onto my salvation, and God was no help. There was no love in Him, only a punishing anger. I tried and tried to feel the truth of God's love that we sang about every Sunday. And when I prodded my heart to see what it had to say, it sighed out in a voice as empty as dry stone, longing for rain, and thirsty.

I sang about love at church—sappy songs about being beloved, about joy and longing for God; I even swayed along. I did devotions; I prayed; I even wrote theological statements in our church newspaper about how God was the love behind all of singing, dancing creation. It was all bullshit. It wasn't a lie; I did believe that this was true for some people. Just not me. I didn't feel it. I didn't feel led. I didn't feel loved. I didn't feel like God had a plan for my life that would lead me to paths of righteousness. All I felt was a dull, muffled thud of despair. The answer seemed so clear: that kind of love isn't for you.

It felt like an extra sick cruelty, a dollop of sadism, that God had made me with the craving for love but not whatever innate quality would win that love. God wasn't just ignoring me, passing me over with a polite "No Thanks;" God was messing with me. Taunting me. What a perverted fuck.

I yearned for escape as fervently as I was convinced that I wasn't allowed it. I had made a promise, after all. *'Til death do us part.* This yearning for freedom, solitude, escape and beauty—this was clearly just my flawed nature trying to pull me away from the right path.

Helen kept looking at me out of those kind blue eyes. Sometimes during our sessions her thin grey cat would come in and delicately leap into my lap as I littered the floor with wadded-up tissues. Her throaty purr worked its way into my knotted stomach like a hot toddy.

"I just can't stop wanting things," I confessed soggily.

"What do you want?"

"So many things!" I wailed. "All bad things. I want—everything I can't have. Definitely not holy things. Expensive shoes. Massages. A big fancy house. To quit my job. A different life. To run away and become an actress."

She was quiet for a second. "What if that longing you feel is *from* God?"

"No, Helen. You don't understand. It's that same longing that's always taken me *away* from God." I didn't tell her the other things I longed for; the secret things.

"I'm not so sure. Maybe He's trying to tell you that he's not the evil terrorizer of your childhood. Maybe those things you long for are taking you toward God." Boom! She dropped her big bag of heresy on the table, and I breathed and waited for her to be struck by lightning. I know it's an expression, but I literally expected her to crumble into a pillar of salt, at least.

She leaned forward, weirdly unpillarized. "What do you really, really want?"

My answer was instantaneous: "I want to leave my marriage. I want to leave the church. I want to feel free." She just gazed at me, smiling a little.

"But Helen, I can't have those things! I'm mmmaaaaaaarrrrrrrried!" I'm sure my mouth hung open. She was almost chuckling.

"Dear girl. I just know that God loves you. And nothing, nothing, nothing, can take you away from that."

—⁓—

Bea had given me a copy of the book *Expecting Adam*, by Martha Beck. I didn't think that a memoir by a Harvard-trained intellectual about having a son with Down syndrome sounded very interesting. But Bea pressed it on me with that bossy passion that distinguishes the true literati—

"No, you HAVE to read it, you just absolutely have to."

"But I'm not even interested in having kids! It'll just make me feel guilty."

"Listen. Read it RIGHT NOW. If you don't read it, I will disown you and pour out all the wine in the city. AND I won't give you any of the jars of pesto."

—so I rolled my eyes and took the book.

It's still my favorite kind of conversation.

You know why they ban books, right? Because they're dangerous. They're the Underground Railroad and freedom fighters and your grandmother's recipes all rolled into one.

That damn book had an electric current running through it. My fingers locked into it and wouldn't stop clutching. I couldn't put it down, couldn't pull my eyes away. I recognized her, this Martha person. She described something so exactly—the rigidness of doctrine as it contorts you—and the insane longing for something, anything else. Her doctrine had been Harvard intellectualism, and mine was evangelical Christianity, but we were fellow travelers, she and I. Even with my stellar missionary-kid bullshit-meter beeping suspiciously, I found that I trusted her as she told the most crazy-sounding stories. She was smarter and funnier than any author I'd ever read, right up there with Anne Lamott, and I tore through *Expecting Adam* in a night, then read it again straight through in a frenzy of yearning. She had miracles! Visions! She had mysterious protoplasmic visitors when she was bleeding to death, for crying out loud! (She called them the *bunraku* puppeteers.)

The book was so beautiful. Wise, sharp, hilarious, heartbreaking.

And BOY was I pissed.

Where were *my* goddamn *bunraku* puppeteers? Why did everyone get something except meeeee?

I huddled on the bathroom floor, that necessary rite of passage for a memoir-writer, and literally wailed out loud with longing and fury. I had to stuff a towel in my mouth. I cried out to God for a sign. (It always worked in the Bible.) Couldn't I have some *bunraku* puppeteers too? Oh please oh please? Hell, I'd take plain old vanilla angels, for that matter, and I wouldn't even complain if they had wings and swords like in those terrible *Piercing the Darkness* books. God, couldn't I know that I was beloved, just once? Couldn't I have something, just a little whiff of the holy spirit? Couldn't a ray of light touch me and make me into one of Jesus's little sunbeams?

Please, please, please, a sign, I begged. *Just let me feel loved for one moment. I just need one moment to sustain me and I will stay. I will stay in the church, I will stay in my marriage, I will stay in the fold and be good. I just need the tiniest flick of your pinkie finger.*

In response, there was a great and resounding silence. An utter void of nonresponse. A cosmic cold shoulder.

If it had had words, it would have said,

That's not how it's going to be for you.

There was something about Martha's book that broke me open. Things started to fall apart. I couldn't hold the illusion together any more. Her book brought my intense yearning out into the open in a way that was so raw, so focused, that it was hard to ignore it any more. Books can do this for us, so wonderfully and terribly—they can rip through what we're pretending and whisper, "You're not crazy. You're not the only one." No wonder people burn them. They're the ESP of the revolution, the wildfire that burns up what needs to go.

Down in my dry parched cells, I wanted to feel loved. I wanted to be a chosen one. I wanted to belong to some group that would have me as I was. But I could no longer deny that I felt no love from God and no love from my husband. The desolation was overwhelming. I was a goat. *For Jacob have I loved, but Esau have I hated.* I was Esau.

I argued with my Bible study leader. I practiced saying "fuck," though naturally only when I was alone. I'd never had more than a glass of wine at a time, but I started drinking whisky because I could knock it back without tasting it. I loved cigarettes most of all because they helped me breathe—they were like a little loving inhaler for my scorched lungs, a little rain in the desert.

I began to punish the loathsome creature of my body, scratching deep lines in my skin, burning myself on hot pans, beating my arms until I was bruised. I never quite had the courage to cut myself (*chickenshit disgusting wimp can't even take a knife* I whispered) but I would bang into sharp corners and twist cords around my wrists until they were raw and chafed. The hurt untwisted the ache inside me for a little while.

But mostly, I just kept thinking about suicide constantly. It was better than booze, even better than pain—the sweet, sweet promise that I could wipe it all out. Killing myself was the only future that made me hopeful:

the possibility that I could stop the utter hopelessness of living as an empty shell for forty or sixty more years. Just stop it all, cut short the suffering.

I fantasized about pills, tall buildings. I stared at subway rails and bridges. I was too afraid of knives and too clumsy to manage a rope, and I was really scared of heights, but pills—ahh, pills. Pills I could manage, I was sure of it. I made plans and checked the medicine cabinet of everyone I knew. I counted. I was always counting.

I think the only thing that kept me from killing myself was the irritating but un-dismissable flicker of a possibility that when I died, I would just end up face to face anyway with that angry fucker. (Father God, Jehovah, Lord Above.) I didn't relish the thought of spending an eternity with him or with his little shithead friend, the devil.

Maybe my contrarian nature saved me.

I'd show 'em—I'd give them the middle finger by staying alive no matter how much they fucked with me.

For my 24th birthday I ordered a coat from J.Crew. I called in the order with my heart beating hard, my credit card going slick with sweat. It was a huge splurge for me at the time, even a wicked splurge, and the coat was so beautiful—silvery blue, soft cashmere, a slim, tailored trench. I thought about it for weeks with a tickle of pleasure as I imagined the pale brown box arriving at my door. It would be such a change from my normal wardrobe, most of which came from the local thrift store. I longed to have one beautiful, quality, classy thing to wear. I craved its thick protection against the bitter Philadelphia winter. I wanted to feel elegant and streamlined. The day it came, I cut through the brown paper tape slowly and pulled it out of the box with glee, luxuriating in the soft nap, the high quality. But when I put it on it was miles too big. The cuffs came down to my knuckles, the neck was floppy and too wide, and no matter how tightly I tied the belt, it was bulky and wadded around my middle.

"Darn." I felt like crying, again. Why couldn't anything go right?

My husband walked in. "What?"

"My beautiful coat. It doesn't fit."

"Yes it does; it's fine."

I held out my arm. "No look, it's way too big."

He looked at me a minute before replying. "Nothing is ever good enough for you, is it?"

Once again I found myself standing in our bathroom, looking at my haggard face in the fluorescent lights. The hollows under my eyes were so deep I could have stored my wedding ring there. I wound the coat tighter around me. It went around me almost twice. I rolled back the cuffs. I would keep it, of course. My husband was right. I always wanted too much. I was so greedy, so insatiable and voracious. There was that awful pit inside me, my yawning hole of ugly *wanting*. That black hole inside me was so wrong, so dangerous. It would wipe out everything and destroy the whole world. It was the very maw of evil.

Here was proof: how could I be so self-indulgent as to send back this perfectly good coat?

I should be so grateful to have such a nice coat.

I nodded dully and scraped the tender inside of my wrist against the bottom of the faucet. *Take that, stupid girl.* The metal was rusty, jagged and rough. I watched red welts bloom against the pale blue veins of my disgusting, contemptible self.

Pills. It was time to gather the pills. I just couldn't do this any more. It hurt too much. I closed my eyes.

It was time.

There was a sudden splitting inside me, a sound like a branch breaking.

The room swayed for a second. Part of me snapped off like a twig. She simply unmoored from my body and floated up to the ceiling. From there she regarded me with her hands on her hips. This self was both me and not me; she was like a very quiet pocket of awareness who hovered near the shower curtain. She watched me holding onto the sink and crying. And she listened to the thoughts pouring through my mind and dripping onto the porcelain.

"I'm so ugly. I'm so hideous. Maybe if I just lose some weight. Maybe I need to be thinner."

This very calm self watched me for a minute. It was sort of nice having her there; I didn't feel quite as lonely. But then she rolled her eyes, shook her head, and swooped back into my body and took over. I felt like I was being lifted, gently cradled in my own arms as I led myself kindly but firmly into the living room. And then I proceeded to have a conversation with myself.

"Sweetheart. Honey. Listen to how crazy you've gotten. You're saying you want to get skinnier even though the coat is too big. That doesn't even make any goddamn sense."

"I have to stay. I should be grateful. I want to die and I have to stay."

"Listen, chicky, this is fucking ridiculous. Let's get out of here."

"I can't. It's forever. Look at all these wedding presents."

"Really? You won't save yourself from imminent mental breakdown because of some dishes? Some glasses? Some goddamn *silverware*? Listen to yourself. Jesus fucking Christ. You are totally batshit crazy right now."

I blinked at her.

It was one of the kindest things anyone had ever said to me.

Very slowly, I tilted my face down into my arms and sighed with recognition. I knew that something momentous had happened. I had just met my authentic self: a part of me deeper than dogma, braver than the scared little girl I'd been for so many years. She was so foreign to me that she felt like something separate from me—less an aspect of me than a completely different entity.

I had already learned two important facts about her. One, she swears a lot. Two, she wasn't going to let me die. She wouldn't even let me sell my soul for some beautiful cutlery.

I already loved her more than anyone I'd ever met.

CHAPTER TWENTY

Sheep go to heaven, goats go to hell.

The first time I heard that Cake lyric, I was slugging back a Pabst Blue Ribbon with my brother Jake in his Chicago apartment. I froze for a second, astounded. The heavens parted and little cherubs and birds twittered in my head and I threw my head back and barked with a manic urgent hilarity that would have mortified me under normal circumstances. Instead, Jake just winked at me, and then he and I hollered along at an unbelievable volume. I whooped in triumph and recognition. There it was! Goats go to hell! I was a goat! I was going to hell—hurray! Let's sing about it!

There was such power in saying it out loud: God does not love me. I cannot stand being Christian for one more minute. The Bible makes me want to throw up. Ahhhhhhh, sweet truth. God was such a fucker anyway, and I didn't even WANT to go to heaven with all the misogynists and Bible-thumpers. The freedom of it! The glee! The *relief.*

For the life of me, I couldn't figure out why it felt so good to renounce (at least quietly, inside my own heart, bellowing along to Cake) everything that I still theoretically believed was actually good and true and right. It wasn't that I came to believe that Christianity was untrue; it was simply that I decided that I'd rather be wrong, and even literally go to hell, than stay the miserable Christian I had become. It was the sweetest truth I'd ever whispered to myself: I'd always been a goat. I'd never been one of Jesus's baby lambs. I was no sunbeam. Nah, I was something else—something distasteful, probably, but I didn't care. I just wanted to tell the truth. I was a goat.

And boy oh boy did the goats know how to frolic.

I had temporarily fled my marriage, and everything else, under the guise of going to visit my brother for two weeks. I had stepped from the tight contortion of my life onto an airplane, and then into another world—into the sweet bubble of my little brother's bohemian apartment.

Jake was only two years younger than me. Our baby sister was still living at home with my parents. Jake was a sophomore at the University of Chicago, living on the south side of the city. (I felt personally responsible for him going to the U of C because the morning of my wedding, I'd almost walked into him in the kitchen. He was just standing there, perfectly still amidst the wedding prep chaos, with a little amused glint in his eye. He handed me a folded piece of paper. It was his acceptance letter. The kitchen erupted into joyful squeals and jumping up and down. I was giddy with pride and glee, and that moment stands out as the happiest bit of my wedding day.) And now here he was, taking classes, working as a security guard at an art museum, my little brother suddenly a real person out on his own. It was the first time we'd spent so much time together without our parents around. And when his big sister suddenly turned up for a two-week visit before Christmas, he generously tucked me into the cocoon of the world he'd crafted for himself and didn't ask any questions.

"Wait, you smoke cigarettes too?"

"Yes!"

"The only people I really like are Christians who smoke," said Tom, our old friend from Japan.

"I'm not sure I'm a Christian," I said.

"That's okay, we know you. You're one of us. We are the goats. Are you having shitty gin and frozen orange juice, or a Pabst?"

"Ummm, another Pabst."

"Besides," Tom continued, "We're all exiles from the Motherland."

"The Motherland?"

"Japan. That place has claws. It gets into you."

That was certainly true. There we were, in Chicago, all missing Japan, our other home—the one that would not grant us citizenship or visas but had claimed a part of our souls, apparently for good. For a moment blue tile roofs and mossy stones and orange persimmons hung in the air between us.

"*Natsukashii ne,*" I said, and we smiled shyly at each other—that untranslatable Japanese phrase that speaks of a kind of sweet ache, a nostalgia that is almost comforting.

"To the land of the rising sun!"

"*Kampaaaaaai!*"

It tasted like home to mix Japanese into my speech; to pretend to talk like Japanese gangsters at bars; and to eat pot after pot of Japanese-style curry rice.

—❦—

Being in Jake's apartment was like inhabiting a Bob Dylan song. The edges were rough and reedy, and some of the transitions were uncomfortable, but the whole thing had a lot of soul. Even the inanimate objects became imbued with a kind of personality, like there was too much feeling for the puny little people to contain, and so it leaked out into all the appliances. The boom box, for instance, was a dilapidated thing that looked like it might have been extremely cool in the 80s, and yet it had a CD player in it that worked nearly all the time. The volume control, however, rarely worked at all, and it played at a constant high roar. Sometimes if we needed to create a quieter ambience than usual, we would set the boom box (we loved calling it a boom box—Hey, dude, like tear it up, yo) out on the porch. So far, none of the neighbors had complained.

Officially my brother lived there with a fellow University of Chicago student. Unofficially, the friend was never there but a waif named Janie had taken up residence. In fact, attractive vagabonds were always sleeping on the couch or other more interesting places. I joined the fray.

One night Dean, an intense guy in a leather jacket, tried in vain to play "Last Dance with Mary Jane."

"There's something wrong with the fucking boom box," he told the waiting masses. A minute later, he marched down the hall and banged on Jake and Janie's door.

Janie opened it. "Hi, sweetheart."

"There's jam on my CD. See these purple fingerprints? And now there's jam in the boom box. Which means that none of our CDs will work. Which means that we are going to need some serious drugs to get through the night."

Janie stared at him. "Oh, that sucks, man." She took the CD from him and licked it. "There, now it's clean."

Dean came sheepishly back to the living room.

I patted his shoulder. "Boy, you sure told her."

"I couldn't do it. I couldn't nail her. It would be like smacking a three-year-old."

"Lots of people smack their three-year-olds." I threw him a pack of smokes. "But not you, hardass."

Furrowing up his brow like he was practicing his Hamlet monologue, he began a thorough and meticulous cleaning of the boom box, using his t-shirt, Windex, and—over my protests—lighter fluid.

Janie liked to play Bob Marley as her wake-up music. The boom box usually spent the night in Jake's bedroom, and no one minded because it helped muffle the sounds of their nocturnal activities. But it also meant that Janie had first access to it in the morning, which meant a whole lot of singing along, and government yards, and Trenchtown.

"I need money, baby. Cigarette money." Janie had her arms around Jake's neck as they swayed and sashayed.

"Okay, baby. Bring us home some smokey treats. And no homeless people this time. Not that I don't like them. It's just that we don't have much booze."

"All right. We'll keep tonight an exclusivity soiree deal. Only our super-special soul sisters. And their brothers can come, too."

"Damn straight."

My brother had brought a *kotatsu* table over from Japan, and we huddled around it on the bitter Chicago nights. A *kotatsu* is a low square table with a heater underneath it and a blanket that drapes around the sides to keep the heat in. Our legs and feet were toasty warm, and we lit our cigarettes with icy fingers.

I kept rolling a word around my mouth. *Divorce.* I was only supposed to be in Chicago for two weeks, and then I'd stretched it to three...and I knew that when I went back to Philadelphia, I was going to pack up a car and leave. I wasn't sure when I had decided that. The knowledge just arrived and took up residence. I didn't want to be a Christian any more. And I didn't want to be married any more. I'd rather kill myself than continue to do those things.

Maybe, I thought idly, I could stay in Chicago. Walk away from all of it—my husband, church, job—and start a new life. The thought was so foreign it stunned me. I'd be dead to all of them, I knew. I'd be evil beyond redemption. I found myself grinning.

Why not? After all, I was a goat. Goats were beyond the pale, and I wouldn't be getting into heaven anyway.

I went into a very expensive hair salon. Since a brief and disastrous bob in college, I'd been growing my hair ever longer, and now it hung down my back, curly and frizzy in turn, lightening to gold around the edges. I sat down in the chair and told my stylist, who had pink hair and wore little booties, that I wanted to look like a different person. I walked out with platinum swirls that floated out around my ears. I looked like a slightly punky Marilyn Monroe. I felt as light and shimmery as champagne.

We were at the edge of Lake Michigan just before dawn. The cops were nowhere to be seen. It felt like the end of the world, the iceberg green of the sky curling into the blue skyline of ice. The water was frozen into waves, white and frothy. I waited in the car, scribbling in my journal. The rest of our crew slipped and cavorted out on the ice, calling to each other, "Don't fall in, kiddo, we won't get to you in time." The sky was shot through with indigo cloud lines. The deep colors broke me awake; in this strange city, in a car near beloved strangers, I was still torn open with joy by the delphinium blue morning.

My people came rollicking back like puppies, and we zoomed away, caught and held in the small racing hub of warm metal. They cracked the windows, lit cigarettes and turned on tinny music against the quiet of the sunrise. I squirmed and concentrated to stay in the blue stillness. This moment, now, this. My hair whipping around my face was tinged purple. The words rolled in with the morning: *nothing is in the way but your fear.*

One night I was alone with Dean. He was skinny, smoked like a chimney, and had a vicious sense of humor that disguised a tender, loyal heart. He said something foul and I felt a strange and unfamiliar sensation well up inside me. It spilled out of me in a laugh. It took me by surprise. How long since I had felt liquid joy burble up in me like this? I stepped close to him and smelled stale cigarettes and a scent that was just him—his ragged leather coat, his sweat—and I felt something inside me swoon. I tipped my head back and looked at him.

"What?" he asked.

I grinned. I stepped closer.

"I think I'm misunderstanding you."

I put my hand on his chest and felt his heart thumping. I reached up and touched my lips to his.

"Oh my god, you're killing me. I would in a heartbeat. But you're the one who's married."

I whispered, "I don't feel very married."

And then I tangled myself in him in every possible way.

Instead of guilt, I was elated. I had crossed a threshold, done something decidedly *bad*, and it felt exquisite. My body was awake, and I couldn't stop laughing. I tackled him in hallways, in empty kitchens, and in his car. He cradled my head and kissed my toes. We tasted every inch of each other. Sometimes I lay there and cried afterward, because I could feel my body again. It had come home to me. It was like standing at the edge of the ocean: like encountering a presence so big and wise and beautiful that there is nothing to do other than greet it with reverence. I marveled at my own skin. I kissed my own wrists and whispered, "I'm sorry." I closed my eyes and just breathed in and out. The air pouring into my lungs felt like an actual miracle.

CHAPTER TWENTY-ONE

I sat across a Formica table from my husband. He had traveled to the midwest, confused about why I hadn't come home yet.

"I'm leaving. I want a divorce."

He used words like "betrayal" and "cruel" and "heartless." I nodded. It was all true; I felt nothing for him. I must be the most cold-hearted person in the world. But I just couldn't care.

When I told Jake, he didn't say much. He lit a cigarette and handed it to me. "Congrats, *nechan*," he said. *Nechan* is an endearment in Japanese that means beloved older sister. That one word was like a love letter. And then he and Janie drove me to Philadelphia, helped me jam the car full of my stuff, and drove me all the way back. That brother of mine doesn't have to say much to communicate with exquisite clarity.

Fast forward a decade for just a minute. You need to understand something about my parents.

When my sister got kicked out of Bible college, nearly ten years later, I was so freaking proud of her. She, like many of her classmates, had not managed to uphold the school's standard of total and complete celibacy.

Unlike many of those same classmates, she refused to lie about it when questioned directly. So they expelled her.

She called my parents in tears. She talked to my mom, of course; my dad has a small quota of words for phone conversations, and runs out quickly.

"Mom? I have something to tell you." She took a breath. "It's bad. I'm...I got...they kicked me out of school. I had sex with my boyfriend." She scrunched her eyes closed, braced for the worst.

"Oh, honey," said my mom instantly, "It's so hard NOT to, isn't it?"

And that was ALL she said about it.

They agreed that Ruth would come home and live with them for a while, and then my mother was seized by an immense and overpowering primal instinct: she went out that very day and bought a new *futon*, pillows, sheets, and blankets. Her baby bird was coming home, and she needed to make a soft nest for her. One of my mother's love languages is bedding.

I understand that this might seem like a normal human parental response, but within our conservative religious community, it was revolutionary. Keep in mind that when I was in high school, my friend's pastor father told her that if she ever had sex, he would tie her naked to a tree and whip her with his belt until she miscarried. Ahhh, good Christian parenting.

To be fair, that particular asshole does not fairly represent the loving people I grew up with. Most of the Christians we knew, who were *not* total sociopaths, would have welcomed home a fallen child with tenderness. But that child would have also been met with deep disappointment, wounded sorrow, and ever-present reminders that they were forgiven.... forgiven in spite of that Very Horrible Bad Thing they had done. So my parent's purely loving response was nothing short of exceptional.

My dad doesn't go in for heart-to-heart conversations; they make him Feel Uncomfortable Things, which he prefers to avoid at all costs. But an hour later he sent my sister the following email:

Dear Ruth, I'm so sorry you're having a rough time. The sakura are blooming here. We can't wait to see you.

Love,

Dad

This is my parents; they are pure love. To me, it seems that their love transcends their belief in Jesus and the Bible; their love is so much bigger than their Christianity. But I know that seems ridiculous to them. They are simply living out what they believe, which is that God is love, and they are loved, and therefore they will love too.

But all this happened nearly ten years later. Back when I was getting divorced, my sister was still in middle school. I hadn't put my parents through the wringer yet, so they were not prepared for my bombshell announcement.

It was at dinner, in the small church house in Indianapolis, where they were living on a yearlong furlough. I cleared my throat. There was no preamble, no way to break it easily.

"Mom. Dad. I'm getting a divorce."

A sick silence.

I kept talking, though I had no idea what was coming out of my mouth. I don't remember what they said; I just remember seeing tears run down their faces. Even my dad, who never cried, was quietly weeping. I couldn't stand it, the destroyed looks on their faces. I wanted to get out of there as quickly as possible, to escape the awful feeling in my chest. They wanted to understand, so they tried to get me to explain. It was so painful to feel their grief and hurt—it twisted in my belly like sick fists—that I took the chickenshit way out: I went back to Chicago, stopped answering their calls, and went dark. They kept reaching in with their tendrils of emotion, their earnest questions, their sorrowful attempts to connect, but I could feel myself rushing away from them so fast that all I could hear was the wind. It was like looking at them from a million miles away.

—⁓—

Dean and I made out silently in the kitchen, on the fire escape, and in his car. We met in the back hall for surreptitious, urgent orgasms. I couldn't stop laughing; the whole world suddenly seemed hilarious. We didn't tell anyone about our affair. Everyone knew anyway. I waited for the guilt to kick in, but felt only a liquid sweaty bliss.

Familial guilt, though— no shortage of that.

The phone rang one night. Jake and I sat there, smoking our cigarettes and reading our books in comfortable silence. It had to be my parents; no one else ever called the land line, and they were back in Japan and had probably just woken up.

"You pick it up," I said.

"No you, you punk," he said. "They want to talk to you, anyway."

I closed my eyes. "I can't. They're so sweet. But they poke around. They fuck up my insides."

"Yeah. I know."

"They want to see the raw spots. But then they want to *talk* about them."

We sat there in mutual misery until the phone stopped ringing.

While my mother was hurt by the distance between us, my father was never one to be stopped by such trifling matters as emotions. One day I received the following email:

Dear children,

Once upon a time, there were three little ships. These ship children forgot their father's birthday. And they sailed across the sea merrily until they drowned.

Love,

Barkley

Barkley was our family cat.

"Jake! Fuck! We forgot Dad's birthday!!!"

"No. No! Shit!" We stared at each other in a panic. Birthdays and Christmas were sacred in our family, estrangement or no estrangement. So we wrote him back immediately:

Dear Barkley,

Please tell Dad that the ship children sent his present by seamail. It should arrive shortly. Probably they ran into a storm at sea and it's taken longer than expected.

Love,
The two eldest Ships

And so it went. Barkley never failed to remind us when we were in danger of stretching the distance too far. She reminded us of birthdays, holiday arrangements, and upcoming visits. And every now and then, if we'd been too uncommunicative, she threatened to burn the treasures we had stored in my parent's storage shed. It became a running joke:

You know those shoji screens you rescued from that house that was going to be demolished? The ones you're sure you'll put into a house someday? Well, I'm going to go sell them all for fish heads if your parents don't hear from you soon.
Love,
Barkley

Late at night when we were all tired and tipsy and too weary to be cool, the Chicago kids would listen to Leonard Cohen. We would light up cigarettes, pour the cheapest gin our pooled change could buy, and all sing along throatily to "Famous Blue Raincoat." It was so restful to stop being ironic all the time and just be earnest. It was the closest to holy I had ever felt.

Sometimes, very late at night, when the stars aligned and the spirit moved and the cigarette smoke swirled up in silent shamanic swoops, we sang Leonard's secret ballad-which-shall-not-be-named-nor-used-in-Disney-movies, "Hallelujah."

There could be no discussion about it. A big deal must not be made. Speaking would have broken the spell.

We might have been total heathens, but we recognized sacrament when we found it.

I heard later that after our divorce, four more couples in our church also divorced in short order. Clearly it was my fault. I had ruined something, apparently. I got some angry phone calls and some poisonous emails, but I felt immune to the uproar. It all seemed so far away, and I just couldn't get myself to care. It was so odd to observe this new self. I had a little bubble around me; a Plexiglas room of simply not giving a fuck. It was so quiet in that Plexiglas room, so peaceful. I wanted to stay there forever.

I had started going to therapy in Chicago. My therapist pointed out that I had used Dean as a bridge to get out of my marriage. I understood the ramifications and nodded solemnly. But I didn't give a rat's ass, and neither did he. He made me laugh and he made me come. I was floating, I was free, and I was beyond the pale.

We were living off our savings, getting wasted every night, laughing and singing, and it was all kind of a mess except for this one crucial, god-damn radiant thing: I never, ever, *ever* thought about killing myself again.

Eventually I ran out of money and got a job at a bookstore. Most of my paycheck came home with me in bags of books. The store let me take over the lapsed kids' story-time, which I conducted from a little plastic chair with my knees up to my chin. The first time, I had a stack of my favorite picture books next to me, sitting by myself on a round carpet like an idiot, wondering if anyone would show, but still trying to play it cool, like I just liked to sit on tiny plastic chairs by myself all the time for fun. Luckily for me, kids did indeed begin to turn up—just a few at first, and then after a few weeks, bunches of them. When I was reading to those squirrely snotty beautiful tiny people, I could feel something in me jiggling, unfurling—a little germ of something golden. Week by week, it was getting bigger in me until it was like a golden egg in my chest. After a month, I looked in amazement at the wiggly circle as I made my way through *Where The Wild Things Are, Lily's Purple Plastic Purse*, and my favorite: *The Gardener*. It seemed so odd and miraculous that the children kept coming. They must not have gotten the memo about what a fuck-up I was!

That story-time was the first thing I had done right in as long as I could remember.

I still had nightmares. I still dreamed of that stitched-together little girl, the one with the furious blue eyes. I woke up soaked in sweat, drowning in terror. I would wake up and be too afraid to get out of bed; too afraid to move and wake Dean in case he would reveal himself to be a monster in the darkness. I could see her grotesque stitches behind my eyeballs. I could feel all the people breathing quietly in the darkness. There was a ferocious growl around the edge of the room. But my therapist had given me a hippie-dippie woo-woo crystal-sniffing CD to play when I went to sleep, and even though I was deeply suspicious and resentful, I couldn't deny that it was shamefully helpful and let me sleep. Slowly the horrible dreams started subsiding.

Then one night, I dreamed a new dream about the little girl.

This time something is different. She has a tiny pair of nail scissors. And she is cutting the stitches with a concentration that is calm but fierce. The skin beneath the stitches has healed clean and whole. With each determined cut, she is growing bigger, like the stitches that had held her together had also kept her small and tiny. She looks up me. Her eyes are a brilliant, blinding blue. I breathe. She smiles.

I could only afford therapy because my parents' supporting church paid for it. This was that same loyal band of Indianapolis faithful that had supported them all these years, that was still sending money to them each month. What a hilarious irony: these loving Christians were paying for the godless therapy that was helping me get strong enough to set out on a life that was completely *against* everything they stood for. But they had a fund set aside specifically for children of missionaries who were "troubled" by their experiences, and I certainly qualified. I was unspeakably grateful for their support. However, I was deeply ashamed to be such a blight on their pristine landscape. They were all sloping green lawns, and big waterfall fountains, and brick cathedrals—and I was an ugly bruised scribble.

I felt pretty guilty about spending their money on therapy while I spent my last few pennies on my divorce, but the other option was to stop therapy, and clearly that would be just stupid.

So I continued thrashing my way through my past within the safe amber walls of my tough, loving, whip-smart therapist's office. It smelled like eucalyptus and burnt sage, and I went through many boxes of tissues while snuggled into the cradling warmth of her leather couch. The thing I couldn't understand was that she kept letting me tell her my dirtiest, most disgusting secrets—and she didn't seem *even a little bit shocked.*

Learning to walk around in my own self was like being in a Cubist painting. There were strange bulges and angles. So many colliding beliefs and realities. I felt pulled and conflicted, and bent into a thousand prisms. As I grew and stretched, new pieces came to the surface, rubbing, clashing. I had never learned to bring all of this, my complicated and conflicted self, to any one situation. I had become very practiced at only showing whichever face seemed appropriate to that context. Trying to plop the whole thing down in a chair for dinner was overwhelming. It was a lot to lug around, and it scared the crap out of most of the people I knew. It was as if I suddenly revealed that I'd been hiding six more heads in my handbag, and they all joined the conversation.

—◊◊◊—

Downtown Chicago, early evening. I sat on a rickety café chair. The couple across from me were venerable, respected in the missionary community, and a little older than my parents. They were loving but stern people, and we all sat there awkwardly out of a sense of duty. After some chitchat, the man dove in.

"Listen, I have to be honest. I don't think that all this therapy is a very good idea."

Although I had officially denounced the faith, I still felt obliged to sit and listen politely to them. It was partly out of respect and affection for these good and virtuous people, who were so truly concerned for my well being. But let's be honest; it was also partly an act of self-flagellation.

"Well, um..." I shifted and squirmed. "I do think the therapy is helping, though."

"Is it helping you go back to your marriage?"

"No. That is not going to happen. We are in the process of getting a divorce."

They sighed in unison, sighs of deep sorrow.

"But here is the thing. When you go to a therapy session, do you feel better afterward, or worse?"

I didn't know exactly how to respond. Usually I felt raw, as if I had vomited up gallons of bile. It wasn't pleasant, to say the least, but it certainly felt better than swallowing it down. Luckily I didn't need to answer, for he sailed on.

"I'm pretty sure that if you feel better after your therapy session, it is not very good therapy. You have to be very careful about self-indulgent New Age psychobabble. Really, therapy can only be doing its job if you feel *worse* afterward." He delivered this pronouncement with the same certainty he delivered his sermons. His wife nodded slowly, but her brow was furrowed.

I just stared at him. Someone inside my head started impatiently tapping her finger on my temple. How much fucking worse did he want me to feel?

It was an honest question.

I pondered the fact that had I felt any worse in the months before I'd left my marriage and started therapy, I would have taken several bottles of pills and chugged them down with some Draino.

The person in my head squinted and tilted her head.

The person on the cafe chair smiled apologetically and got out of there as fast as she could.

I know it might be hard to understand, but my whole world had been so Christian for so long that I agonized over this interaction. Maybe I'd been wrong about it all. Even though I had left the fold rather dramatically, I still felt the sting of being reprimanded. I was an accidental goat, after all; if Christianity hadn't been so agonizing for me I would have stayed in the fold (and in disguise as a faithful sheep) my whole life. And for years, I'd been taught that this man's words had more authority than my experience. Some subterranean part of me still believed that *they* were right and *I* was wrong. Always, always, no matter what.

(Even though being wrong felt so, so good.)

So I felt very guilty about this conversation for a few days, and I told my therapist about it.

She asked if this man had ever been in therapy himself. I highly doubted it. I mean, he was a pastor. They really weren't allowed to have doubts, inner conflicts, or rich inner lives.

She wondered if he knew anyone who had been helped by the therapeutic process.

I couldn't say for sure, but my money would be on "no." After all, this was a group of believers who had denounced couples' therapy at a wedding I'd gone to for an old friend.

During their wedding vows.

"Dearly beloved, we are gathered here to join....and whatever happens, do not be sucked in by the vicious lies of marriage counseling! It is an abomination! It is a lie from the devil designed to distort the natural order of things! Do not go down this dangerous route!"

True story. I was one of the bridesmaids. The bride clutched her flowers to her chest. I had a tiny bottle of wine in my purse, which I chugged down in the bathroom.

So, venerable pastor appreciating the value of therapy? Yeah, no. Probably not.

And then I started laughing. I laughed so hard that I almost peed my pants right there on that gorgeous couch. It was like the walls of Jericho fell down in my mind.

All this light and air and spaciousness rushed into my lungs as old beliefs and obligations crumbled. Why would I listen to this man? He knew nothing about me, or what I was experiencing, or where I was trying to go. Oh my god, the freedom of it!! It wasn't him! It wasn't me!!! It was just that we lived in different realities! Suddenly it seemed ridiculous—unfair, even—that I could expect him to have anything very useful to say to me.

I didn't know what I was doing. I didn't know where all this healing work would lead. But I knew that it was taking me where I needed to go.

—⧉—

My therapist had suggested several times, with varying levels of levity and seriousness, that I might be carrying memories from past lives that caused me to resonate with wounds that I hadn't physically experienced. I rolled my eyes at her, so she said, "Okay, think about it like this. Old family wounds that have been passed down spiritually." Ah. Now that was something that resonated.

As a child, I had thought a lot about torture. I don't even know how I knew what torture was; our media consumption was tightly and benevolently controlled, and it didn't include war crimes. I wasn't terrified of being shot, or killed, or kidnapped, or hit by a car—but I was terrified of being tied up by soldiers and hurt in a long and ongoing way. I felt sure that this would certainly happen to me at some point and I didn't know if I would be able to bear it, or if secrets would come tumbling out of my mouth like a traitor. Did other people think about this kind of thing? I had nightmares about it on a regular basis.

I couldn't handle images of sexual violence, even when I knew it was fake, even when it was supposed to be funny or campy, even when it was clearly a larger metaphor for the blah blah whatever. No. I just felt skewered.

I have been embarrassed about this sensitivity. It feels gratuitous, like I'm horning in on others' pain. But I'm not trying; it just comes to me. Tell me a story and I feel it in my body. Show me an image and I will taste blood. This is just the way it is.

My therapist and I talked about hypnosis, but I didn't want to dig. I believed, and still do, that whatever needed to be healed would come to the surface if it needed to.

Maybe there is a blocked incident of assault or abuse that I can't remember. Maybe the casual cruelty of the Japanese school system, which might have just been an unpleasant memory to a less sensitive kid, imprinted a deep horror. Maybe I'm carrying generations-old ancestral grief down the bloodlines. Maybe it's a Jungian thing, feeling all the rapes of collective Woman. Maybe it's past life memories. Maybe the dissonance between my yearning for a loving God and the fearsome, inconsistent, bloody male God I encountered in Christianity caused a deep despair that feels like a wound. Maybe I'm feeling the grief of our blue planet as we take and take from her. Maybe I'm sensing the great human body crying out for some kind of healing because it is my mission to be a spiritual healer. Maybe I'm a drama queen. Maybe it's all of the above.

Maybe I became human because I wanted to figure something out: how to push my way through to love even when it wasn't handed to me on a platter.

Maybe that's why we're all here.

I was wading through my sorrow, braiding it into something that made sense, but I tasted joy, too. One night we went to that venerable old jazz bar The Green Mill, and Victoria Williams was playing. She had braces on her hands because of her MS, and she was clumsy and frustrated with her fingers, but she banged away at the piano anyway and sang, "You are loved, you are loved, you are reeeaaaaallly loved," and as her voice soared up and came back down, I felt like I had been given back something, like something had come home to roost. She was so incredibly beautiful to me that tears spilled down my face.

The therapy was important but so was all the hedonism. I had been good my whole life, so desperate to be saved, to be loved, to be safe. I'd never done any of the normal drinking, carousing, sneaking out late—not in high school or in college. I was married before I'd ever had more than a few sips of alcohol. I'd been a virgin on my wedding night. I'd worked hard all through college, on my schoolwork but also holding down at least two jobs, often working more than thirty hours a week. I'd been so fucking *good*. There was something incredibly healing in letting all that go completely to hell. I punched in and out of my $5-an-hour bookstore job. I smoked a thousand cigarettes, drank gallons of cheap booze, stayed up late, blew through my savings, had fabulous sex—in short, I was heedless, irresponsible, and full of joy. We went to hear music. We danced. We played cards. We played stupid drinking games. It was perfect. Every puff on a cigarette was better than a prayer, every hangover brought me closer to who I really was, and every orgasm brought me back home to my body. They were good medicine, and exactly what I needed.

There was a huge canyon between my parents and me, not to mention an actual ocean. I knew they still loved me, but naturally they were completely dismayed at the turn my life had taken. It helped that they were now dismayed at my brother, too; he was openly living with his girlfriend now, and I loved him for it. It was such a relief not to be the only black stain on our family honor. Jake and I were in good company; we had each other. Ruth was still at home with my parents, and she might as well have been on another planet.

But my parents hung in there. Their incredible tenacity is completely wonderful and baffling. (I'm taking notes for my own kids' inevitable rebellion, when they decide to vote Republican and denounce feminism.)

It turns out that it's simply impossible to flunk out of my family.

We all still gathered for holidays, pooling frequent flier miles and chasing crazy deals that involved hellish layovers in strange airports on

Christmas Eve. No matter what uncomfortable conversations might have lurked under the surface, we carried on. This was in large part thanks to my sister, who insisted that we adhere to all family holiday traditions to the letter. *No matter what.* We dubbed her the Christmas Dictator, but secretly we were grateful to have instructions.

I don't mean to hurt your feelings, but no family in the world does Christmas as well as my family of origin. We do it with bells on. It was my absolute favorite time of year growing up, when all our engines ran in the same direction. One of my best memories of being a kid is that the night we put up the Christmas tree, my mom and dad would let us kids camp out in the living room so we could fall asleep in the glow of the pink, green, and blue lights. Under the tree perched the little manger scene, which we set up each year in a new cardboard box. We gathered grass for hay; we glued twigs to the roof. Most importantly, we poked a hole in the top and pulled one of the yellow tree lights through it so baby Jesus and Mary and Joseph and the little sheep were illuminated in a golden glow. This might have been a terrible fire hazard, but it made me feel warm and holy inside.

Even now, our traditions are multitudinous. Each year we ceremoniously consume the "trimming of the tree chocolates." We sneak gag gifts into stockings early, because anything spotted before Christmas Eve is fair game. We humor my mother and listen to her read the Christmas story from Matthew and light the Advent candles. We read 'Twas The Night Before Christmas. But all that is mere tinsel compared to the rigidly prescribed routine of Christmas morning. (Stockings first but *only* after everyone is awake; breakfast of sausage, biscuits, and orange syrup; turkey goes in the oven; then we all go get dressed, sit in a circle, and open presents *but only one at a time, people.*)

There was still a lot of love and laughter in these gatherings, even if there were also undercurrents of tension. But inevitably, several years in a row, my mother got sick on the crucial day. It wasn't passive-aggressive; she was well and truly ill, vomiting her brains out or fainting with a high fever. But clearly it was because of the stress of her horrible children. She was truly concerned about our souls, we figured; she worried that we were on our way to doom. So we scrambled around miserably trying to cook the turkey on our own, ruining the gravy, knowing full well that it was our fault—our choices were making her ill. It was all so awful and fraught that most of the time it was easier just to keep them at a distance.

Our phone conversations were something of a wrestling match: my parents tried to pry out as much information as they could, while I clutched my privacy ever closer to my chest. I knew there was love and concern behind their questions, but I couldn't open up myself to them— every time they'd gently inquire, "How are you doing, sweetie?" it sounded to me more like, "Tell us all the ways you are failing."

Also, there was the tiny fact of my anger. The child's anger that came pouring out in therapy sessions was so intense that it scared me, and I didn't know what to do with it. How had they missed so much of what was going on? Why did they spank us, when they were so loving in other ways? Did they know how school had been for me? How could they love such a hideous God? How did they stand such hypocrisy among the missionaries? With all this righteous fury swirling in me, I continued to pick up their calls...some of the time.

After a couple of years, though, something had shifted inside me. Therapy, darlings. It's powerful stuff. I had purged my feelings, made a certain amount of peace with everything that had happened, and I was ready to move on. My therapist said she knew it was my last session when I showed up wearing red patent leather peep-toe high heels. She grinned at me. I grinned back.

But there were still conversations I needed to have. Things I needed to lay to rest. Parts of my past that I needed to bury. Tendrils of longing that still tugged at my heart. I knew, with equal certainty and dread, that I needed to go back to Japan.

CHAPTER TWENTY-TWO

Oh, Japan, that great love affair of mine. She was a place, a presence, a ghost, a mother. No matter where I was on the planet, I could feel a string pulling me back to her red *torii* gates and smoggy streets. There was a smell that would hit you when you got off the plane at Narita, a combination of hot canned green tea and *onigiri* rice balls all swirled into the thick humid soup of the air. Then the blast of stale cigarette smoke, the stench of sour beer, the acrid smell of exhaust. Ahhhh. *Home.*

Before I went back to Japan, I spent ten days on my own in the mountains of Colorado. I stayed in a friend's house, frightened by the bigness and chilled to the bone. It was good for me to feel scared and be brave anyway. I drove twenty straight hours and came back to Chicago to an apartment filled with candles. Every surface flickered with votives, tapers, pillars. The tense, lovely Dean was there. He swept me into his arms and kissed me. I felt bathed in love.

I had brought back a pile of rough Colorado turquoise, the dark green kind. Before I left for Japan, I put one big lumpy stone in my pocket. I gave one to my loving man for him to keep. I took the rest in a small pouch with me to Tokyo. I held it on my lap the whole way there.

Every time I stepped off a plane, the strangest thing always happened. The world I'd just left would completely disappear, as if the two different realities were hermetically sealed off from each other.

In Chicago, Japan was a misty lover, twining herself in my heart, catching me off guard when a fragrance—daphne blossoms, or green tea—would set off earthquakes of homesickness. But it also felt like something I'd dreamed.

The opposite thing happened when I arrived in Japan; Chicago seemed like a mirage, an illusion. My smart tough friends, my sweet lover, my brother and his merry crew—they all seemed like something I'd imagined, something utterly decadent and impossible.

Back in my old hometown, not much had changed at all. I rode my old bike around the neighborhood; I saw my old teachers at the train station and at the bank; throngs of devout high schoolers still met for accountability groups in the local Mister Donut. I tried to remember all the things I had learned from my therapist. *I am a grownup*, I tried to tell myself. *I am safe.* But it was hard to remember. Only the cigarettes I smoked helped ground me; they gave me a socially sanctioned (sort of) excuse to leave any gathering and stand outside by myself, taking deep, slow breaths. I held onto my green turquoise, listened to my Belleruth Naparstek guided meditation each night before I went to sleep, and tried to be brave enough to have The Talk with my mother.

I had persuaded her to sit in the smoking section of the restaurant, because I knew I couldn't get through this conversation without at least a dozen cigarettes. We were sitting at Jonathan's, a "family restaurant" or *famiresu*, and we were surrounded by the smells of thick brown demi-glace sauce, gingered pork with sesame, French fries, soft-boiled eggs. She was sitting across from me, tears running down her face, shaking her head.

"Why? Why didn't you tell me?"

"I don't know, Mom. I really don't know."

"Oh, honey." She gripped my hand. "I thought you were doing so well for a six-year-old, I really thought you were adjusting—"

"I mean I was, I was adjusting to a crazy—"

"Did you think we wouldn't believe you? Were you afraid?"

It is the great mystery of my own childhood. Why didn't I tell my parents how bad school was? Not just first grade in the Japanese school, but the sadistic charismatics—why hadn't I said something?

Why indeed?

Honestly, it just didn't occur to me. School was another world, a kingdom with shifting, contradictory rules completely outside my parents' domain—they didn't know how to navigate it any better than I did (or so I believed at the time). It never occurred to me that they would have had the authority to pull me out of school. They were so at sea when I was little; out of their element, clumsy at the language that pooled so easily into my child's brain, missing a thousand social cues a minute. If I'd imagined it, I might have seen *Sensei* yelling at them, too, them slinking off ashamed and in disgrace like scolded schoolchildren.

But there was another reason. I didn't want to showcase one more way that I was wrong. I assumed the fault was in me, not in anything that was happening. I had come to deeply believe that my own instinctual response was usually the "wrong" one. So my terror, my rage, my misery—these were just more damning pieces of evidence in the case that was always piling up against me.

This is the true cost of indoctrinating children. They come to mistrust their own perception so deeply that they can't tell the difference between real right and wrong. They lose access to their own discernment and no longer trust their own sense of reality. This happens in subtle ways even in healthy, loving families—go kiss Uncle George, honey, oh come on, give him a kiss!—and that inner filament gets skewed. Without that inner compass, they can only mimic what they hope will keep them safe.

All this spooled out between my mother and I, unspoken, unarticulated.

"Maybe I just didn't think there would be anything you could do about it," I finally said. And then my mother said the thing that forever altered the trajectory of our relationship, the hinge upon which our deep friendship still turns:

"I am so sorry. I am so, so sorry."

Never underestimate the power of a true apology. This is one of the gifts of growing up among Christians—a deep experience of the power of forgiveness. That apology from my mother rang into my soul and opened up a dozen padlocks of resentment and anger. We both sat there for a long while, tears running down our cheeks. After a bit, I realized my face was cracked into a smile. It was enough. I fingered the lump of green turquoise in my pocket.

Later, I stood alone on the hot Tokyo street. I clutched the green stone in my pocket again, closed my eyes, and just breathed in the night.

—❦—

My father and I didn't indulge in such excesses of emotion—that's not our way. But one day he and I were standing on a train platform going somewhere, and suddenly we were watching a father lose his temper at his son. The kid was messing around, taunting his father, dangling a foot over the edge, and the father cuffed the side of the kid's head in exasperation. They were awfully close to the edge of the platform, where the train would zoom in at any moment. I heard my dad draw his breath in sharply.

"If that kid gets hurt..." My dad shook his head. "If anything happened, he would never forgive himself," he said. I stayed quiet, and we stood there for a minute. "Do you remember the time you fell off the lake wall?" he asked.

I got very still. This was not the kind of thing my father and I talked about.

I nodded.

"I would give anything to take that back," he mumbled. He blinked hard a couple times, and I felt lightness rising up in me, washing away the old residues.

"It's okay, Dad. It's really okay."

My heart had just grown wing-buds.

—❦—

I buried lumps of green turquoise all over Tokyo and Yokohama, putting to rest the small selves that haunted me. I visited the old Center, which was now a clump of new and ugly apartment buildings. I climbed down into the valley nestled behind it, that quiet green glade. I dug a little hole in this peaceful spot, full of trees and vines, and buried a piece of the turquoise.

I went to my old high school late at night, feeling how it was still girded in righteousness. I sat out on the playground, twirled around the spinning wheel, and thought of all the young souls who passed through this place. I realized how young I was when I was here, how lost, and I buried a lump of turquoise to honor that younger self.

I saved my old Japanese school for last. My brother was in Japan for the summer too, and he came with me for courage. We went on a Sunday, and it was deserted.

We stood on the dusty field and gazed at my first-grade classroom. There it was, the square windows, the prefab beige siding. The metal door set into the wall. I was shaking, I felt cold, I wanted to throw up. I couldn't remember what I was going to do with the turquoise here. I couldn't find any kind of forgiveness. My brother regarded me in his impassive way. With one long gaze, he took me in. I was mortified to be so visibly falling apart. He rooted around in the dirt and handed me a big fat rock, and I laughed.

Of course. The perfect ritual.

I hurled it at the building. I didn't hit a window, no one came out to yell, it was a weak wimpy throw, and I barely thumped the side of the wall, but we turned and ran as if we had just launched a grenade. I was running and running and I left it behind me.

CHAPTER TWENTY-THREE

I was supposed to stay in Japan for two months and then return to Chicago, but I got cast, against all reason, in a professional Japanese stage production. It all happened at once: the phone rang and suddenly I had a rehearsal schedule, a script to memorize, and costume fittings. I would be on tour for several months. I was, in essence, moving immediately back to Tokyo.

I said a fond farewell to the lovely Dean in Chicago over the phone, and he and my brother put my stuff in boxes for me. I rented a tiny shoebox apartment just outside the Tokyo loop, and realized that it was the first time I had ever lived completely on my own. I reveled in it. I made pictures of the moon and painted self-portraits on masks. I hung up my most beautiful clothes on the walls as art. I tacked a swath of butcher paper on the wall and started writing down things I wanted to do and ideas for how to make them happen. I wore exquisite high heels wherever I went.

Such adventures! I got my picture taken, went to parties, drank tons of champagne, and had some mind-blowing sex. I was being paid to go onstage every night and have Lots Of Feelings, and I thought it was hilarious that my old loathed drama queen self was turning out to be quite the cash cow. I signed on for another tour of the play. I was even starting to do a little bit of writing.

And then I was pregnant.

There was no radiant flicker, no "Gasp! A baby!" Instead I felt a deep, awful thud, a clanging warning, a knell of doom. Oh god.

Oh god, fuck you.

—∽—

The first sick inklings of my pregnancy slapped me right back into my cage, to the familiar place of weeping and gnashing of teeth. I wept, grieving a baby I didn't want. I couldn't help thinking that I deserved everything bad that might happen, since I had been stupid enough—and slutty enough—to get pregnant in the first place. In the throes of nausea, pregnant with a tiny speck, I resented the hell out of it. Stupid clump of stupid cells; scary alien tadpole.

I hated it. I felt no love. I wanted to say, "I just can't be a good enough mother." But really I was saying, with every cell in my body, "I won't." This was the deep truth, the only one that let me breathe, but every breath brought an attack of self-loathing.

For years, I had pressed my hand to my heart in moments of fear or desolation to reassure myself that it was still beating, that I still existed. There were moments when my own heartbeat felt like the only thing that anchored me. Other times I was braced with the knowledge of how hard it beat, with what violence of life.

I wanted to have the abortion before a heart started beating.

I loathed and feared the idea of a surgical abortion. It seemed unnecessarily violent, a brutal way to force the body to let go of a pregnancy. I had come to believe, thanks to Dr. Christiane Northrup's wonderful book *Women's Bodies, Women's Wisdom*, that there must be a way to work *with* the body instead of treating it like the enemy. So I tried persuasion. I thought that if I could just attune deeply enough, if I could grope my way back to that primal connection with my own womb, somewhere in the mind-body matrix I would find my gestational motherboard. I was looking for a manual override switch that would let me ovulate, conceive, and flush a pregnancy at will.

I meditated. I willed my period to come. I begged it to come. I held a raggedy séance and asked the invading presence to leave me. But I kept throwing up.

I read about an apocryphal set of acupuncture points called "the forbidden points" that could supposedly end a pregnancy. I turned to the wise, witchy women, certain that they would not let me down. Herbal lore is hard to find and harder to implement, but I was desperate. I tried herbal abortifacients that carried dire warning labels; I put parsley in places it shouldn't go. But the clump of cells stuck. I couldn't dislodge it, and I couldn't welcome it. So I cried and threw up and cried some more, and finally I scheduled an abortion. I cried out to a god I no longer believed in for permission—and for forgiveness. Neither came.

—⁂—

Naturally, I was not the first person I knew to get accidentally pregnant. After all, many of my childhood friends were still Christians. They were trying to be celibate into their mid-twenties. Celibate people, remember, don't carry birth control. And so it happened that, to everyone's great surprise, bewilderment, and sorrow, a lot of girls in my old evangelical community got pregnant.

Shocking! Scandalous! *Those poor, wicked girls.* Some cases were more dramatic than others and involved public confessions and weeping, while other pregnancies were quietly swept under an empire waist wedding dress. But the options available to these girls were few. They could give up the baby for adoption, they could be single mothers with the help of their family, or they could marry the fathers and start their own families.

So most of these girls chose to get married. Some of the women I love most dearly in the world got started in this way as mothers, and they are smart, savvy, patient, and nurturing—even those who got started at the shockingly young end of the age spectrum. That said, there can be problems. I don't know that any of these women resents her children or feels like she was robbed of a more exciting or fulfilling life, but even if she did, I wouldn't hear about it. Because who could ever admit to such a thing without the words Bad Mother appearing on their forehead? In blood??

I, on the other hand, already knew that I would be a Bad Mother. I had left the church but found no community to replace it (my party animal friends notwithstanding). I was drinking quite a bit. I had very little money. Theoretically, I believed that having an abortion might even be a merciful thing to do, since I had already steeped the poor embryo in plenty of alcohol and cigarette smoke. But I wrestled with the idea of closing the door on a potential life. I stewed. I thought about what kind of mother I wanted to be, if I ever was one. Pictures of abused or neglected children tore at my heart, but there was also the frantic desperation I sometimes felt when I didn't know how I would pay my rent. I knew that a crying infant could send even sturdy women into near-insanity. Suddenly it was simple. My children—any child—deserved a better mother than I could be right then.

The night before my abortion, back in Chicago for my brief grim errand, I sat in my grief and defiance. I lit a candle and placed it in front of the collage I had made with images of blood and babies and egg yolks and frightening blue eyes—everything that haunted me, buoyed me, frightened and consoled me. I looked at the prayer that I had scrawled over all of it in desperate black ink: *Let there be light.*

I was hoping for a moment of numinous clarity, an epiphany. The harsh light of the candle only revealed my miserable face, devastated with pregnancy acne. I looked as wretched as I felt. Staring at myself in the mirror, I tried out sentences like, "This is a woman who doesn't want her own baby," and "I am choosing my own life over my child's." I was trying to find a phrase that might break my resolve; I was testing to see whether I would regret my decision. But there I was, reflected back—grieving, unwavering.

I climbed into the bath and got very still and talked to my baby. I didn't feel that the blastocyst, which still looked like a blood clot, was my baby. The baby was the soul perched precariously on this clot, tentative as a moth. It was fluttering at me, asking to be let in. I shook my head. There was no room in the inn. I told her that I couldn't take care of her. I felt her withdraw, I felt her leave, and I felt surrounded by a vast and great silence, a deep darkness waiting to swallow up that tiny phantom heart.

I raged. I blustered. I sent tentative feelers out into that great dark silence. I didn't believe in God, per se, but I didn't believe that there was nothing, either. I didn't believe that we were just chemical accidents. I remembered the gold kernel I sometimes felt in my own heart. I reached out to that blissful energy that had poured through me as a child lying on the grass, the language of the flowers that could fill my body with rosy light. Whatever energy set this world in motion and occasionally flashed into it briefly with love or power—this impulse surely had room in it to take in this one little fluttering moth. If there was nothing out there that moved to the rhythm of compassion, if we were caught in a void or a machine, then we were all so incredibly fucked that there was really no point in going on, I decided. So I sent out a breath. Not to the God I'd grown up with. But to every glimpse of love and grace, to the energy of creation and mothering, to the roar of fire and ocean, to the heart that I sometimes sensed beating out there and even in myself—to all these, I would entrust this little moth. *Ba-dump, ba-dump.* Yes, you, beating heart, I trust you.

And then something broke through. I literally sat up straight in the tub with surprise. If I could entrust this vulnerable little soul to the heartbeat I sensed in the darkness, maybe I could trust myself to it too. I breathed in this remarkable thought, utterly shocked. And then I was enveloped in light. I was in it, of it, covered by it, filled with it. I thudded with its bloody rhythm, the gasps and suckings of its mighty valves.

In that bathtub, bursting out of all names, crying *fuck God, fuck the Lord, fuck the Bible, fuck all that nonsense*—I heard a heartbeat, and that heartbeat was love. Me in the bathtub, beloved. That baby moth, beloved. I the aborter, beloved. The blastocyst, beloved. All beloved. Everything, each atom of this chipped porcelain, each drop of water, each toenail. Beloved aborting, beloved weeping, beloved laughing, beloved enraged and drunk and having orgasms and walking into the ocean. All connected, all adored beyond words, all this love bursting out of the old stories and the old names like a baby from a mother's womb. Brand new, nothing new. I heard a heartbeat, a deep thumping rhythm that cycles everything in and out, giving life, taking it, sucking in, whooshing out. This heart. I trusted this heart. This great heart loved me down to my bones, to my blood and shit, down to my bloated womb and unwanted clump of potential. It loved that clump of cells. But it loved me too, and I understood that it didn't matter, or rather everything mattered a great deal, but it was all the same to the love. The love was the fabric everything else was made of. The love was the heart, and the heart's beating, and the blood rushing through the heart, and all of us veins and arteries and blockages and limbs and lions and mucus and smut were all love too.

They told me I might feel some mild discomfort. That's one word for it. On my back, feet in stirrups, in that posture of humiliation, I refused the woozy drugs because I wanted to know what was happening. Someone held my hand. I cupped my other hand over my womb and kept thinking that the stabbing suction tube was going to puncture through my uterus and skin and gouge right into my fingers.

As I lay on the table, being gutted by the appliance inside me, a bit of knowledge was delivered to me neatly, tied up in brown paper and string. I knew as clearly as if I had heard the words spoken, "I have been here before." I was so glad I was awake, that I hadn't taken any painkillers or Valium. I was there to acknowledge my own awareness and keep it company, like the incredulous witness who swears: I know it sounds crazy, but I saw it with my own two eyes.

I asked to see what was in the metal dish. I looked, I had to look. Just blood clots. *Oh. Oh, thank everything.*

Then I was in the room where other women were waking up. Broken, desolate, violated, and bleeding, I threw up for the last time. Emptied out in every way possible, I lay back on a vinyl reclining chair with a measly sheet to cover my freezing body, and I could not bear to be looked at. I threw the sheet over my head, sat in the whiteness, and sobbed. I placed my hands on my belly, my poor aching torn-up womb, and hacked out the pain and loss of what had just happened.

And the relief. *Oh, the relief.*

I had been ripped, but I was open. I was empty, and I was free. After a while I staggered out into the strange room with the furtive waiting men, past the nurses, through the hateful protesters, and into my loyal friend's car. And then I sat where I would sit for the next good while, in the blood and loss, and cried *thank you thank you* for the new life I had been given.

—⟋⟍—

I was sore and tentative for a day or two, and my soul felt as quiet as a beach after a storm. And that was the beginning of my embarrassing but shameless agnosticism, the one that stays with me still, the persistent and unbidden belief that the universe, in spite of all appearances, is bursting at its seams with love. After struggling for years in the lockstep of Christianity, and after finally turning my back on it with disgust, I had blundered into a surreal realm where I didn't know what I was trusting—certainly not the angry father god of my childhood, and not the Jesus of the misogynistic gospels—but I trusted something. I still don't know what to call it. It doesn't feel like faith, exactly, and the faithful would not claim me. The closest I can come is to say that I feel loved.

Let me assure you, this is not a story that will get much play in any Sunday School I've ever attended.

I knew myself to be loved when I did the one thing, above all others, that I was told was unforgivable. I had always been taught that you could be forgiven for anything—murder, rape—if you just repented. But I am not repentant. My abortion was not an accident, or something that I was forced into, or a mistake made in confusion. It was a sacred initiation that gave me a chance to start a new life.

My words fail me here. No matter where I go in my heart and mind, I cannot escape the Christian imagery that has shaped so much of my life. I want to say, neither this nor that nor anything else can separate us from love; and I want to say, the old shall die that the new may be born again; but I won't say those things because they mean something else to me, with their echoes of Christian trauma. They're so coated in the sludge of the old religion that they leave the taste of metal in my mouth. I need a new wineskin for this new wine, dense as blood. I need the mother-tongue, the one that is deep within, that echoes out in the cosmos. It is as old as forgetting, as new as birth.

CHAPTER TWENTY-FOUR

I honestly thought that after my moment of touching the deep heart in the bathtub, the world would stay imbued with a holy and sacred glow. But it faded. Sometimes I would catch a little pulse, an extra kind of shimmer, but it was fleeting, visible only out of the corner of my eye. I craved more.

I didn't get the bright light of illumination I'd hoped for. Instead, I found myself in that much more feminine element, water. Everywhere I went the world seemed wetter. My insides had been opened up, unlocked, and it seemed to set some primal pump going; my eyes overflowed at the very least provocation. Something funny, something frustrating, something sad or touching or beautiful or horrible—I wept at them all. It was pretty embarrassing. But it also felt so good, like I was marinating, softening. And like all the tears were washing me, bathing me. I felt juicier in lots of ways. I even got wetter, if you know what I mean. But the most astonishing thing was that for every tear I cried, I was soaking up gallons of moisture. Not physically, but spiritually. My parched soul was absorbing, sucking, suckling—taking in great big gulps of nourishment. I would soak in beauty, soak in joy, suck it all up like a parched sponge, and be full and swirling, like a big heavy cloud and then—whoosh—I would cry it all out. And then I would get filled up again—by the trees, the ambience of a bar, the feeling of silk on my skin—all these moments of sensory joy were like drops of water on my parched tongue. It was like learning to breathe again. In and out. I don't know how many years I had gone holding my breath, in a stasis of dryness. Now I was getting drunk nearly every day off the hidden juices of the world around me. It left me reeling.

Things happened that I couldn't explain. Not the sort of things I wanted, mind you. Instead of portents from ravens or gentle whispers from guardian angels, I got cockroaches. The enormous Tokyo cockroaches petrified me, but they also seemed to be weirdly drawn to me. You know how everyone says they're more scared of you than you them? Well, not me. They didn't behave normally around me. They would run toward me. I am not kidding. It was like they were gunning for me. One actually ran up my leg on a Shinjuku street. A friend who was over one night gallantly tried to kill one for me, smiling benevolently at my skittishness. That damn bug eluded him, mocked him, and then laughed at him. My friend shook his head and said, "Something weird is going on here." I laughed, but silently thought, *Oh good, it's not just my imagination.*

Did I neglect to mention that one of them flew at me when I was a child? I had walked into a bedroom, spotted a black spot on the far wall, and it made a beeline for me. It landed in my hair, skittered down my forehead, and plopped on the floor. Then it disappeared. So I was perhaps just a slight bit tenser about them than the average hysteric. I kept seeing things out of the corner of my eye, little dark blurs that would disappear when I whirled to look at them.

And so in a moment of misguided longing for spirit, spirit in any form, I let some kind, well-meaning religious folk do an exorcism on me.

I know. I *know.*

But what can I say? While my friends were out getting their masters degrees, I was getting my PhD in bad decisions.

They were spiritual people who believed in astral travel and faith healings, so I sheepishly ventured to talk about the way that it seemed we were always being watched. I was hoping that they would say, *Oh yes, the eyes of spirit are everywhere, this is very normal, so don't worry about it.*

Instead they got very excited.

They asked me if I could sense anything in the room. Well, of course I could, there was that dark blur that was always with me. There was the sense that I was always being followed by those damn cockroaches. And... other things.

We were at the ocean for the summer. Outside the waves crashed against the cliff.

A man picked up his guitar, strummed it, and prayed under his breath. Someone else started speaking in tongues. It was spooky, but it seemed too late to extricate myself at this point. My brother was with me, watching quietly. The woman put her hands on me.

"I demand in Jesus's name that whatever is troubling this sweet girl will leave her right now. In the name of Jesus..." she swayed and sighed. Her hands were warm and comforting. My body shuddered. It reminded me of the energy work I'd had done a few times; the sense of the body releasing old things.

But even though I was experiencing some very physical sensations, my authentic self was shaking her head. She was shrugging her shoulders, spreading her hands wide, saying, "I mean, it's fine and all, but that's not really it, babe."

Sadly, the exorcism didn't make the cockroaches magically disperse. One night I chased one all over my apartment; I never could catch it, never could kill it. I was frantic with terror and disgust and self-loathing; what was wrong with me that I was freaking out so much about a stupid bug that couldn't hurt me? But it felt like all the horror and malevolence in the world was centered in that one little spot of blackness that didn't run away but advanced and advanced on me until I tried to whack it, at which point it would calmly retreat. I crawled into my bed, itching and feeling phantom crawly legs everywhere, and cried myself to sleep, appalled by my own ridiculousness.

And then in the morning, I went to wash my face. An empty cardboard soap box was sitting on the edge of the sink. And nestled inside it was the cockroach. It was enormous, as big as my cellphone. But I suddenly understood that it was in there as a kind of apology. It wanted me to know that it wasn't going to torment me anymore or pop up weeks later, dead, to scare me again. It either had died or stayed obligingly still for me while I dropped it in the trash and tied sixteen trash bags around it before heaving it out to the stoop.

I went back in and sat at my table and shook my head at myself. I was really losing it. I was interpreting loving messages from big black bugs. Good lord. But then on a strange impulse I pulled out an old journal off my bookshelf, and without much searching, I found a page where I had written down a dream I'd had years before and then completely forgotten. In the dream, I was in my brother's old bedroom and found an enormous cockroach sitting on his windowsill. Revolted, I jumped back and froze against the wall. Then, in that funny dream way, it started snowing. It snowed and snowed. When it stopped snowing, I went back to the windowsill to check on the cockroach and saw that it had turned into a giant white moth. It had emerald green markings on its wings, and I knew that it was powerfully magic. It fluttered up, dropping little crystals of white dust on the carpet, and then drifted out the window.

And since then, no big black bug has ever rushed toward me again.

CHAPTER TWENTY-FIVE

A few years later, I was in Canada for a brief visit, standing in a great field with hundreds of blissed-out music lovers. Emmy Lou Harris had just walked onto the stage. She began to play, and almost immediately my eyes began spurting, because that's just how it was for me that summer. I had so many feelings and they kept coming out of my eyes. It was mortifying, but also weirdly delicious.

My friend Teener and I had made our way to the very front of the crowd and we stood there weeping, swaying, caught up in the sounds of that quavering, ethereal, husky voice. There was a crack of thunder, and a wall of rain moved across us. Emmy Lou kept playing. The crowd swayed and sang along, with rain and tears running down our cheeks, throwing our heads back and chortling, sloshing in mud up to our knees, drenched with joy. A holy heathen baptism.

All those tears, they washed me clean. And then they watered me.

Back in Japan, I grew stronger. I learned to send my emotional roots deep into the fertile earth. I realized that I could pluck nourishment out of the air. I could breathe in particles of beauty, colors and sounds, and be strengthened by them, let them saturate my cells. I was that little girl in the garden again, the gold seeping into me, only this time, I welcomed it. I let myself answer with a hesitant, flickering glow in my midsection.

I never used the word "God" for these moments. It didn't even occur to me. It was just joy, just bliss, just a tangible presence of love that didn't resemble anything I'd ever experienced in church. I didn't pray using words, but I could swirl into the face of a flower and see the whole universe in it.

And then once again I was horking my guts out into a toilet. I knew this feeling all too well: the reeling dizziness, the nausea, the disorientation, and the telltale painful breasts. I was pregnant again. How could that be??? I had been so careful!!!

(I am, apparently, the most fertile of women.)

It didn't make any sense. The guy and I had only been dating for a while; it was clear to both of us that we were not soulmates, though we cared about each other.

I was acting onstage and on camera, a career that lends itself not at all to weight gain, acne, and faintness. And yet, this time, something inside me was clear. *She's mine. I already love her. I am her mother.*

I told the man that I was going to have her, no matter what, and he didn't owe me anything. Upstanding fellow that he is, he said that we would do it together. We would be a family. Neither of us wanted to get married, which was a relief to both of us. We smiled nervously at each other, held together by this most tentative of threads.

During my pregnancy, I discovered that I was watery and fierce in equal measure. I wept at everything—diaper commercials, sunlight, and the little baby alien that Sigourney Weaver kills in the movie *Alien*. But there was a new sturdiness in me too. I could fall apart one minute, and speak clearly the next. I could feel dizzy, weepy, and uncertain—and still articulate exactly the kind of birth experience I wanted. After all those years believing that I was so weak, I was surprised to discover that actually I had some pretty badass muscles too.

As my figure changed, I stopped acting on camera and just did voice-overs. I worked like a maniac, taking any job I could get, stashing away money for my self-funded maternity leave. I worked long hours all over the city, but I didn't mind. I'd throw up between takes, brush my teeth, and hop back into the studio. When I got too dizzy to stand up in the subway, I'd just get off the train and crouch down until I could see again. Impending motherhood had switched something on inside me, and I was on fire.

But when it came to telling my parents, I was as brave as an anemone.

On a cold Saturday, I sat with my mom and dad in our neighborhood donut shop, Mister Donut, the same place where Christian high schoolers still met to confess sins of gossip and sinful thoughts.

"Hey guys." They beamed. I swallowed. It was still tentative, this détente with my folks. I wrapped my icy fingers around the pink mug. The air was thick with sugar and fat.

"So I have some news." My heart was pounding. My mouth was dry. I was every cliché of the nervous daughter. "Don't worry, I'm not getting married."

They blinked and nodded, wary and kind.

"But you're going to be grandparents. I'm having a baby."

On some level I knew they would love me no matter what, would help me and the baby if we needed it—I knew that beyond a shadow of doubt. I would never be that girl on the street, cast out by the horrified and betrayed parents. And yet I expected there to be sorrow there too. I looked for disappointment, maybe shame at their unwed pregnant daughter. They would get past it eventually, I was pretty sure—after all, they had been so gentle with my sister Ruth after her bible college expulsion. But just as they had wept with grief when I told them about my divorce, I expected that the first wave of emotion that would hit them would be disappointment.

They kept staring at me intently for the briefest of moments, quizzically puzzled. It was as if I had spoken to them in German, which we do not speak. Then it hit them.

My dad leaped up.

My mom put her hands over her mouth.

I braced myself. It took me a moment to realize that their faces had creased into identical moonbeams of joy. They whooped, they hugged me, my mom had two rivers running down her face.

They were so loudly joyous that they scared the other donut patrons.

I couldn't stop crying—with relief, with gratitude, with joy. A baby! We were going to have a baby in the family! And oh thank heaven and everything else, they were in my corner.

These are my parents: two fountains of love. They choose love over religious dogma every time. They are the real deal. And so as we welcomed this little beloved being into the world, we also embarked on a new and utterly delightful phase of our relationship.

They brought over a bassinet. Then, delicate Peter Rabbit sheets. Then they arrived with onesies, a stroller, and toys. They drove me places, cooked for me, and were nearly delirious with love for this little being who barely existed yet.

I had fought so hard to become strong. My mother is all tenderness, full of hugs and caresses. She is capable of immense gentleness. I'd scorned that softness in myself; I wanted strength, muscle, boundaries. I'd spent my twenties focused entirely on being tough, learning how to be fierce.

For the first time, I could let myself embrace the great warmth she radiates almost effortlessly. It felt like sinking myself into a deep, hot bath. I relaxed a little, let myself float on the waves of incredible tenderness I felt toward the little being in my belly. I felt the same compassion rushing in from these two parents who beamed more benevolence to me than I'd ever let myself take in before. It was like I got them back in a whole new way.

I grew large and pendulous.

I knew in the deepest possible way that I was having a girl.

And then in a pool of water, on my knees, teetering on the abyss of everything, moaning "I can't do it"—I did. I birthed my baby, and I gave birth to a new self within my body at the same time. I came out a different person. I came out with more love than I'd ever dreamed possible.

CHAPTER TWENTY-SIX

Through the haze of new motherhood, I kept reading voraciously. I read *Women Who Run With The Wolves*, and it was a quickening. It lit me up and woke me up. I loved Skeleton Woman with a fervent, passionate love. I slurped up the stories about embracing the whole cycle of life, even death and rebirth, rather than trying to make all of life be sunshine and midsummer. I actually kissed the pages of that book, adoring the underbelly of myself that it taught me to love, and I could feel the ruthless toothless old crone in me shake out her skirts and commence to rollick. I read about the moon, and the oceans, and the waxing and waning of different energies with our menstrual cycles. It was like getting a transfusion from the wise women.

I wanted more, more, more. I read *Expecting Adam* again, the book that had set so much in motion back in Philadelphia when I'd been so depressed and so married. It was still my favorite book ever in the whole world, and I'd read it at least a dozen times. Out of nowhere a crazy thought popped into my head: *I wonder if Martha Beck has a website.* (Living in Japan meant I didn't watch any American TV or ever see *O: The Oprah Magazine*, so I had no idea she'd become rather a sensation. I was a little slow to figure out the whole internet thing.) Less than a month later, I was signed up for her life coach training certification program, not because I wanted to become a life coach—heavens no, that sounded cheesy and embarrassing—but because I just wanted to know everything this wise, funny woman knew. If she'd had a training on the economic impact of seventeenth-century sausage-making, I would have signed up for that too.

But a funny thing happened. It turned out that I loved coaching people. And people loved telling me their stories. I'd always joked, rather bitterly, that I had "Tell me your secrets" tattooed on my forehead, because everywhere I went people told me their most private stories. This was kind of a bummer at parties, because I spent most of my time huddled in a corner hearing sad tales of trauma and heartbreak, but it turned out to be an immensely useful quality for a life coach.

Suddenly I wasn't alone with my books and my yearning any more. It turned out that there were lots of people like me—and it seemed they were all training with Martha too. (Martha! I called her Martha! Not "Dr. Beck, the Harvard-trained sociologist and *New York Times* bestselling author." It was like meeting God. I was so star-struck that I am actually a bit relieved that I didn't accidentally lick her earrings.) As part of my training, I traveled from Tokyo to Arizona to meet the other coaches-in-training and Martha herself. Martha was even funnier in person than in her books. And the other coaches—I *recognized* them. It was like finding out I had a secret twin, or several dozen of them.

What I do for my work now gets called "life coaching," but in some ways it's closer to being a medicine woman or a spiritual mentor. None of those words is quite right, and sometimes I want to roll my eyes at the fact that I am in what can only be called the "self-help" profession. Unfortunately, this world of lovely healers also contains an unfortunately high percentage of snake oil and sleazeballs who will sell you schlock and call it "*An Ancient and Mysterious Secret*" to make money. I was totally skeezed out by most self-help stuff, all those crystals and feathers and white lights, but at the same time I hungered to talk to someone about what was happening in my secret spiritual life. Was I even allowed to admit that I felt so beloved? Was all this sucking-nourishment-out-of-the-air stuff really healthy? And what about those dark presences that still sometimes pressed on me? None of the airy-fairy woo-woo stuff I read with great skepticism ever mentioned anything like that; it was all supposed to be sweetness and light, but I had the sense that something much more nuanced was going on. I had always thought that I would have to go down to South America and take ayahuasca and have psychedelic vomiting visions in order to deal with all this mystical stuff.

But instead I found a family of fellow mystics much closer to home. Through my new coach friends, I found more teachers. I met a woman named Elena who never mentioned that she was into out-there stuff... but she seemed to be reading my mind. Finally I pinned her down and sat on her until she agreed to talk to me about what she knew. In very simple, practical terms, she described how some of us have extra antennae and can pick up stuff that's being broadcast. Yes, yes, I nodded, I feel like that! And sometimes we feel emotions that aren't actually our own. Oh god yes, I groaned, please help me to stop doing that! And we sometimes get information in ways that don't make any rational sense. Yes yes! All my truest knowings aren't provable! And we can feel energy and presences that most people can't. I got very still. Like...ghosts? "Oh," she said, "call it whatever you want. It's all just energy." Huh. That explained a few things.

Like the dead horse that was in my bedroom one evening. I wasn't hallucinating; my eyes could see that there was nothing physically there. But I could feel it there, dead, decaying, but peaceful. I asked whether it needed anything from me, and I didn't get an answer, so I just waved at it and left it alone. It felt pretty gentle. And a couple of hours later it was gone. I usually never find out what these things mean when they happen. There doesn't seem to be an urgent message that they seem to want me to deliver, like in that movie *The Sixth Sense*. Instead, they just seem to want me to bear witness. So that is what I do. *Okay, I see you*, I say. And then I bring in big white light and they dissolve, leaving a residue of quiet.

These random images were odd, but gentle. More troubling was the door I was always watching over, making sure it stayed closed. There was so much sweetness and light in my life now, but on the other side of that door, I sensed, were ghouls and spirits and ghosts. It took all my force to keep that door shut. Oh, I wouldn't have opened it for anything. I couldn't even stay in the room when people talked about séances and spirits—I couldn't believe that anyone would actually pay money to go to a medium. Were they *fools*? Why would they bring in that scary shit on purpose? I wanted to keep as far away from it all as I could, but the pressure was getting stronger and I wasn't sure how much longer I could hold the door closed.

Now, the thing about life coaches is that they are cursed with an immense curiosity. We can hardly help ourselves, we are such addicts for people's stories. And we get all drooly and hunting dog—point!—when we can tell someone's sitting on something big. So while I was in Arizona for the coaching weekend, an intrepid fellow coach cornered me and sat me down.

"Let's figure out this ghost thing," she said. I looked at her in terror. "Come on. You can't keep being afraid of them."

I reluctantly agreed to use a benign coaching tool, something we call "the metaphor tool," to look more closely at the door holding back whatever was behind it. I agreed to this only as long as it was very clear to everyone involved—I spoke loudly and waved my hands more than was actually necessary—that I didn't want to talk to any ghosts; I just wanted to *look* at them.

You know what? We took a look, and that damn door wasn't even connected to walls. It was just a piece of plywood standing in thin air. "They" had obligingly put it up so I would have something to push against. They were just waiting there politely, behind an invisible line. They could have walked into my space any old time, but they wouldn't do that. That isn't how they worked.

I called a tentative ceasefire. I said I would listen as long as they wouldn't scare me anymore. They nodded quietly.

Many of the mystical woo-woo la-la people I met wanted to sweep around in the ether picking up transmissions from the astral plane. Having already had some unwilling contact with the astral plane, I didn't want any more, thank you very much. I thought they were unwise to mess around with spirits that *might* be good, but on the other hand *might* want to use their bodies for billiard practice. So I asked Elena about evil. I was back in Japan so we were talking over Skype, that magical technology that let us sit in our rooms across an ocean from each other and commune. I was grilling her about whether or not there was actual evil in the world or, as the Buddhists say, it's all just a big misunderstanding.

"Well," she said. "There certainly is evil in the world, and of course people who mess around in mysticism and spirits without knowing what they're doing are foolish. But really, evil isn't something that you yourself will ever have to really worry about, it's very rare for—" and then we lost the connection. My screen went dark. My computer had turned itself all the way off. Even though machines sometimes go wonky around me when I get very excited, I'd never had one actually turn itself off before. A few minutes later I booted back up and she called back.

"Well, honey, this is rather unusual. My machine just turned itself off, which has never happened to me before," she said. "Also, I am getting this very clear directive that I am supposed to talk to you about evil, because you have already encountered it and you just need to know what to do with it."

And at those words, my body slumped in profound relief.

I know it seems nuts—Hurray! I'd encountered evil! Yippee! It sounds ridiculous, I know. But you see, Elena was speaking the truth. And as Martha Beck says in her book *Steering By Starlight*, the truth—no matter how painful—is always a profound relief to the soul.

I soaked up all the wisdom I could find. I worked with a master horse whisperer for one beautiful dreamy day and let some horses teach me how to get into my body and get calm. They did this in a very persuasive way; they simply refused to move if I had any scared, scary, or anxious energy in me. A massive animal towering over you is pretty powerful biofeedback. I learned to get very calm and feel all the way to the edges of my body and tell the horse what to do from my gut. And when I could do that, then it would do what I asked: walk, stop, follow me. It was magic, and I decided that horses might be the only thing in nature I loved more than the ocean and flowers.

I kept learning mystical technologies that helped me start managing my energy instead of being so thrown around by it. I learned to "cloak" myself to give me a clear space free of others' static. I learned to release emotions that weren't really mine, ones I'd absorbed from other people. And most importantly, I learned to tune into my body, that great intuitive master.

I finally admitted to myself that part of the sadness and trauma I carried in my body came from somewhere outside of what had physically happened during my life so far. I resisted this for a long time. Admitting that I believed in past lives just appalled me. It seemed so flaky, so trendy, so wafty. And if reincarnation is the name of the game, I'm not sure that it's literal. But I do think that Jung was catching a thread attached to the fundamental warp and weave of our being when he talked about sharing a pool of consciousness. And also, there is this tiny, awkward, incontrovertible truth: I remember things that I haven't experienced. Lots of them. In fact, when I say the phrase "past lives" to myself, I see a big enormous encyclopedia in front of me. *Oh yes, here I am!* it seems to say. *Which one did you want to see?* I feel immense gratitude to all these stories residing inside me, the ones I can remember clearly and the ones that are hazy glimpses.

When the presences came and pressed on my space, instead of going rigid with terror or eating or drinking until I was numb, I began talking to them. It made me feel ridiculous. I rolled my eyes at myself a lot. But they had interesting things to say. Often they just wanted to be seen. They delivered these hilariously trite messages, like "nothing can destroy us beyond what love can heal" and "it's all love, baby." Whatever energies I was getting transmissions from were obviously taking too much Ecstasy. But it felt so good not to be afraid.

I started a new company; I stopped doing work I had outgrown; I began to write in earnest. My daughter flourished. Things were flowering.

—ᗯ—

Then I had another nightmare. You'd think that by this point I might have figured out that my nightmares have almost always been the bringers of great gifts, but no. They just scared the crap out of me each and every time.

I dreamed of a dusty, desolate landscape. The air was so dry it was leaching the moisture out of me, and I could feel myself withering. I climbed into a red pickup truck with an evil man covered in oozing sores. He was going to kill me, I knew somehow, but I felt drawn to him anyway. I couldn't pull myself away or step out of the truck. A telephone booth flashed by the window as we drove by. He stopped the truck, and I knew he was going to get his knife. I could feel its sharp blade coming for me. Still I didn't run.

I woke up sweating, gasping, terrified. I couldn't shake my fear. I didn't even want to write it down. This one was too big to handle on my own. I called Elena to help me interpret it. Over the phone, we used a dream interpretation method based on Jung's theories about split bits of our consciousness. She helped me to "become" each element of my dream, and in the safety of her presence, I went much deeper. I found myself going into something I can only describe as a trance. Words spilled out of me quickly, as though the dream itself was desperate to tell me its true message.

The killer had indeed come to kill me.

He had come to slit my throat so that I could peel this skin back like a hood and step out of it.

His sores disguised a beauty that could blind.

The dust that had choked me was begging for water. It was longing to be fertile.

The telephone by the road was my direct line to the cosmos should I ever need help.

I found myself cackling with an amazed joy. I would know that laughter anywhere.

I felt a great tangle lift out of my neck. I don't mean this metaphorically. I mean that while on the phone with this great healer, she energetically lifted a mass of snarls up and out of my neck. I felt it leave. I felt a huge rush of emptiness where it used to be.

There was that familiar pain in my core, the wound that I'd felt since I was a child. All the horrors in the world: the infants who they used to operate on without anesthesia, the little girls raped in the war zones, the torture, the violence, the shame, the mourning. I felt it. Instead of pushing it away, this time I breathed in to touch it. I let it fill me. And then I kept breathing until I found the love that was bigger than all that pain.

In, and out. When I let myself fill up with the agony, I could also feel the love. I would hook it with my breath, feel my ribs stretch to bring it in, let it whoosh through me. Then usually I'd lose my concentration and start coughing. I lurched around, finding it and then losing it, feeling totally calm and full of love for a minute and then hunching back into agonized sobs the next. But the longer I held it, the stronger it grew. The more I breathed, the more I could open up wide enough to hold everything in the universe. And when I opened wide enough, there was that great heartbeat underneath everything.

The pain is just what teaches us how big the love is. Call it The Force, The Source, The Universe, What Is, call it anything besides God because that word is too misused and abused.

I said out loud into the air, "Wow. You're really out there, huh."

The laughter burbled. "I'm not out there, sweet pea. I'm *in* there."

And I threw back my head and breathed thank you. Thank you for all of it.

CHAPTER TWENTY-SEVEN

Life in Tokyo was sweet. My baby girl was toddling. I had work I loved: a funny blend of voice work and consulting and even a bit of life coaching. To top it all off, I had begun writing down this story in earnest.

I hadn't had nightmares in so long. But suddenly they were back.

I dreamed I was in labor and there was an angry, impatient obstetrician there. He kept flapping around me, checking his watch, scolding me, saying I was taking too long and doing it wrong.

I woke up livid. This was exactly why I hadn't had a doctor present at my daughter's birth; how dare one come to me at night? I sat scribbling it out in dull resentment that this stupid dream had intruded on me and left me feeling so guilty and ashamed and anxious.

Screw you! I scrawled in fury. *You don't get to come here!*

I waved my pen around a little bit, like an indignant old crone.

And then, right into my living room, a presence swept in.

I could feel her. That's all I can say. She was as real as the table and chair that I sat on.

She was a glorious lion, female, dripping with milk and blood and golden light. Somehow I knew that she was my midwife. She shook her improbable golden mane, and the worried Ob/gyn and all his skittish anxiety just scattered like smoke. She was fierce; she was magic. She looked at me with utter calm and said,

I'm not worried about a thing. This baby will come in its own sweet time.

And then—she just stayed. I know it sounds crazy, but I really feel an incredibly powerful and loving presence nearby almost all the time. If I can't feel her and I need her, I ask her to come, and she does. She is a female lion, but she has a gorgeous golden mane that shakes when she laughs. She laughs at me a lot. When she laughs, little bits of gold fly out of her mane and spatter me until I am lit up with gold too.

I call this presence Madre, though I know that is not her real name. Her name is unpronounceable. It sounds like it will bring the quantum fields crashing upon us. She could have taken any form she wanted: angel, devil, tree, animal guardian—but she comes to me as this majestic female-male lion midwife because, quite simply, it just cracks us both up. It is the biggest, juiciest, most loving joke in the world, this shape she takes. I love her so much. And she is pure love.

Madre's love is like the love I feel for my kids, deep and all encompassing—but without even a shred of the fear or worry that's inherent in the love we feel for our vulnerable babies. She finds us humans utterly ridiculous and also completely endearing. Which is lucky for me, because I am sorry to report that I am a bit of a brat to her.

"Why didn't you come before?" I demand. "All those years, I NEEDED you."

She looks at me with the kindest eyes. And then she winks at me and chortles. She grins, like surely I get the joke. But I do not. I am outraged. I am a toddler stomping my foot.

So then she shows me something that isn't in words— it's a picture of a playground. *It doesn't happen all at once,* she says. *It's not like the goddamn movies. You have to clamber your way through. That's kind of the whole point, kiddo.*

Harumph. I don't like this very much. I want instant gratification and blinding epiphanies and everything to be summed up in a neat tidy little knot at the end. But Madre thinks the mess is gorgeous. She even thinks that messy old me is gorgeous. It's hard to withstand that sort of generous love. It's like trying to stay angry at a laughing baby.

For so many years, I craved some sort of sign from The Universe and as far as I was concerned, I got nothing. All I heard was a great resounding silence, and it broke my heart. I felt like there was no love out there for me. I would read stories of people having visions, visitors, magnificent spiritual experiences, and it just rubbed my nose in the fact that I hadn't been chosen for the divine shoulder tap. So I want to say a word to anyone who feels angry and bereft and wonders where their own Madre is.

I believe that this love is available to us all the time. I think the whole world is turning itself inside out at every minute to try to get our attention, and we are the ones who are blind and deaf to it. But my guess is that the love won't take this exact shape for you. Maybe for you it will be an animal, or a feeling in your chest, or one of those dashing archangels with a proper sword. Maybe it will be dreams. Maybe it will be the love you feel for your spouse, child, parent. One of my clients discovered that if she lies on the earth, she is immensely comforted—somehow, wisdom and instructions will trickle up into her. Another client discovered that the ancient art of belly dancing was all it took to connect her with herself and with the divine. Maybe it will be baking bread or growing things in dirt or doing surgery or nursing your babies. Maybe it will be Excel spreadsheets, even though that possibility actually scrambles my brain. I think it's no accident that Madre swooped in when I started grappling on the page with my own shadows.

I think back to all those signals I got as a child. Working with color or staring at flowers transported me directly and efficiently into that golden bliss that I now recognize as straight-up divine love. Those things WERE loving signals from the universe; I was just so busy looking for a burning bush that I blew right by them. If I had followed any of those blisses, whether into fashion or art or even gardening, I might have gotten here more quickly, without some of the messes I made. *But no matter.* That is what Madre keeps saying. I can feel her grinning at me as I type this. *There's no rush. Sooner, later, who cares? It all makes a good story!* I find her quite scandalous sometimes. But she's not heartless, Madre. She just is radically unconvinced that what I think of as problems are really a very big deal. *So you had some heartbreak? Good! Look what a good healer it turned you into!* she grins.

"But Madre!" I scold. "This is a very messy, inefficient way to get things done! There is a lot of pain, a lot of trauma, a lot of horror in the world!"

And she just looks at me with those deep golden eyes, like I am a beloved but hilarious child, and she rocks me back and forth and says, *Well okay then, baby girl. Why don't you help me make it better?*

I have many excellent suggestions, like ending war, and instant immolation for child abusers, and a kind of peaceful static nirvana world where no one gets hurt.

She says things like, *Those are very nice ideas, darling. But I want to talk to you about pumpkins. Look at those pumpkins! Aren't they just the roundest, plumpest, orangest things you've ever seen????* She cups the pumpkins the way you would cup a beloved toddler's cheeks. And then she looks at me expectantly. Do I get it? *Do I?*

Mostly I do not. And yet suddenly, before I can help myself, I am grinning.

Slowly, slooooowly, I think I am beginning to learn what she is trying to teach me. That I cannot be in enough pain to take away anyone else's. That all my agonizing and empathizing and aching for the hurts of the world only added to the world's pool of pain. She isn't telling me to check out; she's showing me how to tune in. To see the incredible beauty of what is all around me, every minute, every second.

And indeed the more I tune into that, the more I let pleasure and bliss and laughter flow through myself without shame, the more I can feel my healing muscles grow strong and canny. People bring me their problems and instead of getting sucked into them, I can hold a space for them to untangle, stretch, grow, get bigger. It is at once the mightiest and tiniest of work. Helping one woman, for instance, untangle the shame she has around her parenting. Or supporting another one as she gets bold enough to ask for a raise, start her own business, or leave a toxic relationship. It feels like impossibly small and inconsequential work sometimes, in the face of all the horrors out in the world that I believe require my attention. But if there's anything Madre has taught me, it's that size doesn't matter. And as I watch these friends and clients grow sturdier and more steady as they move through the world, I feel like I'm planting seeds for a benevolent revolution.

We are plotting a global takeover by the wise women, Madre and I.

I think that Madre is that same deep beating heart I felt the night before my abortion. But really, I think it's all that heart. When I read (or try to read) the new physics, it all makes a certain kind of bizarre sense. Shapes and forms arising out of a great field of potential. All matter entwined, everything connected with each other. It's that ancient groovy teaching that runs through so many different brands of spirituality—that separation is an illusion. That we are never separate from the divine, we are the divine, we are all that is. And at the same time of course we're not, we're people in these remarkable bodies walking around. This is why so many religions fade into clichés like "it's just a Mystery"—because trying to explain it in words is as impossible as trying to explain the color blue with a handful of straw.

One of my clients said on the phone the other day, "It's the divine blah-blah-blah," and I knew exactly what she meant. This has become our code for one of those things that is so deep and pure and real that it sounds utterly ridiculous when we try to put words to it.

CHAPTER TWENTY-EIGHT

When my daughter was four, we were still living in Tokyo. Her father and I were five years into trying very hard to make it work. We wanted so desperately to be a family for her.

She was sick that morning and couldn't go to preschool. Instead of feeling maternal and compassionate, I was just goddamn fucking pissed. I'd had a full week in the studio doing voice-overs, reading script after script of inane jingles. Today was my reward; I was supposed to get a massage and then have lunch with a friend. All down the toilet, thanks to my darling daughter's cough.

I groused around all morning and finally lay down with her on the bed. I sighed. Motherhood wasn't easy for me; I loved my baby girl desperately, but I hated 97% of the grunt physical labor that it required. I couldn't find the saintly glow that other mothers seemed to have, even as they wiped up shit, fended off snot streams, and handled the laundry, wiping, cleaning, picking up, carrying, and lifting. I thought that every kid should come equipped with its own staff—nanny, house cleaner, cook. I would be the one to kiss the oww-ies and read her stories at night. I was good at that part.

But my little girl was peaked and pitiful, sprawled on the comforter. I curled up around her and stroked her forehead. I silently vowed to be a sweeter mother to her. I peeled my death grip off my cherished "me" day and sank into the sweetness of lying there on the bed with her, all her normal rambunctious energy wilted by her fever. Just as my eyes started to close, I heard a distant rumble. Then the bed lurched.

I sat up; an earthquake, a big one. They happened all the time, and up on the sixteenth floor we were used to some pretty wild swings. Nothing I couldn't handle.

Then the creaking sounds started, and the room pitched sideways like a ship in the storm. Suddenly the whole world was thrashing back and forth. I heard a huge crash from the other room. The creaking sounds grew louder. Before I even knew what I was doing, I whirled both of us off the bed and into the gap between the bed and the wall.

I knew earthquakes. I was so totally not fazed by earthquakes.

This was like no earthquake I had ever felt.

I crawled over her, bracing myself on all fours just like I had done in labor. I put a pillow under her head and smiled.

"I love you, sweetie," I said.

"I'm scared, Mommy."

"I am too, honey. This is pretty scary, huh? But I'm right here with you."

The thrashing grew wilder, the horrendous creaking sound louder. Things crashed and banged, and I waited for the big crunch that seemed inevitable: the ceiling to cave, a beam to crush me. I felt how fragile our bodies were, these thin bones cased in flesh, and I knew that I couldn't protect her. I crouched over her anyway and looked down at her. I loved her so much. I would love her into the great beyond. I knew we were about to die.

...Except that we didn't.

After several minutes, the creaking sound slowed down. Gradually the thrashing slowed. I stood up and walked to the window, expecting to see a city in ruin. But everything looked fine, except for some plumes of smoke in the distance. I pulled up my daughter and we wandered through the house in a daze. The phones weren't working, but the internet was. The posts started flowing through Facebook—*I'm okay, are you?*

An hour later we watched as the tsunami hit the north, and after my first horrified breath I turned the TV off so my daughter wouldn't see it.

The people I loved were okay. The devastation was unreal.

And something inside me had been irreversibly shaken up.

Two days later, my little girl and I got on a plane. We each had a suitcase. We said goodbye to her dad as the airport shuddered in a powerful aftershock. Just for a week, we said, until we find out what's going to happen with the Fukushima nuclear reactors—but just in case, we'd packed all the important documents in my suitcase. He was going to get on a train and go south. Everyone who could had gotten out of Tokyo. There was no bottled water, toilet paper, rice, potatoes, flour, or any sort of food in the grocery stores. The trains mostly worked, but they were erratic. We kept hearing that if it rained, nuclear fallout would pour down as far south as Tokyo. Rolling power blackouts. Melting rods. Possible panic as people tried to flee the city.

The maternal lion in me roared. Madre nodded. I wanted my little girl out of there.

We flew to Portland, Oregon, and stayed with my brother and his fiancée. With twelve hours' notice, they turned their dining room into a sweet little impromptu guest room for us and said to stay as long as we wanted. It was rainy and cold, but crocuses were popping up everywhere, and to my delighted surprise, the city was bursting with fragrant daphne. I'd always thought it only grew in Japan. The lemony sweetness of it buoyed me.

We waited for news on the reactors, but no one knew what was really happening. We were in limbo, and the week on their floor dragged into two months. To my own surprise, I had an immense yearning to stay in Portland. Indefinitely. It was the most bizarre sensation. For the first time in my life, I didn't miss Japan—I wanted to stay in this sweet little green city. Her dad agreed that we should stay; he was drinking imported water and buying all his food at Costco, since no one knew how much radiation was in the Tokyo food. She and I would get a temporary apartment, we decided, and figure out the rest as we went.

We plopped my brother's spare futon on the golden floor of our tiny new apartment. I went to Ikea and bought a sofa covered in pink cabbage roses, some dishes, sheets and a comforter. We hit the vintage stores and bought an old chest for toys and a desk for my laptop. My girl and I, we opened up our suitcases.

We were home.

CHAPTER TWENTY-NINE

In my peaceful green Portland neighborhood, there is one awful corner. People stand around with signs showing tiny severed limbs. I avoid that corner so that my daughter doesn't see an image that will stay with her forever. One day I'm in my car by myself, and I see them swarming the corner like a bunch of vultures. Instantly I am in a red fury. I am so angry, so triggered, it's like I fly out of my own body. I want to stop the car, storm out, scream at them. "Is this how they'll know you're Christians?!?! By your hatred??? By shaming some young women just trying to do the right thing?" I want to write a big sign that blasts, "None of these people will help you AFTER you have your baby," or "These people all voted against the morning-after pill." My hands shake, I grip the steering wheel. I say nothing.

Once my breathing slows down, I can swoop back into my own body. I feel the old sadness in my chest, the impossible gap between me and them. I don't understand how people of faith, and particularly the ones who supposedly follow Jesus, can believe that their God would send innocent aborted souls straight to hell. I don't get why they think a life of being unwanted and uncared-for on earth is better than being sent straight back to their loving God.

Done. I'm done. I can't fight them any more.

And as soon as I step away from the battleground in my own heart, suddenly in my mind's eye I see a horde of peaceful women walking up to the same corner, with a different set of signs.

"Your baby deserves a mother who is ready. You'll get another chance."

"God loves your baby enough to take care of its soul."

"No child should be born into an unsafe home. If you're in trouble, we can help."

"Compassion spoken here."

I won't do it today, or next week. Not yet. This isn't the time in my life to be writing controversial signs. I'm a solo parent now, and my first job is to keep my daughter happy, healthy, and with a peaceful roof over her head. But a time will come for the loving counter-narrative. A compassionate uprising of wise women who can tell a different story than the old one of fear and damnation. And for the moment, this beautiful uprising has at least happened inside me, and I feel its fierce tenderness trickle all the way from my heart down to my feet.

—⋙—

I am building a new life in Portland out of scratch. New friends, new school, new life as a solo parent. I buy some red rain boots to slog through the mud. I start a book club with the moms I meet on the playground. But the visible shifts in my life, though dramatic, are nothing compared to the things that no one else can see.

I decide that I am finally brave enough to face the ghosts head-on. I'm tired of them standing behind that door, however politely. I need to speak to them or do battle with them or send them away or whatever is necessary.

I am deeply concerned that if I open that door, I will become like the woman in the television show *Medium*, with strange people wandering in and out of her bedroom each night, telling her things she does not want to hear. I do not want to be a medium. I'm not sure I believe in mediums. I feel silly for thinking that I could be a medium even if I wanted to. Good grief. I'm sick of this rutted path of thinking.

So with a trusted healer, I settle into my body for about two seconds. She hasn't done any drumming, chanting, or anything remotely shamanic, but immediately the image of the door pops up in my mind's eye. It appears to be as eager as I am to finally have this conversation. My heart pounds, my fists clench, and I almost bail.

"Do you want to stop?" she asks.

"No. It's time to do this." I take a deep breath and open the door.

It's very silent. I can hear my teacher breathing silently, waiting for me to speak. But inside the silence I am laughing, cackling, about to pee my pants.

Her curiosity gets the better of her enlightenment. "Well?" she asks.

"There's no one there! At least, there's this whole line of them going all the way over the hills, lined up like dominos, but they're not ghosts, they're more like feathers."

"What do you want to do now?" she asks, and I can hear a grin in her voice.

"Send 'em to the light. I'm going to give them a little breeze." I take a deep breath and blow gently through pursed lips, and as my breath whooshes out of my body I see them take flight, blown away like dandelion wisps, light as leaves.

I feel relief rush down to my toes like cool air, and I could stand there all day in front of that open door, the sweet breath of the world on my cheeks.

There is a darkness still there, though, sitting just beyond the doorstep like a small boulder. As I look at it quizzically, it begins to change form until it is a wizened old monkey with a bright red butt, just like the ones at the hot springs in Japan. My eyebrows raise even though my eyes are still closed. This has got to be the weirdest message I've received from the universe, if that's in fact what it is.

The monkey nods at me, one brief emphatic nod, then it turns around, waggles its red hindquarters, and walks away. Soon he is gone just like the ghosts, every last flicker dissolved in the dazzling light. I have absolutely no idea what the monkey means. But I like him.

—〰—

It's 9am and I am doing psychic surgery on myself with a trusted teacher. We're clearing out past life contracts, releasing vows, and opening up cages...just an ordinary Thursday morning. She asks me to look into my psychic DNA to find what's causing my current distress. I groan, embarrassed to see more jealousy, victimhood, and self-pity. Today I'm feeling sorry for myself because I can't have another baby. I'm all on my own and my trust fund is so very nonexistent, you see.

My coach snorts. "Please. If you REALLY wanted another baby, you would have one. However unwise, however stupid, if you really wanted this to happen, you'd be pregnant RIGHT now."

I teeter for a moment, on the verge of free falling into defensiveness, hurt feelings, outrage at her unkind statement. But instead a giggle rises up from my very belly. Aw shit, she's right. I could probably go out and get myself knocked up tomorrow, if I really wanted to. You'd be amazed what you can get done with a bottle of whiskey. The truth is, I don't want to have a baby in my current circumstances. That's the choice I'm making, and it's a sound one. And yet I allow this helpless victim story to hang around. It's a pattern I've played for years, taking refuge behind sadness, where I will be unassailable. I can see that I have used sadness like a currency to get out of taking responsibility for what I really want.

When we mourn a true loss, our grief morphs, changes, and eventually sweetens us. What I have been holding on to is something else—an illusion of bitter, wronged, romantic melancholia.

I'm a tad appalled, and a whole lot ecstatic. Because this understanding makes me free.

Grappling with my own ugly parts isn't necessarily my favorite part of this game, but I know by now that it's the fastest way through to freedom. And it does feel like a game, a marvelous, wonderful game that we are all playing: our souls jumping in to have a human experience. It's the most exhilarating game I could imagine—being able to touch things, to kiss, to see colors and sunsets and babies. I am loving this human experience, with skin and heartbreak and eyelashes and salt.

But I also believe that it's just one tiny sliver of our reality. I think we are much more than these human roles we're playing. We're the kids playing on Madre's playground, but we also helped design the playground. It's a little like the story of Jesus, where an all-powerful being decides to deliberately limit that power, to become incarnate in an ordinary human body. I can hardly believe I'm writing this. It takes mental muscle for me to see this parallel in the Jesus stories—it's like pushing magnets together, and I can only hold it for a minute.

But I believe this is what we're all meant to do. To take this body incarnate, understand that it is one temporary arrangement of reality, and enjoy the hell out of it. Some people like to throw parties and make art; some enjoy the game of healing ecosystems, baking pies, or building empires.

Mystics talk about the field of infinite possibility, how everything that we perceive is only one possible version of things. I'd say that's just one more skin of language that we give to something that is beyond words. Ancient religions call it reincarnation. You could say that our subconscious minds branch out of one great joined pool. You could say that on the atomic level, we're all just different vibrations of the same energy. I don't want to put a label on it. I don't need to pin it down. Who was it who said that trying to describe spirit with words was like trying to build the sky with blocks?

I'm working with this teacher, on this Thursday morning, to unwind the tangled stories I've carried from lifetime to lifetime. I can find the victim story easily. That one is comfortable for me, safe, even defensible. I have many memories, in many different skins, where I have been a victim of all sorts of horrors. These old memories are shocking, but they don't press on me the way they used to. They sit in their book to help me understand this part of the human experience. But there's another part to this story, and this one is harder for me to acknowledge. It's agonizing to face the violent archetype in me: the one who is capable of pillage, rape, killing. But when I do, something impossible happens. I see that they're just two sides of the coin. They've been locked in battle since time immemorial, and I'm just one little reflection of this ancient battle. I can't end the battles out in the world, but I can end the one in me.

The two sides face each other, mirror images, yin and yang. I pull light in from the ether, powerful healing light, and both sides burst into a million particles, and where they stood is only light and empty space. I continue to pull light into my body, bathing in it, washing away all the residue (some might call it karma) from this ongoing duel.

Suddenly I remember that dream I had when I was sixteen, the one where Jesus and Satan embraced and walked down the road together, their cloaks flapping behind them as they became one single figure. I had been so horrified by that dream, by the blasphemy of it. But it was just one of those flickers where the illusion fell and I saw into a deeper reality. I didn't know then what to do with them, but as I look back I can see that the flickers were many, and faithful.

I remember the vibrating red tulip I so desperately wanted to capture in my crayon drawing. I see that tulip again as I continue my meditation. This time I cup its petals in my hands and look deeply into it, and the humming noise is unmistakable. I can see everything in that tulip, the red humming of joy, the dark spikes of our stories, the subtle veins that run life through the whole thing. *Sit with this*, Madre says. *Look. Listen.* And this time the humming grows louder, palpable, thrumming through my body until I am tingling with it. It's the song I yearned for in the stars; the thing I would touch sometimes late at night when we sat around and quietly sang Leonard Cohen songs. It had been right there all along. But in those moments when the fabric of existence would rip open and I'd catch a glimpse of that hum, I joined my own sad harmony to it. That was all I brought to the table: my yearning, my sorrow, my minor chord.

This time I understand that I can sing whatever the hell song I want to. Why had I been so committed to this sorrow? I'm ready to let it go now. It isn't a bad song, but it's just one note, and there are so many to sing. I will have to give up my illusion of myself as a victim. I will have to stop taking refuge in the soft cuddle of self-pity.

And in return, I will get everything. I will be awake.

I look back into my own history with new eyes, and new ideas start to trickle in. A friend did some research into Japanese ghosts and wrote me in some excitement. Did I know about the *yuurei*, with their trailing kimonos? And the *hitodama*, those floating orbs of fire? Of course I did. I'd been scared of them my whole life.

But the one I was most afraid of as a child was *yuki-onna*, the snow woman who had a blank white space where there should have been eyes, nose, a mouth. She would come up on travelers lost in the whiteness of a blizzard and they would gasp with relief that they had been found. Yet when she pulled aside her hair and turned around, instead of a woman's face there was just that white empty space. That terrifying blankness was a perfect mirror for how I felt inside: not just invisible but faceless, some essential part of me wiped away. How could the *yuki-onna* see? I wondered. How could she kill (for she always did kill) with no eyes or ears to find her victim? More than the one-eyed ogre, the darting tongues of flame, or the bouncing eyeball, I feared the faceless woman.

I think we are all basically swimming in molecular soup, and our thoughts, dreams, and emotions leave little trails behind us. I wonder if all the things I couldn't say, hear, or even admit to seeing as a child formed their own trail behind me, leaving eddies of disturbed air that I perceived as ghosts. Perhaps the tendrils of my own deep fear were whipping around and tapping me on the shoulder, and I startled at them like an animal afraid of its own shadow.

Or perhaps there was something more malevolent at work, lost or angry energies looking for a porous bit of empathy to latch on to.

Or perhaps my antennae were simply catching a bunch of static: intuitive hits, empathic information, sensory data I didn't know how to process—and so I perceived it all in the only framework I knew, which was that of ghosts and spirits.

I don't really need to know any more. My hunch is that all these explanations are just different metaphors for something that isn't really expressible in words.

One thing I do know is that until I reached my arms around myself, I couldn't feel the love that was also there, in that same soup, the main ingredient. Until that moment in the bathtub when I chose myself, when I declared that there had to be love for me even if I thought I was unlovable, I couldn't taste any other love at all.

—⁓—

I wake up in the middle of the night. Something is present, and I am disoriented. I sit up in the bed. It isn't a dream, or a visitor—it's a new knowing in my chest, a certainty as calm and certain as my own heartbeat. This is how truth arrives in me now. It comes through my body, as sensations and information. Madre blinks calmly.

It's time to go back to Japan.

—⁓—

I talk to a colleague about it. "I'm going back," I say. "I'm going back to the fear."

She has a knee-jerk life coach reaction. "You're not going back, you're going forward. And don't say you're going back into the fear, your language is powerful!"

I understand what she means. Many of my mystical friends believe that our words, those embodiments of our intentions, are incredibly powerful and must be used carefully. In some ways I agree with them; I do believe our declarations are powerful. (No surprise, since my company is named Declare Dominion.) But I also think that like any truth, this kind of thinking can devolve into superstition. Not naming our fears doesn't make them go away. It just makes them the fears-that-shall-not-be-named. I'm devoted now to shining a compassionate light into all my own dark places.

I'm ready to go back to Japan, my old home, and face what scares me.

My daughter's father and I have separated. I wanted it to be peaceful and friendly, and it wasn't entirely, though we did our best. He will always be a big part of her life, but an ocean separates them.

I'm afraid of all the sadness I know my little girl and I will feel upon returning to Tokyo: so many goodbyes unsaid, so many losses not yet mourned.

But instead of recoiling from the fear, I can feel my own tender arms wrapping around my heart. *I know, honey. I know you're scared. It's okay for you to be scared, because you have lots of practice being brave.* And in that moment I can make space for my fear, even treat it gently, because I am so much more than the fear.

I spent years being afraid of my own fear. Afraid it would envelop me, drown me, choke my throat and stop my breathing like the night terrors had done. Maybe that fear was the faceless *yuki-onna*. But when I stopped being afraid of the self who was afraid, then another part of me rose up—a part who was brave, and certain, and true. In this way I finally learned to keep myself company. Not to extinguish that little girl who was so deathly afraid, but to bring a light to her room and offer her a warm bed.

Years after the stitched-together girl with the evil blue eyes first appeared to me, I meet my child self again. I am continuing my quest to greet all the exiled parts of myself, to gather all my parts together into an integrated whole. I close my eyes and go into meditation, ready to confront the girl in the cell, the one who will surely still bear scars from those stitches she had finally pulled out.

Instead, the girl who pops into my mind's eye is grinning. Her curly blonde locks buzz with a mischievous merriment. For a moment I think someone else's inner child has accidentally taken up residence in my psyche. But then I look at her again and she crooks her finger at me.

We walk down a little path through a copse of trees that opens up into a magical sort of library set right into the forest. Moss grows along the tree trunks and bookshelves, and the air hums with a deep peace. Sunlight slants through and pollen drifts gold in its light. She leads me over to a big purple cushion and opens up the ornate leather-bound sketchbook lying on it. She's been writing stories in it, and drawing pictures. She pulls me down on the cushion so we're lying side by side on our bellies and she begins flipping through her book.

I know that she both is, and isn't, the same girl who had been in such agony, imprisoned in her fear and wounds. The healing I've done has worked backward through time, and although I will always remember that girl with her stringy hair in the cell, who was so angry at me, she has transformed into this beautiful, well-loved creature lying beside me now. She has healed. She is complete.

And she has things—oh, such things!—to show me in this great book. She's filled it full of beauty.

It turns out that after years of craving a place where I would feel at home, there had always been a place inside me that I could find my way to. But only the child could take me there, and she had to trust me before she would show it to me.

Now this dreamy forest library is inside me, and I can carry it with me wherever I go.

CHAPTER THIRTY

I'm on an airplane, tracing the familiar arc halfway around the globe. It's been two years exactly since the earthquake, and I'm going back to Japan with my daughter. Her whole world was turned upside down by the earthquake when she was four—she moved abruptly to a new place, where the language, food, and scenery was different. It's not lost on me that this is the story of my own childhood, but in reverse.

Terrible plane food. The flight attendant's hilarious American accent when she makes the announcements in Japanese. My little girl squirms and whines. She doesn't WANT to watch the special Winnie the Pooh movie I'd downloaded for her. She doesn't WANT to draw with her markers. She doesn't WANT to...

Like that, for twelve hours. But mostly I'm just waiting to feel it, waiting for that rush of nostalgia so thick I can taste it—the wet air rushing into the double doors at the airport, the bitterness of that first green tea hot from the aluminum can. The comforting stench of cigarette smoke everywhere, the indefinable loamy richness in the air that you don't get anywhere else.

I wait for it to grip me, the familiar feeling of Japan's hooks in my heart, the deep tug that always begins the second I get on the plane and roils in my stomach as soon as I walk into Narita airport. I am helpless to it; I swoon every time.

Only this time I feel...nothing.

The immigration official opens my passport.

"You have an expired business investor's visa."

"Yes, that's right." That visa had cost me $15,000: the cost to start a company so that I could sponsor myself. "I'm just here on a tourist visa now."

Again, I wait for the grief to kick in, the sense of loss—all that time and money, eight years trudging toward the ten-year permanent residency requirement, and here I am back as a tourist. But it feels fine.

I am confused.

Down the long escalator, scooping up the suitcases, the polite questions from the customs official before the doors slid open and then we are—

Home, I'd always thought.

In Japan, says the voice in my head. Not home any more.

I'm dazed by the oddness of this new way of being there. I am a visitor, someone passing through. It's not my place any more. It's beautiful, overwhelming, crazy, orderly—and I can feel myself apart from it, instead of melting and enmeshing. I test these new, unfamiliar edges to myself. I'd always felt like a sponge, sucking Japan into my very pores—or perhaps I was the one who got sucked into it. My brother and I always called it The Motherland, and it had felt both warm and devouring my whole life, the primal ground of everything. Now it seemed made of the most ordinary materials: metal siding, concrete sidewalks, plastic veneers.

I buy an *ume shiso onigiri* and pull off the complicated plastic wrapper, obediently making my way through tab one two and three so that the firm rice ball sits perfect and pink in my hand. My tongue waters at the tartness, the fresh sour bite of it impossible to find in any American reproduction— but the wave of *natsukashisa*, the desperate nostalgia, doesn't hit.

—∿—

We visit friends, walk along the river by my parents' house, feed the ducks. We have a sweet reunion at my daughter's old daycare, where she can no longer understand a word anyone says. I look around at the cozy room where she'd spent every day of her first few years, the kindly staff bundled up in pink aprons and pink handkerchiefs tied over their heads. What a wonderful place for a child, I think, as though I'm visiting for the first time. I wait for the floods of loss to carry me away, but instead all I get is a gentle lapping.

The chaos of Tokyo is unreal: the incredible crush of people in the trains, the TVs blaring advertisements all the way downtown and then home again. I can't pull a veil between me and the teeming hordes of people in every direction. The noise is constant and cacophonous: announcements in the trains, department stores, restaurants; political vans screaming propaganda; trains trucks buses bicycles whizzing, blaring, clanging.

I'd always thought it so cliché how filmmakers treated Japan in movies. They made it so vivid and surreal that it took on a kind of glazed overlay, the riot of color and flashing turned into a blurry background. How simplistic, I'd thought, how shallow. Now it seems to me that they'd been correct: the mercy of a blur was the only way to move through it with any kind of sanity.

I'd always felt so comfortable in Tokyo, so serene navigating everything, so unruffled by all of it. This time it's awful. I hate it. I feel like I'm in a blender.

I crave the quiet green pocket of my Portland life: the trees out my window, the way people amble instead of rush. I feel defenseless against the frantic whir of my old home country, and I don't want to fight it any more. I just want the peace of my sweet little white apartment with its pink-cabbage-rose-couch. I yearn for my honey-gold floors and the French windows that let in the light and the fresh wet air.

In the Queen Sweep classes I teach, I tell my students that the physical spaces we create for ourselves are powerful reflections of our inner world. When I left the swaying sixteenth floor and came to a sheltered little corner with cherry trees and tulips, I left behind not just the concrete jungle, but the shattered cacophony of myself in it.

Now I wait to feel the tug, the pull of the cord that has bound me to Japan almost as long as I can remember. But it isn't there. I believe that in the great shake-up of my life, the day Japan shook in the earthquake of March 11th, it snapped.

It's like Japan was a bad boyfriend, the kind you can't help but keep going back to, and we'd finally broken up at last.

———✹———

On our last day in Japan, we go with a friend and her two boys to the river out by Okutama. The kids ring the big temple bell, and we drink *Kirin* beer and eat *yakitori* by the river, our butts nestled into a sea of tiny round rocks. There is a strange emptiness inside me where that old cord used to pull so tautly. It's very Japanese, really; I am more aware of it in its absence. There is a little spot of *ma*, of nothingness, of white space.

So I just breathe in and out, making room for that little space, letting each breath make me bigger until I am huge inside—big as a cathedral. The leaves rustle, the kids splash, and the light glints off the water. And my old dream comes to me one last time.

The airplanes are coming in again, and they're still too far away for me to see, but I am standing on the ground waiting with my handful of string. This time I can feel the strings humming. They are alive in my hands. And as I look up, I see that they aren't getting snarled at all. The strings are actually lines of light. As the golden lines cross and touch each other, in a dance that now looks as organic and lovely as seaweed, they simply move through each other, unbroken. The lines stretch way out into the universe, like strands reaching through the ocean. Each one hums with a different sound. Some of them sound like stars, and some like blood, and some like people talking, like telephone lines. And humming down the lines, down into my body and through the soles of my feet, is the thing, the thing— the very thing that I have been waiting for.

CHAPTER THIRTY-ONE

I teach my little girl to feel her feelings all the way through. I tell her that tears help wash us clean. I explain that she's not too sensitive—she just sees things that not everyone can see. Together we make "peace bubbles" around ourselves so that we can have our own emotions and other people can have theirs. I show her how to wash herself clean with all the colors of the world when she is feeling sad, or stuck, or frustrated. And I tell her how much she is loved, just like my mom and dad always told me. I wrap her in the exact same hugs I learned from my parents, soft as an old quilt.

The voice on the phone is hesitant.

"I've never actually said this out loud before. But when I touch trees, I can feel their...energy. Different kinds have different flavors."

"Cool," I say. My voice is calm, though the fine hairs on my forearms have lifted and I feel a little shimmer in my lower back.

"You don't think that sounds crazy?" my coaching client asks.

"Nope."

"Well, and there's more. Sometimes I feel these feelings—and I know they're not mine. I think I'm feeling things that actually belong to other people."

I am grinning. "Uh-huh. And is that a pleasant feeling?"

"No way. It's horrible."

"Where do you feel it in your body?" I ask, as an image floats up of a woman with a golden teardrop in her heart.

"In my chest. In my heart. I don't want it to go away, but I need to be able to manage it. Sometimes it hurts too much and it wears me out."

"Yeah. That's the challenge for most healers. To not be washed away by all the input that's coming in."

"You think I'm a healer?" Her voice is dubious. "I was a lawyer for years."

"Well, Martha Beck calls them 'wayfinders,'" I offer. "Or menders. I think of us as mystics. What do you think the pain is there for? What's it want?"

"I don't know! It feels so urgent! But I don't know what it's telling me." I can hear the agitation in her voice.

"Let's ask it," I say. "This might be simple. It might just tell us."

She giggles suddenly. "Don't we sound like we're nuts?"

"Completely off our fucking rockers."

I ask her to imagine that she is becoming the sensations in her chest. I'm going to ask her some questions, I tell her, but I want her to let the sensations speak for themselves.

"So: Pain. Can you describe yourself for me? What's it like to be you?"

There is a brief silence. I can almost feel my client changing the way she uses her brain as she gropes to imagine herself inside the sensation instead of observing it from the outside.

"I'm...heavy. Hollow. Gray."

"Thank you, pain. And what's your job?"

"I'm here to get Meg's attention."

"And what do you want her attention for?"

There's a snag in her voice. "I don't know."

I try a different question. I soften my eyes so my vision blurs; I concentrate on the palms of my hands. They are dry. I feel a little spurt of compassion for this woman, for this pain she's carrying. "Is there something you want or need?"

"Yes! Yes, yes, yes. I need Meg to send energy out. Stop taking things in. She is supposed to be a sender. That's why I'm pressing on her so hard."

My body begins the slow buzzing that I always feel when a client is having an epiphany. It's like a delicious current is running through me, warming me and waking me up down to my cells.

"And how should she send that love out?"

"She can beam it out like a great big flashlight." I am nodding.

"Okay. Thank you so much, pain. Now, Meg. What do you make of that?"

"Oh my god. Oh my god. Holy fucking shit." She pauses for a minute. "I get it. I can feel it. Even now I'm sending love out, like a giant spotlight of it, and the pain is gone." She starts to cry. "It feels so good in my chest. It's such a relief. I always felt like it was trying to torture me, and now I see that it was just asking me to—to do this thing—I don't know what to call it, but it feels like I can do it, I can beam love out. It's so strong, and it feels so good when I do it." She sighs a deep, relaxed sigh.

Meg is in my new group coaching course. We're talking by phone because she, like the twenty-nine other women in the group, is halfway around the globe from me. They've all put down a chunk of change and suspended their skepticism to take a class called "Practical Magic for Secret Mystics." They're here to learn how to stop feeling so raw, tap into their own intuition, and learn to feel more at ease in the world. We talk about setting boundaries with people and getting grounded. We talk about setting up a circle of energy around themselves and filtering out any toxic crud they encounter. We talk about what to do with all the information that comes in through their invisible antennae. Most of them are highly sensitive, empathic, and intuitive. I teach them what has worked for me.

I spend my days sitting on my cabbage rose sofa talking on the phone to these soulful, smart women about magic. Again and again, they say to me, "I just thought I was crazy! I thought I was the only one!"

And I grin. "I know," I say. "I know."

—◊—

There was a phrase that I heard from the pulpit my whole life. The idea was that there was a dichotomy between Love and Truth. The theology went that Love without Truth is a lie, and Truth without Love is too harsh. I could see them in my mind's eye: Love was a radiant light, a quiet sphere of gentle laughter. And the Truth was a sword. A great gleaming sword made of ice.

This sword of Christianity had lopped off my head, slashed through my heart, and chopped my arms and legs like firewood. I felt hatred in that sword, and rage, and disgust for what I was.

Pastors preached that The Old Testament was truth without love—judgment, punishment, failure. And The New Testament was Jesus coming as love and truth. But, they cautioned—beware! The great fallacy of our time was an attempt to have the Love without the Truth. People wanted the soft fuzzy feel-good part without the discipline of the sword. I felt despair in my stomach, for it was true—I did crave that golden sphere of laughter. And I no longer wanted to be chopped up.

If I could go back to that girl sitting in church, trying to accept that Love and Truth were locked in battle, I would take her by the hand. I would smile in a friendly way at every one of those pastors, who in their Christian way did honestly want to help people, and give them a friendly middle finger. I would take myself by the hand and walk her out of church. I would lead her out under the stars and tell her to tilt her head back.

And out in the cold night, outside the stuffy rooms with their dusty hymnals and dogma, I know she would feel what I feel now. It would start as a quiet longing. If only she could have the love without the destruction. Impossible, of course. But I'd tell her to keep looking up at the stars. To forget the words in books between bloody leather covers, and listen to what the earth is whispering directly into her ear.

She would be quiet for a long time. Suddenly I'd hear her chortle. She'd look over at me and grin.

No WAY.

I'd grin back. Way.

All of it?

Yes.

She'd be laughing hard now, groaning, waving her hands. *Oh my god! It's such bullshit! And I believed it for years!!!*

I know! I'd yell. I'd grab her hands and we'd do an undignified celebratory dance. The fear and shame and guilt suddenly would be the most ridiculous things in the world, compared to what we would both feel as firmly as the ground beneath our feet.

Love isn't locked into a battle with Truth. It's not the crazy rebel forces that need to be held in check by the sharp threat of judgment. If anything, it's the other way around. Love is what is. It's the starlight that pours down from the sky. It's the atoms that hum in the dirt we stand on. It's the joy that pushes through the ground every spring as green growing things, it's the quiet embrace of snow, it's the tango of the planets. It is what we are made of.

The great palace lie is that there is any part of us that isn't loved. The great deception is that we are ever outside of love.

—∞—

There was never any giant finger from the sky singling me out. No teacher who came to find me and said, "You! Youuuuuu." Instead I'd gotten my own strange story, my own messy miracles—a heartbeat in a bathtub, a life raft of books, seeds of turquoise forgiveness that I planted myself. And a radiant little girl in my arms, the most astounding gift of all.

I know it might sound absurd, but my current working theory is that I designed this particular human lifetime for myself because my soul thought it would be such an amazing adventure; a great obstacle course to figure out; a fascinating puzzle to crack. (My soul tends to forget what it's like to actually be in a body, apparently. I can just imagine her cackling mercilessly, going, "Oooooh, missionaries and ghosts—yes! It's just too hilarious!") My plan for next time is to leave instructions including hot sex, scads of money, and the ability to fly.

But this go-round, I set it up so that the first couple decades of my life I couldn't feel the truest thing that there is. I came in as Esau, to see if I would eventually realize that there is no such THING as an Esau. My soul wanted to know what it would feel like to push through a thick gauze curtain of delusion and fight to know the truth for herself. I must admit that I treasure this truth all the more because it wasn't handed to me on a gilded platter. And maybe I'll carry those fighter muscles into my next lifetime. I surely hope so.

—◦◦◦—

Imagine for just a moment that this is true for you, too. Pretend that your life is a playground that you designed for yourself. What were you trying to figure out? Who were you trying to become? What colors did you want to taste? Who did you come to save? What's the story you wanted to hear...badly enough that you jumped in to live it?

Reach inside yourself for what you yearn to be true. Reach out to the cosmos for the love you hoped was there. Reach down into the earth for its bright joys and beautiful sorrows. If you can't feel anything, just start with trees, and stars, and music, and cake and dirt and freshly made beds. You will be amazed at the joyful humming you can hear in them if you listen in close.

I think that maybe we get the God we believe in.

Maybe we even deserve the God we believe in.

So dream up a good one, dearest heart. The whole universe is holding its breath, hoping you will. It's got all the candles and sparklers and tiaras held behind its back, just aching to burst into wild celebration when you stick to the truth you know— or the one you WANT to know. Because if you long for it, it's yours. Claim it. Go get it. Declare dominion over this gorgeous life. And wrap your arms around your sweet self, because the deepest truth I know is that we are all beloved. Oh so dearly.

I never got the radiant illumination I'd asked for. And I never got a burning bush. But all this time, I'd had it ass-backward. I didn't need to be called—my longing *was* the calling.

My whole life I'd been waiting to be chosen, to be wanted, to belong. I kept waiting for someone to tell me that I was included. But instead it turned out that *I* was the one who got to do the choosing. *I* got to decide what was going to belong to *me*.

So here's what I decided:

All the beauty and love in the world are mine.

And I am theirs.

ACKNOWLEDGMENTS

As you have seen, it turns out that it is simply impossible to flunk out of my family. This was very good news for me, because I put my parents through the wringer so many different times over the years (don't worry! I don't think there are any left!). THEN, I went and broke our family code of communicating mostly using *ma*, unspoken white space, which we learned from so many very touching Japanese soap operas—and I went and wrote an intimate memoir full of squirmy family stories. For some reason, they love me anyway and gave me their blessing. Mom and Dad, I hope you can feel the love in these pages— the love I feel for you, and the love I received from you. I'm rrrrrich because of your care and persistence, and I damn well know it. You two are living, breathing incarnations of love, and the heroes of this whole story. Thank you to my brother and sister for so graciously allowing me to share their tales along with mine, especially the juicy ones. And thank you both for letting me crash on your floors (literally and metaphorically) so many times over the years. Love you. Woof woof.

This book literally wouldn't exist without Betsy Rapoport. Fierce mama bear, loyal champion, exquisitely skilled book midwife, and yet somehow always hilarious and kind. Thank you for putting up with all my weepy emails and never giving up on me.

I'm grateful to Alexandra Franzen and the cohort of women I met at her retreat in Hawaii, where the final draft of this book was completed. Alex, you're a gorgeous powerhouse and I'm infinitely grateful for your support. I'd especially like to thank Theresa Reed and Alexa Fischer, who stood watch with me at dawn as I pressed "send" on a very scary email.

Thank you to Lissa Rankin, Susan Hyatt, and Pam Slim for reading early versions of this book and offering their encouragement and support. Your generous words kept me afloat in many a dark hour.

My gratitude to Melissa B, who believed in this project before it even existed. To Erin MB, who first handed me Anne Lamott's book *Bird By*

Bird and told me it was okay that I wanted to be a writer, and maybe I should just get started. To Julia R, who was there for me when I needed it most. To Jenny S and Kristen K, staunch allies for many years.

To all the teachers and church folk whose hearts are so much bigger than your official religion: I see you out here in this field beyond the—you know. To all the coaches, writers, energy healers, and spiritual teachers I've worked with who helped me find my true religion as a heathen mystic: thanks for being the real deal. And to Madre: I thought I'd lost you a few times there. Thanks for reminding me that we're never really lost.

To The Mamas of Portland, the literati, the true hearts, you of the deep cackle and the fancy cocktail stroller and the gourmet picnics in the park—you are my village, and I couldn't have done this without you. I love you and miss you more than you can imagine.

To all the agents and gatekeepers who turned me down: thank you. You turned me into an epic fucking badass who had to believe in myself even when no one else did.

To the radiant kindred spirits who joined my Patreon community: you will probably never know how much your faith and trust mean to me. Did you know that I was ready to just put this whole thing in a drawer? But you took a risk, you showed up, you said, "Let's just do the damn things ourselves," and you know what? We did it!!! And oh, dearhearts, we're just getting started. We're going to make SO MANY BEAUTIFUL THINGS together. I love you.

To my beloved private clients, from whom I learn so much: I'll tell you a secret. I'd coach you all for free if I didn't have all these children to feed, that's how much I adore you. Don't tell anybody.

To my children, Adventure, Danger, Epic, Wilde, and Mayhem: what goes around comes around. If you decide to write your own memoirs one day, I promise to be as good a sport as my parents were. You make my heart bigger every day. Oh, also, no means no and your body is your own and be kind and brave and yes I will keep embarrassing you forever.

And finally, and most of all, to Nick—my true love, my partner, my soulmate, my best friend, the hottest man alive—you were the greatest surprise of my whole life, but honey, you were worth waiting for. You and me, babe. All the lifetimes. (I promise to never make you be a tree again.) I love you always and forever and even after that. I can't wait to write the next chapter of our story.

.

ABOUT THE AUTHOR

Katherine North became a life coach because she realized that she'd always had "tell me your secrets" tattooed on her forehead in invisible ink anyway and hell, maybe it was time to go pro. Her clients are ambitious, successful, and too smart for most of the self-help aisle—but they secretly yearn for terribly mortifying things. Things like more magic, more peace, and more grit (oh god). She helps them be bigger and braver than they ever thought they'd need to be...sometimes bigger and braver than they wish they HAD to be. She calls this "Declaring Dominion" and she did exactly that by changing her name to Katherine North at age 42 just because she wanted to. (Is that allowed?!? It is!!!) She's a queer feminist, mother of five, and she grew up as a missionary kid but now she's a foul-mouthed heathen mystic. She also might be the only life coach in the world who doesn't believe in the law of attraction. More than 3,000 women have used her **Queen Sweep** program to clear their lives of clutter, she teaches sensitive empaths to set energetic boundaries in **Practical Magic for Secret Mystics**, and she helps kindred spirits become epic f*cking badasses in her **EFBA** programs. You can find more about Katherine's work at DeclareDominion.com. She and her husband, Nick North, made an award-winning documentary about their big queer blended family called Just Another Beautiful Family. Her Patreon community funds her creative work, including this memoir, and is open to all.

Find Katherine online:
Instagram, Facebook, Twitter, etc:
    @declaredominion
    http://DeclareDominion.com

CPSIA information can be obtained
at www.ICGtesting.com
Printed in the USA
LVHW031358090720
660209LV00003B/295

9 781734 952902